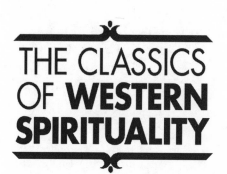

THE CLASSICS
OF WESTERN
SPIRITUALITY

THE CLASSICS OF WESTERN SPIRITUALITY
A Library of the Great Spiritual Masters

The Pilgrim's Tale

EDITED AND WITH AN INTRODUCTION BY
ALEKSEI PENTKOVSKY

TRANSLATED BY
T. ALLAN SMITH

PREFACE BY
JAROSLAV PELIKAN

PAULIST PRESS
NEW YORK • MAHWAH

Cover art: NICHOLAS T. MARKELL lives in Edina, Minnesota, where he makes his profession as an artist. Nicholas majored in visual art at the University of Saint Thomas in Saint Paul. In 1992, he received a master of arts degree in theology and a master of divinity degree from the Washington Theological Union in Washington, D.C. Working in a variety of media, Nicholas conveys a deep understanding of religious thought and spirituality in his art. Applauded for his artistic excellence, Nicholas's original art has won national awards and has been exhibited in numerous shows, galleries, churches and academic institutions in Minnesota, Maryland, Virginia and Washington, D.C. His stained-glass window designs can be found in numerous churches across the United States. Nicholas is currently illustrating IlluminationBooks, a series on contemporary spirituality also published by Paulist Press. Of this cover icon, he states: "Perhaps no other art form has influenced me as deeply as the tradition of icon writing. Within this tradition, Russian iconography and spirituality holds a special place. The very nature of icon painting is one of prayer and ministry, for an iconographer is more a minister than artisan, and an icon more a sacramental than painting. When I create an icon I am called to journey deeper into a life of Christian humility and service, ever seeking a glimpse of eternity and the face of the living God."

Library of Congress Cataloging-in-Publication Data

Rasskaz strannika, iskatelia molitvy. English.
    The pilgrim's tale / edited and with an introduction by Aleksei Pentkovsky ; translated by T. Allan Smith ; preface by Jaroslav Pelikan.
        p.   cm. – (The classics of Western spirituality : #95)
    "A translation of the text of the Optino redaction. A translation of a new redaction of the three supplementary tales is given in the appendix. These translations are made on the basis of texts published in 1922" – Introd.
Includes bibliographical references (p.   ) and index.
    ISBN 0-8091-3709-7 (paper); ISBN 0-8091-0486-5 (cloth)
    1. Spiritual life—Orthodox Eastern Church. I. Pentkovsky, Aleksei. II. Smith, T. Allan. III. Title.   IV. Series.
BX382.R3713   1999
248.4'819—dc21   99-35236
                                                                                              CIP

Published by Paulist Press
997 Macarthur Boulevard
Mahwah, New Jersey 07430

www.paulistpress.com

Printed and bound in the United States of America

Contents

Editor of This Volume

ALEKSEI PENTKOVSKY currently resides in Moscow. He has studied at both the Moscow Chemical Technological Institute and the Moscow Theological Seminary of the Russian Orthodox Church. He received a doctor of oriental ecclesiastical sciences degree from the Pontifical Oriental Institute in Rome in 1996. At present, Dr. Pentkovsky is a reader at the Moscow Theological Academy of the Russian Orthodox Church and serves as executive secretary of the foundation, Russian Initiative for Culture. He plans to continue his research into the spirituality and liturgical tradition of the Russian Orthodox Church.

Translator of This Volume

T. ALLAN SMITH was born in Brampton, Ontario, in 1953. After receiving his M.A. in Russian literature at the University of Toronto in 1977, he entered the Congregation of Priests of St. Basil and was ordained to the priesthood in 1983. Specializing in the history and theology of the Russian Orthodox Church, he earned his doctorate in theology at Friedrich-Alexander Universität Erlangen in 1988, with a thesis entitled *The Volokolamskii Paterik, A translation, study and commentary*. He has published articles on Russian monasticism, Orthodox spirituality and ecclesiology. He is the editor and translator of Sergei M. Soloviev, *Russian Society under Ivan the Terrible*, Academic International Press, 1996. A second volume, *The Tsar and the Patriarch*, is in preparation. Dr. Smith taught church history at Newman Theological College in Edmonton from 1994–1998. He is currently Associate Professor of Church History and Director of Advanced Degree Programs at the Faculty of Theology, University of St. Michael's College, in Toronto.

Author of the Preface

JAROSLAV PELIKAN received his Ph.D. in 1946 from the University of Chicago, where he also taught from 1953 to 1962. Since 1962 he has been a member of the faculty of Yale University, where he is now Sterling Professor of History. He was editor of the American edition of *Luther's Works*. His five-volume *The Christian Tradition: A History of the Development of Doctrine* is a well-respected contribution to the history of Christian doctrine. More recent publications include *Faust the Theologian, Mary Through the Centuries: Her Place in the History of Culture* and *The Illustrated Jesus Through the Centuries*.

Preface

*I*t is a highly instructive exercise, not to say an edifying one, to read, side by side, this English translation of *The Pilgrim's Tale* and its Russian original, *Rasskaz strannika*. For not only has the translator preserved the special mixture of spiritual naïveté and speculative power in Mikhail Kozlov's text, but at many points he has clarified obscure passages, emended faults in the printed version of the Russian, and provided explanatory notes that elucidate references or allusions over which even an experienced reader might be tempted to pass without noticing. The learned and incisive introduction by Aleksei Pentkovsky, which constitutes a miniature monograph in its own right, assembles a vast amount of historical and literary material in convenient compass, providing detailed information about the checkered history of the text itself; and I have neither the inclination nor the erudition to go beyond it. Instead, I want to highlight several features in *The Pilgrim's Tale* of which any reader, and especially a Western reader whose language is English, needs to be reminded.

Perhaps the most striking such feature is what present-day literary criticism would call its *intertextuality*, which is a needlessly abstract term for the habit, characteristic of Eastern Christian spirituality and theology but by no means confined to it, of constructing a treatise by stringing together quotations and references from earlier sources. By far the most frequently cited such source here is the *Philokalia*, an eighteenth-century work by two Greek monks, Saint Nikodimos of the Holy Mountain (of Athos) and Saint Makarios Notaras, which was published for the first time in 1782 (in Venice). The *Philokalia* was itself a compilation of quotations and references from earlier texts of Patristic and Byzantine spirituality. Thanks to the scholarly efforts of Bishop Kallistos Ware and his colleagues, we now have a reliable and usable translation of it into English. The translation of it into Slavonic, soon after its publication in Greek, was the work of starets Paisii Velichkovski. According to the historian of Russian Orthodox spirituality, Father George Maloney, this translation, titled *Dobrotoliubie*, "had perhaps the greatest influence after the Bible in keeping alive the traits typical of Russian spirituality."

The linkage of Bible and *Philokalia* pervades *The Pilgrim's Tale*. "Sacred Scripture," the work says near its beginning (12), "is a brilliant sun, and the *Philokalia* is the necessary piece of glass which facilitates our access to that most sublime luminary." The reason is not hard to find, for "[i]n the *Philokalia*, all the instructions about the practice of the prayer of the heart are drawn from the Word of God—from the Holy Bible" (44). Therefore the pilgrims report later in the work: "We spent all the rest of the time sitting in lonely woods reading the *Philokalia*" (68). And more than once we are told that "I read my *Philokalia* to fortify my soul" (83, 92). Our edition very helpfully identifies passages from the *Philokalia* (that is, from the English translation of the Greek original) that are quoted verbatim, but so much of the vocabulary and texture of the tales being recited here comes from the Slavonic/Russian version of it that the pages would have to be peppered with footnotes to document the dependence. Also present, whether directly or through later collections, are quotations from Symeon the New Theologian (177), from *The Ladder of Divine Ascent* by John Climacus (130), and other texts in the tradition of Eastern Orthodox spirituality and liturgy (49).

Much less explicit, but nevertheless far more pervasive than the overt references to it would indicate, is the conflict over who had a legitimate claim to that tradition of Eastern Orthodox spirituality, and therefore the contrast with and polemic against the thought and spirituality of the Old Ritualists *(Staroobriadtsi)* or Old Believers. Mikhail Kozlov was himself a convert from the Old Believers to the Orthodox Church, and in many of the conversations and debates may well have been striving, at least implicitly, to make the point that, despite its notorious revisions in the liturgical books, Russian *Pravoslavie* had not abandoned authentic ways of worshiping and praying. The most vigorous polemic, however, is reserved for the opposite ends of the ideological spectrum, the "so-called spiritual, pseudosophisticated *(lzhemudrikh)* philosophers" (122) who disparage the power of prayer.

For to a degree that many Western Christians, both Roman Catholic and Protestant, may find surprising, prayer, which "constitutes universally the essence or soul of every religion" (135), performs a function here that is so comprehensive as to include not only the sacrificial and fervent communication of human petition, praise, and thanksgiving to God, but a divine and indeed sacramental communication of grace to the human condition: "I consider prayer to be the most important and necessary means of obtaining salvation and the primary duty of every Christian. Prayer constitutes both the first step and the crown of a devout life" (106). Especially does all of this apply to the Jesus prayer, "Lord Jesus Christ, Son of God, have mercy upon me," which "is an abridgment of the entire Gospel" (24). Cruelly and unfairly caricatured by Tolstoy in a chapter of *Resurrection* that was originally suppressed by the censors, the Jesus prayer is interpreted here as "a most Christian and wholesome action" (76). It is the fulfillment of the apostolic injunction in 1 Thessalonians 5:17, to pray without ceasing, which was neither a hyperbole nor an allegory, but a requirement.

What I called earlier the special mixture of spiritual naïveté and speculative power in this work owes some of its effectiveness to the narrative structure and to the familiar organizing principle of the pilgrimage. But in its use of pilgrimage as a root metaphor, Kozlov's *The Pilgrim's Tale* is far closer to Bunyan or to Comenius than to Chaucer. While acknowledging what Chaucer documents so unforgettably, that "many of our brother and sister pilgrims wander because they have nothing to do or because they are lazy" (63), it describes the journey of the soul to God in the language of the pilgrim's journey to Jerusalem. And it could well have closed, though it does not, with the words of Bunyan about Mr. Valiant-for-Truth: "So he passed over, and the trumpets sounded for him on the other side."

Introduction

From "A Seeker of Unceasing Prayer" to "The Candid Tales of a Pilgrim" (notes on the textual history and authorship of *The Pilgrim's Tale*)

*I*n 1881 the superior of Saint Michael the Archangel monastery of Cheremis in the diocese of Kazan, Hegumen Paisii Fedorov, published in Kazan four tales of a certain pious pilgrim. The tales described how the pilgrim obtained the gift of praying the Jesus prayer unceasingly and the edifying and instructive events that happened to him while he wandered at length across the limitless expanses of Siberia. The book was called "The Candid Tale of a Pilgrim to His Spiritual Father."[1] In 1882 the Russian monastery of St. Panteleimon on Mount Athos published an abbreviated and reworked version of the Pilgrim's Tales, under the title "The Remarkable Tale about the Grace-giving Effects of the Jesus Prayer," which subsequently was reprinted on numerous occasions.[2] In 1883, Hegumen Paisii Fedorov produced a new edition of the 1881 text, under the title "Candid Tales of a Pilgrim to His Spiritual Father."[3] Next year, in 1884, the monastery of Saint Michael the Archangel made a new edition of the text, published in 1883 by the superior.[4] It was this revised and edited text of the Pilgrim's Tales that subsequently received universal distribution.

Repeatedly reissued in Russian and in numerous translations, the tales of an unknown pilgrim became not only one of the most famous works of Russian spiritual literature but also one of

1

the fundamental sources for the study of Russian spirituality. The attention of both readers and researchers has been concentrated on the content of the tales. The authenticity of the image of the pilgrim did not give rise to any doubts and thus no particular importance was attached to questions concerning the provenance and history of the text. Already in 1971, however, S. Bol'shakov noticed that in the correspondence of elder Amvrosii of Optino the author of the Pilgrim's Tales is mentioned. Bol'shakov also suggested that "the original of this manuscript" might be found in the Panteleimon monastery on Mount Athos.[5] Shortly afterward, in the library of Panteleimon monastery, he discovered the sought-for manuscript, which contained a manuscript redaction of Four Tales. After comparing the text of the manuscript with the text of the 1884 edition and finding some fragments that were absent from that edition, the researcher no longer doubted that the text he had discovered was the author's redaction, and he supposed that the unknown pilgrim had written down these tales for the father confessor of Panteleimon monastery, the priest-monk[6] Ieronim (Solomentsov).[7]

The priest Vsevolod Roshko formulated a new theory about the original text. He had discovered and published a fragment of the unknown printed text that closely resembled the concluding portion of the First Tale.[8] Proceeding from the variant readings of the fragment of the text he uncovered and of the corresponding text in the edition of 1884, the publisher reached the conclusion that the fragment belonged to an unknown first edition. In his article, Father Roshko drew attention to the involvement of Bishop Feofan the Recluse in editing the 1884 version and advanced the conjecture that Bishop Feofan edited precisely that version of the Pilgrim's Tales, a fragment of which he had discovered. Touching on the question of authorship of the text he was investigating, Father Roshko suggested that the four fundamental and three additional tales[9] belonged to various authors. Without being more precise about the authorship of the fundamental text, the researcher suggested that Elder Amvrosii of Optino was the compiler of the last three tales.

INTRODUCTION

Substantial changes in the notion about authorship and the history of the text of the Pilgrim's Tales were introduced in 1987 by the priest-monk Vasilii Grolimund, who reported on a note by Father Pavel Florenskii in a copy of the 1884 edition. In this note Father Florenskii identified the anonymous author of "Candid Tales of a Pilgrim to His Spiritual Father" as the superior of Holy Trinity monastery in Selenginsk, Archimandrite[10] Mikhail.[11] Father Florenskii based his conclusion on evidence from the correspondence of Archbishop Veniamin of Irkutsk in which a manuscript of Archimandrite Mikhail, "A Seeker of Unceasing Prayer," containing the tales of a certain pilgrim was discussed.[12] Father Vasilii Grolimund did not agree fully with the note of Father Florenskii concerning the authorship of Archimandrite Mikhail, the evidence about Archimandrite Mikhail's manuscript from the letter of Archbishop Veniamin and the remark of the publisher of the correspondence, K. V. Kharlampovich, concerning the authorship of Archimandrite Mikhail. The researcher cautiously suggested that only the note and the editorial work on the tales of the unknown pilgrim belonged to Archimandrite Mikhail; later, during his stay on Mount Athos, Hegumen Paisii Fedorov became acquainted with Father Mikhail and copied the manuscript he had compiled. At the same time, Father Grolimund reported on a manuscript newly discovered in the library of the Russian monastery of St. Panteleimon on Mount Athos to which S. Bol'shakov made reference. A comparison of the text of the manuscript with the text of the 1884 edition convinced the researcher of the correctness of Bol'shakov's observations and prompted him to return to the 1881 edition. Comparison with this version showed both the closeness of the texts and the large number of variant readings. Further searching allowed Father Grolimund to draw the following conclusion: at first Hegumen Paisii published a text known on the basis of the fragment published by Father Roshko and only then did the 1881 edition appear.[13]

In 1989 Father Grolimund gave more precision to his conclusions. In the introductory article to a publication of the principal variant readings of the text of the Pilgrim's Tales from the 1881 edition and the manuscript of the Athos Panteleimon monastery, he noted that the text of the fragment discovered and published by Father Roshko belonged to an abbreviated redaction first published in 1882, and did not depend on the 1881 edition.[14] Of special interest were the nine fragments of text from the Athos manuscript published by Father Grolimund,[15] which owing to the inaccessibility of the manuscript, are the sole source for the characteristics of the text contained therein.

The conjectures made by Fathers Florenskii and Grolimund about the degree of participation of Father Mikhail Kozlov in the composition of the Pilgrim's Tales, attractive in their simplicity, received further development in an article by I. Basin. Not only did Basin not doubt the authorship of Father Kozlov; he even included the first Kazan edition of the Pilgrim's Tales in his list of the published works of Father Kozlov.[16] In doing so the researcher, like his precursors, disregarded the differences between the texts of the Pilgrim's Tales from the known printed editions and the Athos manuscript.

* * *

Fundamental changes in the existing ideas about the provenance of the text of "Candid Tales of a Pilgrim" and the interrelation of the different redactions were made in 1992 when the texts of the manuscript redactions of the four basic and three additional tales were published.[17] The publication of the texts was accompanied by an article that examined the different manuscript and printed redactions of the Pilgrim's Tales and their interrelationship.[18] On the basis of that analysis the following conclusions can be drawn:

1. The earliest known redaction of the text of the Four Tales of a pilgrim is found in two closely related manuscripts from the Optino hermitage, Opt 455[19] and Opt 456.[20] This redaction has been called *Optino* on the basis of its place of origin. The distinguishing features of the Optino redaction are its name ("The Tale of a Pilgrim, a Seeker of Prayer" [absent in Opt 455]), the dating of each of the tales (12, 20, and 23 December 1859, respectively [in Opt 456 the date of the First Tale, 6 November, was added

later]), and the heading of the First Tale ("The Tale of a Pilgrim, how he acquired the gift of interior unceasing prayer of the heart"), which are absent from all the other known redactions. The pilgrim began his search for explanations of the apostle's words concerning unceasing prayer either in Kiev or Kazan, since he heard a sermon in the cathedral church on the Sunday of the Publican and the Pharisee, and another on the Sunday of the Veneration of the Cross in the church of the Theological Academy. The location of the conversations themselves is Irkutsk, for at the end of the Third Tale, while referring to Irkutsk the pilgrim uses the spatial qualifier "here" and he calls the merchant who gave him money to complete his pilgrimage to Jerusalem "a local merchant." We note especially that in this redaction references to his "spiritual father" are entirely absent. Based on the dates for the tales contained in the text, it follows that the Optino redaction originated no earlier than 1859. The text of the Optino redaction, however, is not the authorial redaction of "A Seeker of Unceasing Prayer" of Father Mikhail Kozlov, which remains unknown to the present day. (For more details, see below.)

2. On the basis of results obtained from a comparison of the texts of the manuscript and printed redactions, the existence of an *Athos redaction* has been postulated, although there are no known copies of it. The text of this redaction, which in many ways is close to the Optino redaction, was assumed as the basis for the 1881 Kazan edition prepared by Hegumen Paisii Fedorov. In the foreword to the second Kazan edition (1883) Hegumen Paisii pointed out that he prepared his edition on the basis of a manuscript that he copied on Mount Athos.[21] For this reason the redaction of the text used by Hegumen Paisii for his 1881 edition has been called the Athos redaction.

3. As a result of the changes introduced into the text of the Athos redaction, there arose the *Sergiev redaction*, whose text is preserved in two manuscripts—Sergiev and Panteleimon. The first manuscript is found in the archives of Professor Archimandrite Kiprian (Kern), kept in St. Sergius Theological Institute in Paris.[22] The text of the Four Tales of a Pilgrim found in the manuscript is called "Tale of a Pilgrim (concerning the Jesus Prayer)" and

the author of the text, indicated on the cover, is Hegumen Tikhon from the Vyshensk hermitage.

The second manuscript is found in the library of the Russian monastery of St. Panteleimon on Mount Athos.[23] It is the very text made known by S. Bol'shakov and from which Father Grolimund published nine text fragments.[24] The short description of the Panteleimon manuscript contains no information about its title or author.[25] At the present time it is impossible to establish the exact interrelationship of the texts of these two manuscripts because of the inaccessibility of the Panteleimon manuscript. From the published fragments it follows that the text of the Panteleimon manuscript, in comparison with the Sergiev manuscript, contains independent omissions; however, the Panteleimon manuscript has an afterword, missing from all other copies and redactions.[26]

For the comparison of the different redactions of the Pilgrim's Tales, the text of the Sergiev manuscript was used, and this determined the title of the redaction (Sergiev). The characteristic features of the Sergiev manuscript are the abbreviations of the text at the beginning of Tales Three and Four. In addition, the names of the Second, Third, and Fourth Tales in the Sergiev manuscript have been replaced by numbers.

4. The absence of the text of the Athos redaction does not permit a more accurate determination of the origins of the *Abbreviated redaction*, first published in 1882. Its text represents an abbreviated retelling of the Four Tales.[27] The probable source of the text of the Abbreviated redaction is either the Athos redaction or, more likely, the Sergiev redaction.

5. In 1881 the text of the Athos redaction, significantly reworked with respect to both style and content, was published in Kazan. Its publisher, Hegumen Paisii Fedorov, gave a new title to the text—"The Candid Tale of a Pilgrim to His Spiritual Father"—and appended to it a selection of texts by the holy fathers dealing with the Jesus prayer.[28] Besides the changes in style and meaning caused by the editor's personal relationship with the published text and by the demands of the censors, the dates for all the tales and the title of the First Tale are absent

from the first Kazan edition of 1881. One of the most substantial alterations made by Hegumen Paisii was the exclusion of the tale about the miraculous deliverance from a wolf with the assistance of the elder's prayer beads and the discussions about the mechanism for materializing spirits (in the Second Tale), which follow that tale.[29]

6. The most significant changes were introduced into the text of the second edition of the Pilgrim's Tales, which was published in Kazan in 1883. Bishop Feofan the Recluse, who participated in the preparation of this edition, substantially "corrected and supplemented" the text published in 1881. Bishop Feofan's treatment of the text was not fortuitous. Undoubtedly, the tales of the pilgrim interested the compiler and editor of the Russian *Philokalia*, inasmuch as they exposed the living experience of an "unsophisticated" practitioner of the Jesus prayer.

The Vyshensk Recluse's familiarity with the edition of Hegumen Paisii could have arisen in various ways. First, the editor himself sent a copy of his edition to the Vyshensk hermitage, as Bishop Feofan's letter of 26 November 1882 to N. V. Elagin attests. This letter reports that Hegumen Paisii had printed and sent a certain "Tale of a Pilgrim who sought the Jesus Prayer." Bishop Feofan further reports that he "corrected and supplemented" the text sent to him and forwarded it for reprinting.[30]

Second, the Pilgrim's Tales printed in 1881 provoked both interest and doubt among readers about the correctness of the exposition of the doctrine concerning the Jesus prayer, which were grounds for appealing to the Vyshensk Recluse. One of the doubters was the priest-monk Nikon Rozhdestvenskii, future bishop of Vologda and Tot'ma and publisher of three supplemental tales (Five, Six, and Seven).[31]

Well known, however, to pious readers and editors of spiritual literature alike were not only the printed versions of the text published in Kazan but also its different manuscripts. In the correspondence between Archbishop Veniamin of Irkutsk and Archbishop Vladimir of Kazan, cited by Father Florenskii, reference is made to the fact that the Irkutsk bishop not only recommended that everyone read the manuscript of Archimandrite

Mikhail, but he also sent via the Kazan bishop a copy of the text of the tales (the manuscript "A Seeker of Unceasing Prayer") to his own brother, a monk in the Vyshensk hermitage, for clarification of the opinion of Bishop Feofan the Recluse about it.[32]

Questions linked with the text under examination were put to the elders of Optino hermitage too. Thus, the nun Leonida Frizel', bursar of Vlakhernskii Spasskii monastery in the Dmitrov district of Moscow province, who had studied the Jesus prayer and whom Elder Amvrosii of Optino exhorted to pray, asked the elder's opinion about "a manuscript which indicated a simple method for going through the Jesus prayer with the mouth, the mind and the heart, belonging to some peasant from the Orel province, who had been taught this by an unknown elder," dated 1859.[33] In written replies from 7 November and 11 December 1879 and 8 February 1880, Elder Amvrosii asked her to send him this manuscript, and reported receiving and copying it, and sending back the original.[34] In a postscript to the letter of 8 February 1880, Elder Amvrosii communicated his opinion about this manuscript: "I do not know when I intend to write you again, therefore I will say a few words about the manuscript of the pilgrim now. There is nothing offensive in it. The pilgrim lived as a pilgrim and led a wanderer's life, not obliged by any anxieties or cares, and he freely practiced the prayer as he wished...."[35] Two years later, in a letter dated 27 April 1882, Elder Amvrosii again recalled the Pilgrim's Tales and reported on the edition produced by Hegumen Paisii.[36]

Judging by all this, in the letters the question concerns the Optino redaction, since the tales of this very redaction are dated 1859. Elder Amvrosii's testimony about preparing a copy of the manuscript sent to him by the nun Leonida in Optino hermitage has particular significance because it explains the origin of the two Optino manuscripts containing the Pilgrim's Tales. These manuscripts go back to the original sent by Leonida.

The evidence introduced above (that of Bishop Feofan the Recluse, Elder Amvrosii of Optino, Archbishop Veniamin of Irkutsk, and others) illustrates that already in the seventies and eighties of the nineteenth century different redactions of the

INTRODUCTION

Pilgrim's Tales were known to readers of spiritual literature. It is likely that the popularity of the manuscript and printed versions of the Pilgrim's Tales, containing generally accessible descriptions of the practice of the Jesus prayer in the heart, was one of the chief reasons determining the special relationship of the Recluse from the Vyshensk hermitage with the text published by Hegumen Paisii, into which he introduced changes that to him seemed necessary. But the "emendations" of the most reverend redactor amounted to more than this or that stylistic and orthographic correction and minor explanatory insertions. (We are supposing that all the corrections to the 1881 text were made by Bishop Feofan, since it is hardly likely that someone else would resolve to introduce changes into a text prepared by the bishop-recluse himself for reprinting.) First of all, a few fragments were excluded from the text:

1. From the First Tale:
a) The narrative about the pilgrim's quests for an answer to the question concerning the method of attaining uninterrupted prayer in harmony with the apostle's command, which contains latent criticism of some aspects of the theology from the Synodal period.[37]
b) Two quotations from the fourth chapter of a work by Dmitrii of Rostov, "The interior person, alone in the closet of his heart, who studies and prays in secret,"[38] and the unsuccessful attempt to explain them by the superior of the monastery with whom the pilgrim was conversing.[39]

2. From the Fourth Tale:
a) The details of the pilgrim's temptation in the post station.[40]
b) The description of the common meal at the home of the parish priest.[41]
c) The tale of the old woman pilgrim concerning her miraculous deliverance from the assault on the forest road.[42]

The following passages relate to the "additions" made by Bishop Feofan the Recluse:

INTRODUCTION

1. A fragment from the Second Tale containing the narrative about the pilgrim's miraculous deliverance from a wolf with the aid of the elder's prayer beads and the exposition of a conversation with a writer and a teacher concerning the mechanism for materializing spirits, which follows this narrative.[43]

2. Insertions in the Third and Fourth Tales which make clear that the pilgrim was talking with none other than his spiritual father, not with some other person [printed in italics]:

a) *Before my actual departure from Irkutsk, I visited my spiritual father once more, with whom I had had the conversations, and said to him*:

Here I am actually on the road to Jerusalem! I have come to say farewell and to give thanks for the Christian love shown me, an unworthy sinner.

He said to me:

May God bless your path! But it's too bad that you didn't tell me anything about yourself, who you are and where you come from. I have heard a great deal from you about your travels, and I would be interested to learn about your origins and life prior to your pilgrimage.[44]

b) The Russian proverb is correct: man proposes, but God disposes,—*I said, coming once again to see my spiritual father*. I supposed that right now I would be on my way to the holy city of Jerusalem, but it has turned out otherwise.[45]

c) All the while God and His Holy Providence govern our deeds and intentions, as it is written: "Both the willing and the doings are God's work."

Hearing this my spiritual father said:

I am sincerely glad, dearest brother, that the Lord has arranged for me to see you so soon and unexpectedly.[46]

d) *When I finished these tales, I said to my spiritual father:*

Forgive me, for God's sake. I have been chattering away long enough <...> our journey for the good.

With all my soul I wish, beloved brother, that the abundantly loving grace of God may spread as a canopy over your path and accompany you as the angel Raphael went with Tobias![47]

INTRODUCTION

All the insertions, which were to witness to the conversation with none other than the spiritual father, as well as the other changes and additions made by Bishop Feofan as he was preparing the 1883 edition, were introduced directly into the text of the 1881 edition and do not depend on any other texts. The narrative concerning the miraculous deliverance from a wolf and the conversation in the inn with the writer and teacher, restored to the 1883 edition, are the only exceptions. The sole possible source for this major insertion is a manuscript text of the Pilgrim's Tales that had to be at Bishop Feofan's disposal. Proceeding from textual peculiarities of the restored fragment, we can surmise that Bishop Feofan used the text of the Sergiev redaction, inasmuch as the corresponding text of the Sergiev redaction is for the most part close to the fragment under examination.

Therefore, Bishop Feofan had at his disposal not only the first edition but also a manuscript version of the Pilgrim's Tales which he used to restore a fragment omitted from that edition. The origin of the manuscript used by Bishop Feofan is unknown, but it is hardly probable that it was the manuscript sent to the Vyshensk hermitage by Archbishop Veniamin of Irkutsk, since it contained the original text of the composition by Father Mikhail (more details below).

In preparing a new edition, the selection of ascetical texts, published in the 1881 edition, was also subjected to significant changes and additions; however, since these texts are absent from the manuscripts containing the Pilgrim's Tales and only enter into the composition of the printed redactions, they will not be examined here.

Summing up the textual study of the known manuscript and printed versions, the following conclusions can be made: No earlier than 1859 (the date preserved in the Optino redaction) Father Mikhail Kozlov composed "The Seeker of Unceasing Prayer," the text of which is unknown. The earliest known text deriving from Father Mikhail's composition is "The Tale of a Pilgrim, a Seeker of Prayer" (Optino redaction). The text of the Athos redaction, which is close to the Optino redaction, was used by Hegumen Paisii for the 1881 edition, where it was printed with abbreviations and changes made by the editor. The next redaction of the manuscript text was the Sergiev redaction, but the next redaction of the printed text was that of Bishop Feofan the Recluse (the 1883 edition), during the preparation of which he made use of one of the manuscript redactions. The abbreviated redaction of 1882 was published independently of the 1881 edition; its text derives from either the Athos redaction or the Sergiev redaction.

* * *

In comparison with all the redactions of the Pilgrim's Tale, the least is known about "The Seeker of Unceasing Prayer" composed by Father Mikhail Kozlov. The sole source of information about the original redaction is the reference to "The Seeker of Unceasing Prayer" in the correspondence of Archbishop Veniamin of Irkutsk. In his letter of 18 March 1881 he reports independent information concerning the manuscript composed by Father Mikhail Kozlov: "The Seeker of Unceasing Prayer" is "tales of a certain pilgrim" that relate how the narrator initially performed a great many prostrations by himself without guidance and then "under the guidance of an elder performed thousands of prostrations with the Jesus Prayer." This became his preferred method for acquiring unceasing prayer, since "he [the narrator—A. P.] indicates no other method for acquiring the prayer." Finding their way into Father Mikhail Kozlov's text were also "the pilgrim's references to sermons" which Archbishop Veniamin "understood to mean that he [the narrator—A. P.] did not find in them what his soul was searching for," that is, explanations of the apostle's words about unceasing prayer. The experiences of unceasing prayer were portrayed "in persons, in simple and lively conversations."[48]

All the elements entering into the composition of the text being described by Archbishop Veniamin are contained in "The Tale of a Pilgrim, a Seeker of Prayer" (Optino redaction) as well. But Archbishop Veniamin expressly noted that in Father Kozlov's manuscript there was no mention of "the external effects of the prayer of the heart,"[49] the description of which constitutes one of the characteristic features of the Four Tales of a Pilgrim. This key observation by Archbishop Veniamin compels us to return to the text of the Optino redaction, the earliest known redaction of the Four Tales of a Pilgrim.

On the face of it the text of "The Tale of a Pilgrim, a Seeker of Prayer" seems to be sufficiently homogeneous; all the large and small tales are linked to each other, creating the appearance of integrity (we note that even the texts of the printed editions of 1881, 1883, and 1884 provoked no doubts among readers and researchers). Nevertheless, analysis of the text draws attention to independent repetitions in the depiction of the sensations and effects of the Jesus prayer as well as in the exposition of the technique for its performance. Consequently the text under consideration is not homogeneous; there existed a special source underlying the repetitive passages or the textual fragments close to each other. This source is "The Recollection of a Life of Prayer of Elder Vasilisk, a Monk and Hermit in the Siberian Forests"[50] written in the form of a missive to a certain beloved brother in Christ. "The Recollection" contains annotated descriptions of various effects of the Jesus prayer experienced by Elder Vasilisk of Turinsk and his disciple, Petr Michurin, as well as a collection of "the results of interior prayer" made on the basis of the Slavonic text of the *Philokalia*.

A comparison of the text of "The Recollection of a Life of Prayer of Elder Vasilisk, a Monk and Hermit in the Siberian Forests" with "The Tale of a Pilgrim, a Seeker of Prayer" (Optino redaction) leads to the conclusion that precisely this text was one of the basic sources for the additions made to the original text of Father Mikhail Kozlov. The following segments trace their origin to "The Recollection of a Life of Prayer of Elder Vasilisk": the description of the twelve-thousand rule in the First Tale; the systematization of the delightful effects of the Jesus prayer and the discussions concerning "saving pretense" in the conversation with the peasant girl in the Second Tale; the pilgrim's great quotation from the holy fathers and the reference to the prayers of Indian and Bukharan monks in the conversation with the manager in the Second Tale; the descriptions of the effects and sensations produced by the Jesus prayer, among which figure sweetness, pain, warmth, a sweet bubbling heat, the prayer's warming effect in the cold.

Thus, the Four Tales of a Pilgrim differed substantially from Father Mikhail Kozlov's "Seeker of Unceasing Prayer." These differences, however, cannot be reduced to simple additions or borrowings from various sources, one of which was "The Recollection of a Life of Prayer of Elder Vasilisk." As a result of the compiler's labor, all the additions became integral parts of a new text, itself the result of significant reworking of the original text. It is possible to expose all the additions and alterations introduced into the original text only through a comparison with Father Kozlov's "Seeker of Unceasing Prayer." Unfortunately, the location of that text is unknown. Nevertheless, on the basis of the borrowings already detected, it is now possible to assert that Father Kozlov's original text was significantly shorter.

The features of the textual history of the Pilgrim's Tales examined above permit the isolation of two layers of text in the Four Tales: the primary text (first layer) belonging especially to "A Seeker of Unceasing Prayer" (authorial redaction of Father Mikhail Kozlov), and a supplementary text (second layer), belonging to the compiler of the Four Tales. These conclusions, based on textual criteria, are corroborated by an analysis of the doctrine of the Jesus prayer contained in the Four Tales. Here too a two-layered structure may be detected: the first layer contains the basis for the vocal Jesus prayer and various examples, while the second layer exposes the doctrine and describes the experience of the Jesus prayer in the mind or heart. Moreover, we observe a correspondence between the layers, themselves defined on the following basis: the adherence of the texts to the original or later redactions, and the description of the various types of Jesus prayer.

The first layer, in which the vocal Jesus prayer is described, contains an account of the pilgrim's quest for an explanation of the apostle's words on unceasing prayer, followed by some simple and vivid examples of the vocal Jesus prayer; these include a tale about deliverance from temptation in the inn or the old woman pilgrim's tale about how she was miraculously saved from assault

on the forest road. This layer corresponds to the first, fundamental layer, determined on the basis of textual criteria. Thus, it
belongs to "A Seeker of Unceasing Prayer," the authorial redaction
of Father Kozlov. The original text expounded the doctrine of the
vocal Jesus prayer alone; the beginning of the First Tale attests to
this too. In his very first words the pilgrim reports that his entire
possessions consist of a sack of bread crusts and a Bible with which
he checked everything he heard during sermons and conversations. The pilgrim does not mention the *Philokalia*, which was his
basic guide for the mental Jesus prayer. The first reference to the
Philokalia appears only in the concluding section of the First Tale,
but in the Second and Fourth Tales, which give an account of the
intellective Jesus prayer in the heart, the *Philokalia* becomes the pilgrim's basic book. It is noteworthy that Mikhail Kozlov (in religion,
Meletii) describes in one of his books the practice of just this vocal
Jesus prayer, which in many ways assisted his conversion from the
Old Ritualists[51] to the Russian Orthodox Church.[52] The conversion
determined the subsequent life and activity of Father Kozlov whose
principal occupation became missionary work among the Old
Ritualists. It is likely that even then he did not abandon the vocal
Jesus prayer, but missionary activity is scarcely compatible with the
practice of the intellective Jesus prayer in the heart, a necessary
condition of which is solitude.

The second layer of text of the Four Tales of a Pilgrim has
to do with the Jesus prayer operating in the mind or heart.
This layer originates chiefly in "The Recollection of a Life of
Prayer of Elder Vasilisk" and belongs not to Father Mikhail
Kozlov but to the compiler of the Four Tales, who was familiar
with the practice of the mental Jesus prayer. The text of "A
Seeker of Unceasing Prayer," containing the basis and description of the practice of the Jesus prayer in the mind, was the
ready form into which the compiler of the Four Tales only
needed to pour new contents associated with the mental Jesus
prayer. Given the absence of the text of "A Seeker of Unceasing
Prayer," however, it is practically impossible to divide the text
into two independent layers or parts, inasmuch as neither layer

exists independently of the other in the text of the Four Tales but each passes smoothly and almost imperceptibly into the other.

To conclude this discussion, some brief biographical information about Archimandrite Mikhail Kozlov, the author of the original text ("A Seeker of Unceasing Prayer"), is in order. Makarii Kozlov was born around 1826 in the town of Sychevka, Smolensk province, in a family of Old Ritualists. In 1846 he joined the Orthodox Church, thanks largely to the influence of Archpriest Matfei Konstantinovskii, the father confessor of N. V. Gogol'. In 1854 Makarii Kozlov became a postulant in the Edinoverie[53] monastery of the Protection of the Theotokos in Starodub'e, Chernigov province. In 1857 he transferred to the Russian monastery of St. Panteleimon on Mount Athos, where in 1858 he was tonsured as a novice and received the name Meletii. In 1860 his first book, *Letters to my Friends from Mount Athos*,[54] was published. That same year Meletii was sent to Russia to collect offerings for the monastery. In 1864 he returned to Mount Athos, where on 29 October 1866 he was tonsured into the little habit and received the name Mikhail. In 1874 Mikhail Kozlov returned to Russia, was ordained to the priesthood, and entered the monastery of the Theotokos in Sviiazhsk in the eparchy of Kazan. There he took up missionary activity throughout the eparchy among the Old Ritualists. It is noteworthy that at the same time and in the same eparchy Hegumen Paisii Fedorov, the superior of the monastery of St. Michael the Archangel and future editor of the Pilgrim's Tales, devoted himself to missionary activity among the Cheremis. In 1879 Father Mikhail was elevated to the rank of archimandrite and appointed superior of Holy Trinity monastery in Selenginsk. He then headed the Trans-Baikal Mission to the Old Ritualists. Archimandrite Mikhail Kozlov died on 30 January 1884.[55]

* * *

It is appropriate to examine separately the question concerning the authorship of "The Recollection of a Life of Prayer of Elder Vasilisk, a Monk and Hermit in the Siberian Forests," which was used to supplement "A Seeker of Unceasing Prayer." The primary sources for "The Recollection" are the works of

Zosima Verkhovskii, a disciple of Elder Vasilisk: a manuscript entitled "A Narration concerning the Effects of the Prayer of the Heart of Elder Vasilisk the Hermit,"[56] and the biographies of Elder Vasilisk and Petr Michurin published in 1849.[57] Yet another source is the Slavonic version of the *Philokalia*.[58]

"The Recollection of a Life of Prayer of Elder Vasilisk, a Monk and Hermit in the Siberian Forests" may be reliably dated to the fifties of the nineteenth century, since it was this text to which Elder Makarii of Optino referred in his famous "Warning to the readers of spiritual books of the fathers and to those wishing to study the mental Jesus Prayer." At the beginning of his "Warning," Elder Makarii notes that one of the two reasons that induced him to write his "Warning" was "the manuscript of an unknown author in which are explained various effects of prayer and spiritual consolations which the Siberian elder, Vasilisk, contrived <...>. Although the manuscript is found in the hands of only a few people and is known only to the odd person, still it is impossible to remain silent about it. It is written convincingly, its evidence adapted from books of the fathers."[59] A biography of Elder Makarii reveals that he wrote his "Warning" shortly before his death in 1860.[60] There is no doubt that "the manuscript of an unknown writer" was in fact "The Recollection of a Life of Prayer of Elder Vasilisk, a Monk and Hermit in the Siberian Forests," since the "Narration concerning the Effects of the Prayer of the Heart of the Elder Vasilisk the Hermit," compiled by Zosima Verkhovskii contained only the description of seventy-five effects of prayer and did not have any "evidence from the books of the fathers" (that is, the *Philokalia*), which attracted the particular attention of Elder Makarii of Optino.

As follows from the text of his "Warning," Elder Makarii did not know "the unknown writer" who compiled "the manuscript" about which it was "impossible to remain silent," but in the "manuscript" itself the name of the author was absent. We observe that the name of the author is not indicated in the copy of "The Recollection" known to us and preserved in the Bibliothèque Slave de Paris. Therefore, in the absence of direct information about the authorship of "The Recollection," one of the possible methods for attributing the text is to compare it with similar compositions dedicated to the Jesus prayer, or thematically linked with the Jesus prayer.

First of all, we ought to point to the affinity of the separate fragments from "The Recollection of a Life of Prayer of Elder Vasilisk, a Monk and Hermit in the Siberian Forests" with the collection of letters to a certain "beloved brother" that are united under the general title "On the Christian Enjoyment of Life on Earth." A copy of this work was kept in the manuscript collection of the Optino hermitage.[61] Peculiarities of the interrelation of the fragments that coincide with or are close to each other bear witness not only to the priority of the letters "On the Christian Enjoyment of Life" with respect to "The Recollection," but also indicate that these texts belong to one compiler. The letters are dated 1859–1861, but the name of the compiler is missing.

As indicated on the first leaf of the manuscript and as follows from the text itself, the letters are the eighth part of a certain "Ascetical Miscellany," which was probably a selection of works dedicated to prayer and asceticism. The seventh of the fifteen parts comprising the "Ascetical Miscellany" has been preserved in the manuscript collection of Optino hermitage, and is a treatise entitled "The Doctrine of Prayer."[62] It contains a theoretical introduction and a description of the techniques for performing the Jesus prayer, as well as a description of the gracious effects that arise during its performance. On the last leaf of the manuscript is found the entry "Excerpts from Orthodox Fathers of the Greek Church concerning Interior Prayer, collected by the unworthy Arsenii in the month of March, 1827, while he was living in St. Simon monastery. Begun on 8 March, in the second week of the Fast, the day after my humble cell burned down."[63] This date is mistaken, since in 1827 the second week of the Great Fast was 21–27 February, and 8 March was Tuesday of the fourth week of the Great Fast. An entry found in the autobiographical "Notes for my sinful, accursed and feeble memory," compiled from 1824 to 1828 by a certain Valentin Troepol'skii, a resident of the St. Simon monastery in Moscow, allows us to eliminate the copyist's error and to give a more accurate date for the composition of the Treatise on Prayer. In the midst of events for the year 1827 the following was noted: "The same year, on Tuesday of the third week of the Holy Fast, God visited upon me a trial, revealed by divine dispensation in the burning of my humble cell. After this I put together a book on the Jesus Prayer, which was completed on 4 March with the blessing of my beneficent elder. Lord Jesus Christ, Son of God, have mercy on me a sinner!"[64]

In 1827 Tuesday of the third week of the Great Fast fell on 1 March. Thus, the "Book about the Jesus Prayer," which is the same as the "Treatise on Prayer" from the "Ascetical Miscellany," was compiled between 2 and 4 March 1827. Because the contents of these two entries coincide, there is no reason at all to doubt that they refer to one and the same event and that they were written by one and the same person. Consequently, the compiler of the autobiographical remarks, Valentin Troepol'skii, who entered the Moscow St. Simon monastery in May 1825 and whose cell caught fire on 1 March 1827, and the "unworthy Arsenii" who composed the "Treatise on Prayer" in 1827 in St. Simon monastery, are one and the same person. The compiler of the "Treatise on Prayer" (the seventh part of "An Ascetical Miscellany") was the monk Arsenii (born Valentin) Troepol'skii.

The thematic and stylistic affinity of the "Treatise on Prayer" with the letters "On the Christian Enjoyment of Life on Earth" on the one hand, and their belonging to "An Ascetical Miscellany" on the other hand permit us to surmise that Arsenii Troepol'skii owned not only the seventh part of "An Ascetical Miscellany" but also its other parts, for example, the letters "On the Christian Enjoyment of Life on Earth," and that he put together the entire collection.

In order to corroborate this assumption, it is necessary to turn to the other compositions known to be the work of Arsenii Troepol'skii. The manuscript collection of Holy Resurrection-New Jerusalem monastery contains the autograph of "Four Books on Prayer" compiled by Arsenii Troepol'skii.[65] In the first book, "On Prayer in General," a definition of prayer is given and an etymological analysis of the word for prayer in different languages is undertaken. The second book is dedicated to interior prayer in various religious traditions of the East and West. The third book contains a brief essay on the history of interior prayer. Among the practitioners of mental prayer in the sixteenth century the compiler mentions the Spaniard Ignatius of Loyola, who was "a former soldier turned monk" and "established the Jesuit order."[66] The fourth and concluding book is devoted to a defense of interior prayer against various objections and attacks.

One more collection of letters compiled by Arsenii Troepol'skii and dealing with various themes such as interior prayer, inner quietude, and the remembrance of death is found in a manuscript from the library of Optino hermitage.[67] Included in this collection are "A Letter on the Fruitfulness of Observing Useful Thoughts," twenty-seven letters grouped under the title "Arguments for Taking Up Interior Prayer," "Letters containing a reminder about attentiveness, in which is depicted its necessity, methods and possibility," "Letters on spiritual dryness wherein methods for overcoming it and preservation from despondency are portrayed," "Letters on visiting God's temple, wherein are presented the need for this and its usefulness," "Letters on the remembrance of death, containing an incentive to practice it," and "An observation about edifying thoughts relating to inner quietude." These letters were composed in different Russian monasteries and are dated between 1834 and 1859. Those dated 1858 and 1859 were written in "the monastery of Venerable Pafnutii," which we may identify as the monastery of Saint Pafnutii Borovskii in Kaluga province. The archives of this monastery have preserved some brief biographical information about the monk Arsenii that coincides with what is contained in the Letters, autobiographical remarks and other compositions of Arsenii (Valentin) Troepol'skii.

Arsenii, the infirmarian priest-monk of Pafnutii Borovskii monastery in Kaluga province, was born in 1804 of a noble family. He studied at the Philological Faculty of Moscow University. In 1826 he became a postulant to the Moscow monastery of St. Simon, where on 3 March he received monastic tonsure. On 12 January 1831 he was ordained a deacon and in 1832, to the priesthood. In August 1833 he was appointed to the Kozel'sk Optino hermitage, and in 1835 transferred to the Kievan Caves Lavra. In

January 1837 he was moved to the Trinity-St. Sergius hermitage not far from St. Petersburg, whose superior at the time was Archimandrite Ignatii Brianchaninov; however, in December of the same year Arsenii was transferred to Zaikonospasskii monastery in Moscow. In 1842 he was moved to St. Simon monastery in Moscow, where he carried out the duties of sub-prior. On 12 September 1847 he was appointed to the St. Savva Visherskii monastery in Novgorod province. While there, Arsenii was sent on official business to a squadron of the Baltic fleet at sea, where he was chaplain for one of the units. In 1852 he was appointed to the Balaklava St. George monastery in Crimea and in 1854 he was transferred to St. Nicholas monastery in Maloiaroslavl in Kaluga province. From there he was moved on 16 March 1857 to Pafnutii Borovskii monastery. In this monastery Arsenii spent the last part of his arduous life.[68] He died on 7 July 1870 in the village of Naro-Fominskoe in the Vereiskii district of Moscow province (modern-day Naro-Fominsk in Moscow region).[69]

The coincidence of biographical information and of textual fragments allows us to attribute to Arsenii Troepol'skii one more text dedicated to the Jesus prayer: "The Candid Missive of an eremitic Anchorite to his Elder and Mentor in Interior Prayer."[70] This work was composed at the beginning of 1870 and represents the final composition of Arsenii Troepol'skii. It contains a description of his own lifelong practice of the Jesus prayer. Written on the basis of journal entries and earlier works, "The Candid Missive" begins with a description of his experiences with the Jesus prayer that took place in the summer of 1833 in Optino hermitage. The biographical information contained in the text—for example, a reference to the death of his father, information about his moving from one monastery to another, as well as the list of basic events in his life appended to the end of the manuscript[71]—fully coincides with the facts of Arsenii Troepol'skii's life. In addition to this, the text of "The Candid Missive" mentions his compiling four books on prayer. These books should be associated with the "Four Books on Prayer" examined above.

A few times in "The Candid Missive" Arsenii Troepol'skii alludes to the biography of Elder Vasilisk and to a description of how he practiced prayer. In one of those references, the description of the effects of prayer bears the title "A Description of Elder V[asilisk]'s Visions in Prayer and of many fathers of the Philokalia, presented in their totality," and it is also mentioned that this text belongs to "An Ascetical Miscellany." Following this reference Troepol'skii cites a fragment of a description of three types of delights in prayer (reflected in feelings, in the spirit, and in revelations), which resembles the corresponding passage from "The Recollection of the Life of Prayer of Elder Vasilisk."[72] "The Description of Visions in Prayer" referred to in "The Candid Missive" and "The Recollection of the Life of Prayer of Elder Vasilisk" are undoubtedly one and the same text.

"The Candid Missive" did not remain unanswered. At the end of the manuscript is found "The Mentor's Answer to the Candid Missive of His Disciple"[73] the text of which matches in many ways letter 23 from "Arguments for Taking Up Interior Prayer," a miscellany of letters by Arsenii Troepol'skii.[74]

Thus, the priest-monk Arsenii Troepol'skii, who wandered across Russia from monastery to monastery in the second third of the nineteenth century, is the compiler of "A Treatise on Prayer," "Four Books on Prayer," "The Recollection of the Life of Prayer of Elder Vasilisk," "The Candid Missive," and other works devoted to prayer in general and to the Jesus prayer in particular, as well as a series of works with ascetical themes, such as the letters "On the Christian Enjoyment of Life on Earth." A feature of the literary creations of Arsenii Troepol'skii is the absence of the author's name in practically all of his compositions.

The attribution of "The Recollection of the Life of Prayer of Elder Vasilisk" and the exposure of other works belonging to Arsenii Troepol'skii permits some serious refinements in the existing suppositions about the origin of the Four Tales of a Pilgrim. First of all, in comparing the Pilgrim's Tales and the works of Arsenii Troepol'skii it is impossible not to notice their affinity and the similarity of style. This cannot be accounted for on the basis of simple borrowings from "The Recollection of the Life of Prayer of Elder Vasilisk," composed by Arsenii Troepol'skii. For a more precise characterization of the interrelationship between the Pilgrim's Tales and the works of Arsenii Troepol'skii, we should compare the text of the Optino redaction, which is the earliest known redaction of the Four Tales, with the texts of Arsenii Troepol'skii.

As has already been observed, the work entitled "A Seeker of Unceasing Prayer" composed by Father Mikhail Kozlov did not contain any descriptions of the external effects of the Jesus prayer; the descriptions of these effects found in the Four Tales of a Pilgrim derive from "The Recollection of the Life of Prayer of Elder Vasilisk" of Arsenii Troepol'skii. "The Recollection," however, was not the only text of Arsenii Troepol'skii used in the composition of the Four Tales. For example, in the Fourth Tale there is the narrative about a blind man of prayer who was a tailor before losing his sight and who used to say the vocal Jesus prayer, which he learned about in the *Philokalia*. In the miscellany of letters on the Jesus prayer, "Arguments for Taking Up Interior Prayer," compiled by Arsenii Troepol'skii, there is a catalogue of "the miraculous effects of invoking the name of Jesus Christ." Under number 10 the following "effect" is noted: "A peasant tailor who, while reading a book on prayer would utter the name of Jesus Christ, became a man of prayer."[75] There can be no doubt that the catalogue predates the Pilgrim's Tales, since it entered the body of a letter dated 23 June 1851. Furthermore, the instructions of an elder concerning the Jesus prayer from the First Tale of a Pilgrim very closely resembles the style and content of the instructions about the Jesus prayer in the biography of Elder Ilarion by Arsenii Troepol'skii. Ilarion was the father confessor of St. Simon monastery and Arsenii's teacher.[76]

The affinity of the texts by Arsenii Troepol'skii and the Four Tales of a Pilgrim did not happen by chance. To all appearances, Arsenii Troepol'skii was familiar with the text composed by Father Mikhail Kozlov. In "The Candid Missive" there is a reference to his reading a certain text at the end of 1862 that was devoted to the vocal Jesus prayer. "At the end of December [1862], while reading <...> a description of the graces which unexpectedly result from invoking the name of Jesus Christ, at different times and in different places, I was startled by the power of the name of Jesus and the Father's divine mercy, recalling that in all the cases mentioned the Jesus prayer had been uttered externally, only with the lips, without an intensification of one's attentiveness or its being absorbed in the heart, and that even with distraction <...> it revealed such tangible and swift boons!"[77]

The opinion of Arsenii Troepol'skii about the "description" that he read coincides in many respects with the characterization of the composition of Father Mikhail Kozlov made by Archbishop Veniamin of Irkutsk. This allows us to associate the anonymous "description of the graces which unexpectedly result from invoking the name of Jesus Christ" with Father Mikhail Kozlov's "Seeker of Unceasing Prayer." But Arsenii Troepol'skii was familiar not only with the original redaction of the Pilgrim's Tales ("A Seeker of Unceasing Prayer"). He thoroughly knew the text of the Four Tales as well, evidence of which is given in the borrowings from the Pilgrim's Tales found in "The Candid Missive." The description of the experiences of performing the Jesus prayer vocally and of moving on to its mental performance, and also the description of some effects of grace produced by the Jesus prayer in the hermitage of the St. Savva Visherskii monastery from "The Candid Missive" originate in the concluding part of the First Tale.[78] Furthermore, the same method was used to compose the Four Tales that Arsenii Troepol'skii used when he wrote "The Recollection of the Life of Prayer of Elder Vasilisk": the existing text, chosen as the basis of the new text, was supplemented and reworked, and fragments of his own compositions were used for the additions. This method was typical for Arsenii Troepol'skii, for he used it also when composing other works, such as various letters and "The Candid Missive."

Facts about Arsenii Troepol'skii, his works and their mutual interrelationships on the one hand, and the material about the Four Tales of a Pilgrim and their correlation with the works of Arsenii Troepol'skii on the other hand, provide a sufficient basis for determining the authorship of the Four Tales of a Pilgrim. To demonstrate this we will select three texts from those examined above: "The Recollection of the Life of Prayer of Elder Vasilisk," the Four Tales of a Pilgrim, and "The Candid Missive."

Not only does a common subject matter—namely, prayer, the Jesus prayer, and different types of Jesus prayer—unite the three texts; they also demonstrate a single method of composition and textual parallels. With respect to their time of creation, the texts follow one another chronologically. Fragments of the preceding text are used in each subsequent text. The first and third texts, that is, "The Recollection of the Life of Prayer of Elder Vasilisk" and "The Candid Missive," belong to Arsenii Troepol'skii. Therefore, the second text, the Four Tales of a Pilgrim in the Optino redaction, also belongs to Arsenii Troepol'skii.[79]

The analysis of the texts published in the appendix to the first printed edition of the Pilgrim's Tales (Kazan, 1881) supports our conclusion about the authorship of Arsenii Troepol'skii. In the appendix of the 1881 edition several texts were published that contain instructions on the Jesus prayer:

1) Three keys to the inner treasure of prayer (found in the spiritual riches of the holy fathers);[80]

2) An instruction of the holy fathers on how to sink inside oneself, that is, how to bring the mind into the heart and to keep one's attention there, so that one may pray with the heart unceasingly and attain holy sweetness in interior prayer;[81]

3) Observations during a repeated reading of the fathers on interior prayer, dated 16 February 1849;[82]

4) The Instruction on attentiveness, dated 10 December 1848.[83]

Three of these texts can be confidently attributed to Arsenii Troepol'skii. Thus, in "The Candid Missive" repeated mention is made of "Three keys to the inner treasure of prayer" that are repeatedly proved by practical action.[84] "The Instructions of the holy fathers on how to sink inside oneself" belong to Arsenii Troepol'skii, since the description of the practical methods for performing the Jesus prayer given in this Instruction coincide with the corresponding text from "The Recollection of the Life of Prayer of Elder Vasilisk."[85] Finally, "The Instruction on Attentiveness" also belongs to him, because the information presented at the beginning of this text concerning the place and time of its composition coincides with facts from his life. "The Instructions on

Attentiveness" were written down on 10 December 1848 in "the monastery of venerable Savva," after he returned from his tour of duty with the Russian fleet in the Baltic Sea.[86] In addition to this, "The Instructions on Attentiveness" that were incorporated into the "Ascetical Miscellany" refer to "The Candid Missive."[87]

Thus, the editor of the first Kazan edition of the Pilgrim's Tales, Hegumen Paisii Fedorov, had at his disposal not only a copy of one of the redactions of the Pilgrim's Tales but also other works by Arsenii Troepol'skii. Among them undoubtedly was "The Candid Missive," since the title of the first Kazan edition of 1881, "The Candid Tale of a Pilgrim to his Spiritual Father," echoes the title of the final work of Arsenii Troepol'skii, "The Candid Missive of an eremitical Anchorite to his Elder and Mentor in Interior Prayer."

Hegumen Paisii Fedorov's familiarity with "The Candid Missive" allows us to formulate our theory about the origin of the reference to the Athonite "elder–monk of the great habit,"[88] found in the foreword to the second Kazan edition of 1883, in whose cell the Pilgrim's Tales were copied.[89] This reference sometimes serves as the basis for identifying the Athonite "elder–monk of the great habit" with Archimandrite Mikhail Kozlov, author of "A Seeker of Unceasing Prayer." In fact, in 1867–1869 Paisii Fedorov was twice on Mount Athos: from 16 June to 3 November 1867, and from 14 August 1868 until 25 April 1869. In his travel journal he noted that on 24 September 1868 a meeting took place with a certain monk of the great habit, Mikhail, who had earlier been an Old Ritualist.[90] It is possible that this monk of the great habit was Father Mikhail Kozlov. If, however, Paisii Fedorov copied the text published in 1881 while with Mikhail Kozlov, he must have copied and edited the text of the authorial redaction of Mikhail Kozlov. But as was shown above, the text of the Pilgrim's Tales compiled by Arsenii Troepol'skii was used for the 1881 edition. Thus, Mikhail Kozlov could not be the "elder–monk of the great habit" to whom belonged the manuscript of the Pilgrim's Tales copied by Paisii Fedorov.

The information reported in the foreword belongs to Paisii Fedorov, but an analysis of the contents of the foreword demon-

strates that we have sufficient grounds for handling this information with caution. For example, while discussing the circumstances that compelled the pilgrim to relate his search for unceasing prayer, the author of the foreword insists that when the pilgrim stopped in Irkutsk and "had some free time, in keeping with
his custom and need he searched for and found a spiritual
father,"[91] an issue that became the motive for all four tales.
However, the author of the foreword had knowledge of the manuscript where there were no allusions of any sort to a spiritual
father. Further ground for doubting the existence of the Athonite
"elder–monk of the great habit" is the allusion to him found in
the foreword to the edition containing the text redacted by Bishop
Feofan the Recluse. It cannot be ruled out that reference to the
manuscript's origin on Mount Athos and to an Athonite elder
would have confirmed the authenticity of the published text and
that the appearance of this reference could be linked with the
wish or instruction of the redactor.

Nevertheless, it seems that the reason that there is an allusion to the Athonite elder in the foreword lies in the works of
Arsenii Troepol'skii. As has already been noted, "The Candid
Missive" and the other works by Arsenii Troepol'skii used by
Hegumen Paisii Fedorov were anonymous, but the elder's answer
to his disciple's missive makes mention of their joint presence on
Mount Athos.[92] This allusion too could underlie the suggestion
that "The Candid Missive" and, accordingly, other works dedicated to the Jesus prayer, belonged to one of the Athonite monks.
Similar suggestions evidently were a certain ground for the ensu-
ing conclusion that the Pilgrim's Tales were transcribed in the cell
of an Athonite "elder–monk of the great habit."

At the present time it does not seem possible to indicate
where and when Hegumen Paisii Fedorov received the manuscript
of the Pilgrim's Tales for his edition. Still, the suggestion that this
manuscript originated on Mount Athos cannot be eliminated since
it is known that the Athonite monastery of St. Panteleimon acted
as patron for the monastery of St. Michael the Archangel, whose
hegumen was Paisii Fedorov. One piece of evidence of this patron-
age is the gift of an icon of the holy megalomartyr Panteleimon and

a particle of his relics, which the Athonite monastery sent to the Cheremis monastery in 1873.[93] In the same way, some manuscripts of the works of Arsenii Troepol'skii could also have been sent, including the Pilgrim's Tales, provided that these texts were known to the Athonite monks.

* * *

The history of the text of the Four Tales of a Pilgrim, composed by Arsenii Troepol'skii, did not come to an end with the appearance of new printed and manuscript redactions, that is, the 1884 edition (redaction of Bishop Feofan the Recluse) and the Sergiev redaction. In 1911 Bishop Nikon (Rozhdestvenskii) of Vologda and Tot'ma published a compilation containing three new supplementary tales of the pilgrim.[94] These tales were published on the basis of a manuscript copy discovered in the papers of Elder Amvrosii of Optino.[95] Unfortunately, the manuscript used by Bishop Nikon has not been preserved, and it is possible to judge it only on the basis of the published text, which belongs to a later redaction in comparison to the text of three supplemental tales from a manuscript recently transferred to the Optino hermitage.[96] The manuscript, which was returned to the monastery, was discovered in the cell of the priest-monk Rafail (Sheichenko), spiritual son of Optino Elder Nektarii and one of the last monks in the Optino hermitage. He passed away on 19 July 1957 in the town of Kozel'sk.

The newly discovered manuscript redaction differs substantially from the one published in 1911. In the Fifth Tale there is an instruction "On the Intonation of the Jesus Prayer," which is missing from the printed text, and in the place of "The Confession of an Interior Person"[97] is found a brief instruction on the Jesus prayer from the Florilegium of Abba Dorotheos.[98] In the Sixth Tale are found discussions of the special grace "imparted" to objects and words, as well as a reference to the book *Magnum Speculum*,[99] which are missing from the printed text. The Seventh Tale contains a fragment of a text, missing from the printed edition, in which magnetic attraction is likened to the attraction of spirits.[100] And finally, the text of a prayer for one's neighbors from the concluding part of this tale does not coincide with the text of the prayer published in 1911.[101]

From their composition and stylistic features, the three supplementary tales, despite the presence of evident thematic links, are easily divided into two approximately equal parts: the Fifth Tale, which contains the pilgrim's narrative concerning events that occurred since the time of his "last" meeting, and the Sixth–Seventh Tale, which contains various dialogues about prayer where the pilgrim figures as an interlocutor. But despite this division and independently of their belonging to the manuscript or printed redactions, both the Fifth and the Sixth–Seventh Tales occupy a similar position with respect to all the works of Arsenii Troepol'skii and to the text of the four basic Pilgrim's Tales. It is, of course, beyond doubt that each of these parts is secondary with respect to the four tales; however, the fact that each part has common elements that are found in the works of Arsenii Troepol'skii leads to some unexpected conclusions. Let us examine in more detail the texts of the supplementary tales.

It is not difficult to notice that the Fifth Tale has a definite stylistic similarity with the first four tales and offers a new tale of the pilgrim about events that happened over the course of the year following the "fourth meeting" on 23 December 1859. As was true of the Fourth Tale, one of the sources of the Fifth Tale is the already-alluded-to catalogue of "miraculous effects from invoking the name of Jesus Christ," compiled by Arsenii Troepol'skii. In number 7 of this catalogue the following "miraculous effect" is noted: "A shepherd who was searching for his ewe and lost his way in the forest at night, unwittingly received the gift of prayer."[102] The village shepherd's tale about unexpectedly discovering the gift of the Jesus prayer from the Fifth Tale is obviously dependent on the short entry in the catalogue of "miraculous effects," but the image itself of the kneeling shepherd youth and his narrative about the pilgrim's presence in Kiev derive from a source that is independent of the works of Arsenii Troepol'skii. This source was the narrative about Saint Serafim of Sarov, widely disseminated in Russian spiritual literature. The beginning section of "A Story about the life and ascetic feats of Elder Serafim," composed by one of the elder's disciples, contains a description of the pilgrimage to Kiev of the young Prokhor (the secular name of Elder Serafim), during which he visited Dosifei the Recluse, who was practicing asceticism in the Kitaev hermitage and received from him an instruction concerning the Jesus prayer and a blessing to stay in the Sarov hermitage.[103] The narrative from the Fifth Tale about the pilgrim's stay in Kiev follows the plot line of the biography of Elder Serafim: the pilgrim arrives in Kiev, meets his father confessor in the Kitaev hermitage, receives from him an instruction on the Jesus prayer and then, with the blessing of his confessor, sets out for Pochaev Lavra.

If the Fifth Tale seemingly continues the pilgrim's narrative, the Sixth–Seventh Tale has no direct thematic link either with the Fifth Tale or with the first four tales. This is no longer the pilgrim's tale but some dialogues devoted to prayer that are linked with the first four tales only by a common theme and the participation in them of the "pilgrim" and his "spiritual father." In these dialogues the pilgrim is not the principal participant but only listens to the different edifying stories and discussions. He writes down the most interesting of them. To all appearances, it seems that the Sixth and Seventh Tales originally were independent of the Fifth Tale with which they were later united. Once the two texts had been united, the pilgrim's pious traveling companion in the Fifth Tale became the Professor of the Sixth and Seventh Tales or Dialogues. But even here, despite some stylistic differences between Tales One through Four and Tale Five, there are borrowings from the works of Arsenii Troepol'skii. At the beginning of the Sixth Tale the pilgrim is copying gratefully from a small treatise entitled "The Mystery of Salvation, Revealed by Unceasing Prayer" that the monk of the great habit, one of the new participants in the conversation, had read out to his grateful audience. The text of "The Mystery of Salvation" contains quotations from the First Tale, after which follow allusions to a certain "seeker" with a copy of the *Philokalia*, and a "mentor," who reveals to him the mystery contained in the continuousness of the prayer. Consequently, "The Mystery of Salvation" was composed under the immediate influence of the

Four Tales. In the closing section of the Sixth Tale the monk of the great habit is reading one more text that he prudently "carried with him." In reality the monk is reading Letter 24 of Arsenii Troepol'skii from the miscellany of letters "Arguments for Taking Up Interior Prayer,"[104] which, as has been noted, was used in the composition of "The Candid Missive" as well as the Fourth and Fifth Tales.

The consonance and borrowings thus detected cannot be accidental, so it is possible to suppose with sufficient confidence that the three supplementary tales also belong to Arsenii Troepol'skii. Nevertheless, a definitive answer to the complicated question about the authorship of the supplementary tales can be given only after bringing to light and carefully studying all the works of Arsenii Troepol'skii.

* * *

At the present time it is difficult to characterize fully the influence of the Pilgrim's Tales and other works of Arsenii Troepol'skii on Russian spiritual literature of the end of the nineteenth and beginning of the twentieth centuries. The manuscript portion of this extensive literature is practically unstudied, and a preliminary catalogue does not even exist for the printed editions. Even now, however, it is impossible not to notice the influence of the Pilgrim's Tales on the composition and contents of one of the best-known works produced in a monastic circle of Athonite "Idolaters of the Name"—the famous Conversation of Hermit Elders on Inner Union with the Lord through the Jesus Prayer.[105] This was composed by the monk of the great habit Ilarion, a hermit in the Caucasian mountains. Ilarion's composition, first published in 1907 and subsequently reissued on numerous occasions, was one of the reasons for the revival of the polemic around the veneration of the divine name at the beginning of the twentieth century and for the subsequent eviction of a number of monks from the Russian St. Panteleimon monastery on Mount Athos. It is worth noting that the publisher of the three supplementary tales, Bishop Nikon (Rozhdestvenskii),[106] was among the participants in the expedition that was sent to St. Panteleimon monastery in

1913 aboard warships to explain to the monastic Idolaters of the Name the correct doctrine on veneration of the divine name, and which concluded with the eviction of some of the monks.

The Pilgrim's Tales were known not only in monastic circles. At the beginning of 1900, Vladimir Sergeevich Solov'ev presented M. A. Novoselov with "A Pilgrim's Notes," which was cited in the first issue of *A Library of Religious Philosophy* published by M. A. Novoselov.[107] From the textual features of the quotation it appears that Solov'ev gave him a copy of the 1884 edition. This very quotation was used by Pavel Florenskii, a student at the Moscow Clerical Academy, in one of the sections of his thesis.[108] Florenskii soon afterward acquired a copy of the Kazan edition, since in *The Pillar and Confirmation of Truth*, the complete version of his master's thesis, published in 1914, he cites this quotation from the 1884 edition.[109] On the title page of a book belonging to him, Father Pavel included an excerpt from the correspondence of Archbishop Veniamin of Irkutsk, published in 1913, concerning the authorship of Father Mikhail Kozlov. It was this note of Father Pavel that gave rise to Father Vasilii Grolimund's suggestion about the authorship of "The Candid Tales of a Pilgrim."

* * *

The history of the text of the Pilgrim's Tales is typical of Russian spiritual literature of the eighteenth and nineteenth centuries, which originates in the literature of medieval Rus' and continues its traditions. In this essentially medieval literary tradition, texts were not only transcribed or, at a later date, reissued; they were also redacted, supplemented, abbreviated, and used in the composition of new works. One of the typical figures of this literature was that of the pilgrim or wayfarer, journeying toward Jerusalem. The description of a pilgrimage was one of the typical genres, and pilgrimage itself was one of the characteristic phenomena of the Russian Orthodox tradition. Generally speaking, the mystic whose life is dedicated to searching for God is compared with the wayfarer or pilgrim, and the spiritual life is compared with a journey or pilgrimage, both commonplaces in many religious traditions.

In the twelfth century Daniil, "a hegumen of the Rus' land," completed a pilgrimage to Jerusalem, and his "Journey to the Holy Land" was one of the first such descriptions of travel in the Russian literary tradition.[110] Six centuries later, at the beginning of the fifties of the nineteenth century, the Siberian peasant Iakov Lanshakov set off on a journey to Jerusalem. His mystical visions were copied down in 1853 by Alimpii, a priest-monk in the Kievan Caves Lavra.[111] At the same time the monk Parfenii, who likewise called himself a pilgrim, compiled and published his *Stories about my Journey and Travels around Russia, Moldavia, Turkey and the Holy Land*.[112] Converting from Old Ritualism like Father Mikhail Kozlov, Parfenii put together a detailed description of his life and lengthy travels, in which were included both his narrative about the life of a practitioner of the Jesus prayer, Elder Ioann of Moldavia,[113] and his biography of the Siberian ascetic, Elder Daniil of Aginsk.[114] A comparison of the works of Parfenii the monk with the Pilgrim's Tales uncovers many similar elements. For example, Parfenii the monk describes at length his meetings and conversations with Elder Ioann of Moldavia, the practitioner of the Jesus prayer, whose instructions greatly changed his life. At the beginning of his travels, Parfenii completed a pilgrimage to the Kievan Caves Lavra. In this case, however, it is a question of using common traditional themes and not of the influence of one text on the other or of borrowings.

Thus, in the nineteenth century too, pilgrims made their way across Russian territory, carrying on an ancient tradition. They would head for Jerusalem, thereby signifying their quest for and perhaps their discovery of "the city above" on account of which they had abandoned their worldly lives. Of course, their relationship to the wandering mystics was far from simple, but it was precisely the pilgrim, and not the hermit, the recluse, the reverential priest, or the pious peasant who became "a seeker of unceasing prayer." Here both Mikhail Kozlov and Arsenii Troepol'skii were following a stable tradition whose foundation lies in the Christian culture of medieval Rus', which was handed down to the nineteenth century thanks in many respects to the culture of the Old Ritualists.

Old Ritualist culture was familiar to Archimandrite Mikhail Kozlov, the composer of "A Seeker of Unceasing Prayer," since he was born and raised in an Old Ritualist milieu. In the individual apocalyptic-minded Old Ritualist circles, pilgrimage received a particular interpretation. Among the priestless communities, that is, Old Ritualists having neither hierarchy nor priesthood, there were some numerically rather strong communes of clandestine pilgrims who called themselves "the truly Orthodox Christian–Pilgrims."[115] They created an original literary and book-writing tradition which, by virtue of the particular conservatism of its creators, traced its origins directly to Old Russian writing culture. They preserved miscellanies (*florilegia*) of the pilgrims, containing excerpts from the books of Sacred Scripture, works of the holy fathers, historical and literary works. These testify to the great erudition of their compilers.[116]

Literary activity did not cease in the monasteries of the Russian Orthodox Church either. Monks continued to translate, transcribe, and prepare new editions of the works of the holy fathers, and to compile new texts and miscellanies. One of the best-known spiritual and literary centers was the Optino hermitage,[117] to which Arsenii Troepol'skii came in 1833 at the very start of his long journey among the monasteries of Russia and in whose manuscript collection were preserved the texts of the Pilgrim's Tales and his other works. The variety of manuscript and printed redactions of the Pilgrim's Tales and texts derived from them, right up to the monk of the great habit Ilarion's composition about the spiritual activity of hermits, testifies that the Pilgrim's Tales continually attracted the attention of monastic bookmakers. Compiled from the middle of the nineteenth to the beginning of the twentieth centuries by Russian monks who were practitioners of the Jesus prayer, all of these compositions belong to that special and little-known, little-studied circle of Russian spiritual literature. There is documentary evidence of the depth and richness of the Russian spiritual tradition. In these works is concentrated the profound mystical experience of many Russian ascetics, such as St. Serafim of Sarov, whose prayer consisted in the invocation of the name of Jesus Christ. Of course, a central place among these works is occupied by the tales of "a shelterless pilgrim," whose sole possessions consisted of a sack of bread crusts, a Bible, and the *Philokalia*.

* * *

In conclusion, it is fitting to dwell on the history of the text of the Pilgrim's Tales in the twentieth century. In 1930 the publishing house YMCA-Press republished the 1884 Kazan edition, edited with an introductory article by B. P. Vysheslavtsev.[118] This edition has a series of variant readings that are the result of editorial activity, as well as separate misprints and omissions. The second edition was published in 1933 (printed in Riga). The same year in Vladimirova na Slovensku the three supplementary tales were republished, under the editorial supervision of Hegumen Serafim.[119] The published text was also subjected to a systematic correction. In 1948 in Paris, Professor Archimandrite Kiprian Kern united the texts of the first four tales, published under the editorial supervision of B. P. Vysheslavtsev, and the three supplementary tales, published by Hegumen Serafim. He published this compilation with all the changes and misprints introduced into it, under the general title of *Candid Tales of a Pilgrim to His Spiritual Father*. He also added his own foreword.[120] The 1948 edition was reproduced in phototype in 1973 and in 1989 it was supplemented with an afterword by Father Vasilii (Grolimund) and the publication of variant readings from the Panteleimon manuscript and the 1881 edition.

Thus, the text of the Pilgrim's Tales, reissued many times in the twentieth century, not only was not checked against the original, but was also subjected to systematic emendations. Editorial activity in many ways determined the conviction about the poor quality of the Kazan editions, which was formulated by Bishop Nikon thus: "It [the book, here it is a question of the first Kazan edition—A. P.] was published, one can say, in an illiterate fashion; no one took the trouble to correct even grammatical errors."[121] Unfortunately, precisely this "emended" text received the greatest distribution and renown in the West, where translations were made from this text.

What is presented here is a translation of the text of the Optino redaction. A translation of a new redaction of the three supplementary tales is given in the Appendix. These translations are made on the basis of texts published in 1992.[122]

Notes to Introduction

[1] *Otkrovennyi rasskaz strannika dukhovnomu svoemu ottsu* [The candid tale of a pilgrim to his spiritual father] (Kazan, 1881). Hereafter *Tale* 1881.

[2] *Zamechatel'nyi rasskaz o blagodatnykh deistviiakh molitvy Iisusovoi* [The remarkable tale about the grace-giving effects of the Jesus prayer] (Moscow, 1882).

[3] *Otkrovennye rasskazy strannika dukhovnomu svoemu ottsu* [Candid tales of a pilgrim to his spiritual father] (Kazan, 1883). Hereafter *Tales* 1883.

[4] *Otkrovennye rasskazy strannika dukhovnomu svoemu ottsu* [Candid tales of a pilgrim to his spiritual father] (Kazan, 1884). Hereafter *Tales* 1884.

[5] S. Bol'shakov, *Na vysotakh dukha: Delateli molitvy Iisusovoi v monastyriakh i v miru* [On the heights of the Spirit: Practitioners of the Jesus prayer in monasteries and the world] (Brussels, 1971), p. 35.

[6] [The priest-monk or hieromonk is a monk who has received ordination to the presbyterate, normally to meet the liturgical needs of his monastery. A monk with the rank of deacon is known as a deacon-monk or hierodeacon. Trans.]

[7] Bol'shakov, *Na vysotakh dukha*, p. 37 (see n. 5 above).

[8] Priest Vsevolod Roshko, "Neizvestny fragment «Otkrovennykh rasskazov strannika»" [An unknown fragment of "The Candid Tales of a Pilgrim"], in *Simvol* no. 15 (Paris, 1986), pp. 201–8.

[9] *Iz rasskazov strannika o blagodatnom deistvii molitvy Iisusovoi* [From the Pilgrim's Tales about the grace-giving effects of the Jesus prayer] (Sergiev Posad, 1911). Hereafter *From the Tales* 1911.

[10] [An archimandrite originally was a hegumen chosen by a bishop to oversee the monasteries in his eparchy. Very quickly, however, the title was given to the heads of all the large or important monasteries

of an eparchy. In 1174 Polycarp, the hegumen of the Kievan Caves monastery, became the first figure in Russian church history to receive the dignity of archimandrite. Trans.]

[11]Hieromonk Vasilii (Grolimund), "«Otkrovennye rasskazy strannika dukhovnomu svoemu ottsu»—novye otkrytie raznykh redaktsii teksta" ["Candid Tales of a Pilgrim to His Spiritual Father"—New discoveries of different redactions of the text], in *Tysiacheletie Kreshcheniia Rusi. Mezhdunarodnaia nauchnaia tserkovnaia konferentsia «Bogoslovie i dukhovnost' Russkoi Tserkvi», Moskva, 11–18 maia 1987 goda* [The millennium of the baptism of Rus'. An international scholarly church conference "The Theology and Spirituality of the Russian Church," Moscow, 11–18 May, 1987] (Moscow, 1989), p. 319.

[12]K. V. Kharlampovich, "Pis'ma Veniamina, arkhiepiskopa Irkutskogo (+1892) k Kazanskomu arkhiepiskopu Vladimiru" [The letters of Veniamin, Archbishop of Irkutsk (d. 1892) to Archbishop Vladimir of Kazan], in *Chteniia v Imperatorskom obshchestve istorii i drevnostei rossiiskikh* [Readings in the Imperial Society of Russian History and Antiquities], book 4 (247) (Moscow, 1913), pp. 134, 143 (third pagination).

[13]Hieromonk Vasilii (Grolimund), "«Otkrovennye rasskazy strannika dukhovnomu svoemu ottsu»", p. 320 (see n. 11 above).

[14]Hieromonk Vasilii (Grolimund), *Posleslovie* [Afterword], in *Otkrovennye rasskazy strannika dukhovnomu svoemu ottsu* [Candid tales of a pilgrim to his spiritual father], 5th ed. (Paris, 1989), pp. 301–302.

[15]Hieromonk Vasilii (Grolimund), *Glavnye raznochteniia iz pervogo kazanskogo izdaniia 1881 goda i Afonskoi Panteleimonovskoi rukopisi No. 50/4/395* [The principal variant readings from the first Kazan edition of 1881 and the Athos Panteleimon manuscript No. 50/4/395], in *Otkrovennye rasskazy strannika dukhovnomu svoemu ottsu* [Candid tales of a pilgrim to his spiritual father], 5th ed. (Paris, 1989), pp. 311–32.

[16]I. Basin, *"Avtorstvo «Otkrovennykh rasskazov strannika»"* [The authorship of "Candid Tales of a Pilgrim"], in *Simvol* no. 27 (Paris, 1992), pp. 167–90.

[17]*Rasskaz strannika, iskatelia molitvy (Podgotovka teksta i publikatsiia A. Pentkovskogo)* [The tale of a pilgrim, a seeker of prayer. Preparation of the text and publication of A. Pentkovsky], in *Simvol* no. 27 (Paris, 1992), pp. 7–74 [hereafter *Tale* 1992; *Rasskaz piatyi, shestoi, sed'moi (Podgotovka teksta i publikatsiia A. Pentkovskogo)* [The fifth, sixth, and seventh tales. Preparation of the text and publication of A. Pentkovsky], in *Simvol* no. 27 (Paris, 1992), pp. 79–135. Hereafter *The Fifth* 1992.

NOTES TO INTRODUCTION

[18]A. Pentkovsky, "Ot «Iskatelia neprestannoi molitvy» do «Otkrovennykh rasskazov strannika» (k voprosu ob istorii teksta)" [From "A Seeker of Unceasing Prayer" to "Candid Tales of a Pilgrim." The question of the history of a text], in *Simvol* no. 27 (Paris, 1992), pp. 137–66.

[19]The Department of Manuscripts of the Russian State Library (Moscow) [hereafter OR RGB], f. 214 [f. = fond (collection) here and throughout], No. 455 [from the library of the Optino hermitage, the former number: otd. I, No. 65].

[20]OR RGB, f. 214, No. 456 [from the library of the skete of Optino hermitage, the former number: otd. I, No. 239] (see n. 19 above).

[21]*Vmesto predisloviia* [In place of a foreword], in *Tales* 1883, p. 3 (see n. 3 above).

[22]Paris, L'institut Saint Serge, archives of Professor Archimandrite Kiprian Kern, No. A–57, old numbering, 47-2-1.

[23]Library of the Russian monastery of St. Panteleimon on Mount Athos, No. 50/4/395; old numbering, XVII/3/47 or 317/1883.

[24]Hieromonk Vasilii (Grolimund), *Glavnye raznochteniia*, pp. 311–32 (see n. 15 above).

[25]Hieromonk Vasilii (Grolimund), "«Otkrovennye rasskazy strannika dukhovnomu svoemu ottsu»," p. 319 (see n. 11 above).

[26]Hieromonk Vasilii (Grolimund), *Glavnye raznochteniia*, pp. 331–32 (see n. 15 above).

[27]*Zamechatel'nyi rasskaz* (see n. 2 above).

[28]*Tale* 1881, pp. 108–29 (see n. 1 above).

[29]Ibid., p. 45.

[30]*Sobranie pisem sviatitelia Feofana*, vyp. VII [Collection of letters of Bishop Feofan] (Moscow, 1900), p. 164.

[31][Bishop Nikon], *Iz rasskazov strannika*, p. 3 (see n. 9 above).

[32]Kharlampovich, *"Pis'ma Veniamina,"* pp. 134, 143 (third pagination) (see n. 12 above).

[33]*Sobranie pisem Optinskogo startsa ieromonakha Amvrosiia k monashestvuiushchim*, vyp. 2 [A Collection of Letters of the Optino Elder, Hieromonk Amvrosii, to those pursuing the monastic life] (Sergiev Posad, 1909), p. 119.

[34]Hieromonk Amvrosii (Grenkov), *Pis'ma k Leonide (Frizel'), kaznachee Vlakhernskogo Spasskogo monastyria Dmitrovskogo uezda Moskovskoi gubernii* [Letters to Leonida Frizel', bursar of Vlakhernskii Spasskii monastery in the Dmitrov district of Moscow province], OR RGB, f. 213 (archive of the Optino hermitage; see n. 19 above), kart. 55, ed. 4, l. 80–83 ob.; l. 88; l. 90 ob.–91 [ed. = unit, l. = folio, ob. = verso here and throughout].

[35]Ibid., 1. 90 ob.–91 (see n. 34 above).

[36]Ibid., 1. 103 (see n. 34 above).

[37]*Tale* 1881, pp. 4–10 (see n. 1 above). Cf. *Tales* 1883, pp. 5–6 (see n. 3 above). Hereafter the 1884 edition is used for comparison, not the 1883 edition.

[38]Bishop Dmitrii of Rostov, *Sochineniia* [Works], part 1 (Moscow, 1852), pp. 153–54.

[39]*Tale* 1881, p. 12. Cf. *Tales* 1884, p. 7.

[40]*Tale* 1881, pp. 96–98. Cf. *Tales* 1884, pp. 95–96.

[41]*Tale* 1881, p. 99. Cf. *Tales* 1884, p. 97.

[42]*Tale* 1881, pp. 101–3. Cf. *Tales* 1884, p. 99.

[43]*Tale* 1881, p. 45. Cf. *Tales* 1884, pp. 41–45.

[44]*Tales* 1884, p. 61. Cf. *Tale* 1881, p. 61.

[45]*Tales* 1884, p. 66. Cf. *Tale* 1881, p. 66.

[46]*Tales* 1884, p. 68. Cf. *Tale* 1881, p. 68.

[47]*Tales* 1884, p. 103. Cf. *Tale* 1881, p. 107.

[48]Kharlampovich, "Pis'ma Veniamina," pp. 143, 144 (third pagination) (see n. 12 above).

[49]Ibid., p. 144.

[50]"Pamiat' o molitvennoi zhizni startsa Vasiliska, monakha i pustynnika Sibirskikh lesov (Podgotovka teksta i publikatsiia A. Pentkovskogo)," [The recollection of a life of prayer of Elder Vasilisk, a monk and hermit in the Siberian forests. Preparation of the text and publication of A. Pentkovsky], in *Simvol* no. 32 (Paris, 1994), pp. 279–340. Hereafter "Recollection" 1994.

[51][The term "Old Ritualists" or "Old Believers" refers to those members of the Russian Orthodox Church who rejected the reforms of Patriarch Nikon and were condemned at a church council in 1666. Their leader, Avvakum, and many others were burned to death as heretics and criminals in 1682. Adherents fled into the northern forests, where they survived clandestinely. Soon after the schism, the Old Ritualists split into two groups: the priestless sect, or *bespopovtsy*, who renounced the priesthood and sacraments after the last clergy ordained before 1666 died out, and the priest sect, or *popovtsy*, who retained both. A further schism among the Old Ritualists gave rise to the *beglopopovtsy*, who attracted disaffected or fugitive clergy to their cause. In 1847 an important segment of the Old Ritualists retaining the priesthood and sacraments was reorganized by the former Greek Orthodox metropolitan Ambrosios of Sarajevo, who consecrated two bishops for them. The tsarist government continued to persecute and

exile Old Ritualists until an Edict of Tolerance in 1905 granted them official recognition as a religion. That edict also suppressed the term "Schismatic" in favor of their own name, "Old Ritualists." Trans.]

[52]Monk Meletii (Kozlov), *Pis'ma k druz'iam s Afonskoi Gory i razgovor s prezhde byvshimi edinomyslennikami, mnimymi staroobriadtsami, o Pravoslavnoi Tserkvi, ee tainstvakh i obriadakh* [Letters to my friends from Mount Athos and a conversation with my former kindred spirits, alleged Old Ritualists, concerning the Orthodox Church, her mysteries and her rituals], part II (St. Petersburg, 1860), p. 356.

[53][*Edinoverie* (one faith) refers to the segment of Old Ritualists who were compelled by the lack of their own hierarchy to enter into union with the Russian Orthodox Church in 1800. The terms of the union permitted them to retain their old uncorrected liturgical books. Trans.]

[54]Monk Meletii (Kozlov), *Pis'ma k druz'iam s Afonskoi Gory* (see n. 52 above).

[55]*Dvadtsatipiatiletie episkopskogo sluzheniia Vysokopreosviashcheneishego Veniamina, arkhiepiskopa Irkutskogo i Nerchinskogo* [The twenty-fifth anniversary of episcopal service of Most Reverend Veniamin, Archbishop of Irkutsk and Nerchinsk] (Irkutsk, 1888), pp. 56–71; "Pamiati arkhimandrita Mikhaila" [In the memory of archimandrite Mikhail] in *Irkutskie eparkhial'nye vedomosti* [Reports of the diocese of Irkutsk], 1884, no. 10, pp. 125–32.

[56]OR RGB, f. 214, No. 404, 450 (see n. 19 above).

[57]*Zapiski o zhizni i podvigakh Petra Alekseevicha Michurina, monakha i pustynozhitelia Vasiliska, i nekotorye cherty iz zhizni iurodivogo monakha Iony* [Notes on the life and ascetic feats of Petr Alekseevich Michurin, the monk and hermit Vasilisk, and a few traits from the life of the monk Iona, a fool for Christ] (Moscow, 1849).

[58]*Dobrotoliubie ili slovesa i glavizny sviashchennogo trezveniia, sobrannye ot pisanii sviatykh i bogodukhnovennykh otets* [*Philokalia* or discourses and chapters on sacred moderation, collected from the writings of the holy and theopneumatic fathers], 2nd ed. (Moscow, 1822).

[59]Hieromonk of the Great Habit Makarii (Glukhov), *Predosterezhenie chitaiushchim dukhovnye otecheskie knigi i zhelaiushchim prokhodit' umnuiu Iisusovu molitvu* [A Warning to the readers of spiritual books of the fathers and to those wishing to study the Jesus prayer of the mind] in *Sobranie pisem blazhennyia pamiati Optinskogo startsa ieroskhimonakha Makariia (pis'ma k monashestvuiushchim)* [A Collection of the letters of the Optino elder and hieromonk of the great habit, Makarii of blessed

memory (letters to those living the monastic life)] (Moscow, 1862), pp. 361–62.

[60]Hieromonk Leonid (Kavelin), *Skazanie o zhizni i podvigakh blazhennyia pamiati startsa Optinoi pustyni ieroskhimonakha Makariia* [The Story of the Life and Ascetic Feats of the Elder of blessed memory from Optino hermitage, Hieromonk of the Great Habit Makarii] (Moscow, 1861), p. 48.

[61]OR RGB, f. 214, No. 656 (see n. 19 above).

[62]OR RGB, f. 214, No. 655 (see n. 19 above).

[63]Ibid., l. 22 ob. (see n. 34 above).

[64]OR RGB, f. 214, No. 449, l. 97 ob.–98 (see nn. 19 and 34 above).

[65]The Department of Manuscripts of the State Historical Museum, Collection of the Voskresenskii monastery, No. 147. A description by Archimandrite Amfilokhii, *Opisanie Voskresenskoi Novoierusalimskoi biblioteki* [A description of the library of Holy Resurrection-New Jerusalem monastery] (Moscow, 1876), p. 180.

[66]Ibid., l. 247 (see n. 34 above).

[67]OR RGB, f. 214, No. 411 (see n. 19 above).

[68]Russian State Archive of the Ancient Documents (Moscow) [hereafter RGADA], f. 1198, op. 2, ed. khr. 5430, l. 1–1 ob., 8, 14–14 ob., ed. khr. 5682, l. 1–2 [op. = inventory list, ed. khr. = archival unit here and throughout] (see nn. 19 and 34 above).

[69]RGADA, f. 1198, op. 2, ed. khr. 5788, l. 1 (see nn. 19, 34, and 68 above).

[70]OR RGB, f. 214, No. 715 (see n. 19 above).

[71]Ibid., l. 243–244 (see n. 34 above).

[72]Ibid., l. 162 ob.–163 (see n. 34 above).

[73]Ibid., l. 229–242 ob. (see n. 34 above).

[74]OR RGB, f. 214, No. 411, pp. 104–8 (see n. 19 above).

[75]Ibid., p. 10.

[76]"Ocherk zhizni startsa Ilariona, ieromonakha i dukhovnika Moskovskogo obshchezhitel'nogo Simonova monastyria" [A sketch of the life of Elder Ilarion, Hieromonk and Father Confessor in the Moscow Cenobitic Monastery of St. Simon], *Strannik* (April 1863), pp. 11–15.

[77]OR RGB, f. 214, No. 715, l. 63–63 ob. (see nn. 19 and 34 above).

[78]Ibid., l. 9 ob.–12 ob. (see n. 34 above). Cf. "Rasskaz strannika, iskatelia molitvy," pp. 19–20 (see n. 17 above).

[79]For more information, see A. Pentkovsky, "Kto zhe sostavil Optinskuiu redaktsiiu Rasskazov strannika?" [Who composed the Optino Redaction of a Pilgrim's Tales?], in *Simvol* no. 32 (Paris, 1994), pp. 259–78.

NOTES TO INTRODUCTION

[80]*Tale* 1881, pp. 108–13 (see n. 1 above).

[81]Ibid., pp. 114–24.

[82]Ibid., pp. 120–25.

[83]Ibid., pp. 125–29.

[84]OR RGB, f. 214, No. 715 l. 7–7 ob., 13, 15, 226 (see nn. 19 and 34 above).

[85]*Tale* 1881, pp. 122–23 (see n. 1 above). Cf. "Recollection" 1994, p. 283 (see n. 50 above)

[86]*Tale* 1881, p. 125 (see n. 1 above).

[87]OR RGB, f. 214, No. 715, l. 189 (see nn. 19 and 34 above).

[88][In Byzantine monastic practice two degrees of fully professed monks and nuns exist, the so-called monk/nun of the little habit and the monk/nun of the great habit. Normally, the great habit is donned by a monk or nun who has lived a blameless life for many years; not infrequently, however, the approach of death moves a monk or nun to enter this higher degree of monastic perfection. The candidate renews his or her solemn profession of vows, and is tonsured anew. The great habit differs from the little or ordinary monastic habit by the addition of a scapular decorated with the instruments of the passion of Christ. The monk or nun of the great habit is dispensed from manual labor and some of the choir duties in order to pursue the contemplative life with greater ease and to practice a much more austere form of asceticism. Since its inception sometime in the eighth century, theologians have criticized this gradation of monastic profession into the less and the more perfect, often on the grounds that just as there is only one baptism so there can be only one monastic profession. Their words have been largely ineffectual. Trans.]

[89]*Vmesto predisloviia* [In place of a foreword], in *Tales* 1883, p. 3 (see n. 3 above).

[90]*Dnevnye zametki vo vremia puteshestviia po sviatym mestam Vostoka Sarovskoi pustyni ieromonakha Paisiia, 1866 goda, a nyne nastoiatelia igumena Paisiia Mikhailo-Arkhangel'skogo Cheremisskogo muzhskogo monastyria Kazanskoi gubernii Kozmodem'ianovskogo uezda* [Journal entries during the journey to the holy places of the East of Sarov hermitage hieromonk Paisii, 1866, who is now superior and hegumen Paisii of St. Michael the Archangel men's monastery in Cheremis, Kazan province, Kozmodem' iansk district] (Kazan, 1881), pp. 18, 66, 140, 144, 177.

[91]*Vmesto predisloviia* [In place of a foreword], in *Tales* 1883, p. 4 (see n. 3 above).

[92]OR RGB, f. 214, No. 715, l. 240 (see nn. 19 and 34 above).

NOTES TO INTRODUCTION

[93]*Kratkoe opisanie Mikhailo-Arkhangel'skogo cheremisskogo muzhskogo monastyria Kazanskoi gubernii Kozmodem'ianskogo uezda* [A brief description of St. Michael the Archangel men's monastery in Cheremis, Kazan province, Kozmodem'iansk district] (St. Petersburg, 1874), pp. 37–39.

[94]*From the Tales* 1911 (see n. 9 above).

[95]*From the Tales* 1911, p. 4 (see n. 9 above).

[96]The manuscript was given over to the Optino hermitage in 1990 by Elizaveta Bulgakova. The text is *The Fifth* 1992, pp. 79–135 (see n. 17 above).

[97]*From the Tales* 1911, pp. 17–22 (see n. 9 above).

[98]*The Fifth* 1992, pp. 90–91 (see n. 17 above). Cf. *From the Tales* 1911, pp. 18–19 (see n. 9 above).

[99]*The Fifth* 1992, pp. 105–6 (see n. 17 above). Cf. *From the Tales* 1911, p. 39 (see n. 9 above).

[100]*The Fifth* 1992, p. 133 (see n. 17 above). Cf. *From the Tales* 1911, p. 69 (see n. 9 above).

[101]*The Fifth* 1992, p. 135 (see n. 17 above). Cf. *From the Tales* 1911, p. 71 (see n. 9 above).

[102]OR RGB, f. 214, No. 411, p. 10 (see n. 19 above).

[103][Hegumen Georgii], *Skazanie o zhizni i podvigakh startsa Serafima, ieromonakha Sarovskoi pustyni i zatvornika, izvlechennyia iz zapisok uchenika ego* [The Story about the life and ascetic feats of Elder Serafim, a hieromonk and recluse in Sarov hermitage, drawn from the notes of his disciple], vol. 16, book 32, *Maiak* (St. Petersburg, 1844), pp. 61–62.

[104]OR RGB, f. 214, No. 411, pp. 108–16 (see n. 19 above).

[105]Monk of the Great Habit Ilarion, *Na gorakh Kavkaza. Beseda dvukh startsev pustynnikov o vnutrennem edinenii s Gospodom nashikh serdets, chrez molitvu Iisus Khristovu, ili dukhovnaia deiatel'nost' sovremennykh pustynnikov* [In the Caucasian Mountains. The conversation of two hermit elders about inner union with the Lord of our hearts through the prayer of Jesus Christ, or the spiritual activity of contemporary hermits], 2nd ed. (Batalpashinsk, 1910).

[106]For more details about Bishop Nikon (Rozhdestvenskii), see Metropolit Manuil (Lemessevskij), *Die Russischen Orthodoxen Bischöfe von 1893 bis 1965* [The Russian Orthodox bishops from 1893 until 1965] (Erlangen, 1987), 5:250–61.

[107]M. A. Novoselov, *Zabytyi put' opytnogo bogopoznaniia* [A forgotten path of experiential knowledge of God], in *Religiozno-filosoficheskaia biblioteka* [A library of religious philosophy], vyp. 1, Vyshnii (Volochek, 1902), pp. 31–34.

NOTES TO INTRODUCTION

[108]P. A. Florenskii, *Stolp i Utverzhdenie Istiny* [The pillar and confirmation of truth], *IX. Pis'mo vos'moe: Tvar'* [IX. Letter Eight: Creation], in *Religiia i zhizn'* [Religion and life] (Moscow, 1908), p. 60.

[109]Priest Pavel Florenskii, *Stolp i Utverzhdenie Istiny* [The pillar and confirmation of truth] (Moscow, 1914), pp. 316–17.

[110]M. A. Venevitinov, *Khozhdenie igumena Daniila v Sviatuiu Zemliu v nachale XII veka* [The journey of Hegumen Daniil to the Holy Land at the beginning of the twelfth century] (St. Petersburg, 1877).

[111]OR RGB, f. 214, No. 453 (see n. 19 above).

[112]Monk Parfenii, *Skazanie o stranstvii i puteshestvii po Rossii, Moldavii, Turtsii i Sviatoi Zemle* (Moscow, 1855).

[113]Ibid., part I, pp. 209–11, part II, pp. 5–36.

[114]Ibid., part III, pp. 148–83.

[115]I. Piatnitskii, "Istoriia sekty strannikov" [The history of a sect of pilgrims], *Bogoslovskii vestnik* [Theological messenger] 2 (July–August 1906), pp. 383–416; "Uchenie strannikov" [The doctrine of the pilgrims], *Bogoslovskii vestnik* 3 (September 1906), pp. 1–25; "Organizatsiia i bogosluzhenie sekty strannikov" [The organization and divine service of a sect of pilgrims], *Bogoslovskii vestnik* 3 (September 1906), pp. 189–211; "Byt sekty strannikov" [The daily life of a sect of pilgrims], *Bogoslovskii vestnik* 3 (November 1906), pp. 403–30; "Smysl sekty strannikov" [The meaning of a sect of pilgrims], *Bogoslovskii vestnik* 3 (December 1906), pp. 724–59.

[116]A. A. Amosov, N. IU. Bubnov, *Arkheograficheskie èkspeditsii Biblioteki AN SSSR v Kargopol'skii i Plesetskii raiony Arkhangel'skoi oblasti (1975–1976 gg.). Materialy i soobshcheniia po fondam Otdela rukopisnoi i redkoi knigi Biblioteki Akademii Nauk SSSR* [An expedition to Kargopol' and Plesetsk region for the study and publication of early texts sponsored by the Library of AN SSSR, 1975–1976. Materials and reports in accordance with the reserves of the department of manuscripts and rare books of the Library of the Academy of Sciences of the USSR], Leningrad, 1978, pp. 262–98.

[117]Archimandrite Nikodim, "*Startsy otets Paisii Velichkovskii i otets Makarii Optinskii i ikh literaturno-asketicheskaia deiatel'nost'*" in *Zhizneopisaniia otechestvennykh podvizhnikov blagochestiia 18 i 19 vekov. Sentiabr'* [The elders, Father Paisii Velichkovskii and Father Makarii of Optino and their ascetical literary activity. In Biographies of homeland ascetics of piety of the eighteenth and nineteenth centuries. September] (Moscow, 1909), pp. 454–582.

NOTES TO INTRODUCTION

[118]*Otkrovennye rasskazy strannika dukhovnomu svoemu ottsu* [Candid tales of a pilgrim to his spiritual father], 1st ed. (Paris, 1930).

[119]*Iz rasskazov strannika o blagodatnom deistvii molitvy Iisusovoi* [From the Pilgrim's Tales about the grace-giving effect of the Jesus prayer] (Vladimirova na Slovensku, 1933).

[120]*Otkrovennye rasskazy strannika dukhovnomu svoemu ottsu* [Candid tales of a pilgrim to his spiritual father], 3rd ed. (Paris, 1948).

[121]*From the Tales* 1911, p. 3 (see n. 9 above).

[122]*Tale* 1992, pp. 7–74 (see n. 17 above); *The Fifth* 1992, pp. 79–135 (see n. 17 above).

The Tale of a Pilgrim,
a Seeker of Prayer

The Tale of a Pilgrim
How he acquired the gift of interior unceasing prayer of the heart

*B*y the mercy of God I am a Christian; by my deeds, a great sinner; and by vocation a homeless pilgrim, a man of mean estate who wanders from place to place. These are my belongings: over my shoulders I carry a pouch of dried bread crusts, and in my breast pocket a Bible. That is all.

One day [it was the twenty-fourth Sunday after Trinity Sunday[1]] I went to church to pray at the liturgy. They were reading the Epistle, from the Letter to the Thessalonians, pericope 273, where it says *"Pray without ceasing."*[2] These words planted themselves firmly in my mind, and I began to wonder how anyone could pray without ceasing when merely to stay alive demanded so much of each individual. I checked in the Bible and found the same thing: it is necessary to pray without ceasing, to pray at every moment in the spirit,[3] and to raise one's hands in prayer in every place....[4]

I thought and thought but could find no answer. So I asked a cleric:

"What does it mean to pray unceasingly and how does one do it?"

He replied: "Just pray as it says."

I asked again: "Yes, but how do you pray unceasingly?"

"You're still asking?" said the cleric and left.

I went to see the parish priest.

"How do you pray unceasingly?" I asked him.

The priest replied: "Go to church often, pay attention to

49

the readings and hymns, perform thanksgiving prayers, light candles, make more prostrations to the ground...."

"And where does it say that in the Bible?" I asked.

"What business do you have in reading the Bible, you boor? You aren't allowed to read the Bible; only we are allowed to read it." After saying this, he left me.

What am I to do? I thought. Where can I find someone to explain this to me? Let me visit the churches that are famous for their good preachers, for surely there I'll hear something that makes sense to me.

I went to the cathedral church on the Sunday of the Publican and the Pharisee. The bishop himself was delivering a sermon on the text "*The Pharisee stood up and was praying in himself in this way.*"[5] The entire sermon consisted of a discussion about what was needed for true prayer and how unworthy was prayer without due preparation. For example, he said: "If you wish that your prayer be true, that it bear fruit leading to salvation and that it not be rejected but heard by God, then first of all, acquire a solid faith, purify your mind of all evil thoughts and lay aside all cares of life. Make your heart a temple for the Holy Spirit. Drive out of it every passion and renew it with purity and zeal. Tame the flesh with fasting and continence and kill all fleshly desires. Be gentle with everyone, preserve peace and holiness in your heart, and when you have been fortified with such feats of asceticism, bring your gift to the sanctuary, offer your pure prayer at the divine altar; and your prayer will be heard and it will save you. Otherwise, if you dare to set about praying distractedly and coldly without having prepared yourself by means of the prescribed virtues and without having cleansed yourself beforehand by repentance and a continent life, you will deprive your prayer of its "wings" and you will not give it the strength to operate. Such prayer not only will be ineffectual; it will also be insulting to God and baneful for you, and it will turn into sin for you, as it is said in the Psalms: '*And let his prayer be counted as sin.*'"[6]

When I heard this I became frightened and thought: What shall I do? Nothing has been prepared for prayer within me, and even for the future I do not see in myself any hope for these pre-liminary labors. Thus I left the church despondent in spirit.

When I reached my room I checked my Bible and verified what I had heard from him: "Acquire first of all a solid faith...." But how do I acquire it, when faith is not from us? For it is God's gift.[7] In order to receive a gift, it is necessary to ask for it, to pray for it. *Ask and it shall be given to you;*[8] but he said: "First acquire faith and then pray." That is the exact opposite. And then he added "solid." But the apostles themselves did not have such faith, and they asked: Lord! *Increase our faith.*[9] He also said: "in order to pray truly, cleanse your mind of thoughts, repudiate the cares of life." But in the Bible it is said: *For the inclination of the human heart is evil from youth,*[10] *and the Lord has given to humans wicked intentions, and they do not avoid even worse things.* Because of this you ought first to pray so that your irrepressible mind may be cleansed of thoughts; but if you seek to purify your mind of thoughts by your own efforts and wait until it is pure, then you'll never pray at all. This is not how he put it. Furthermore he said: "Renew your heart with purity and zeal for real prayer." Is it possible for anyone to remake their heart when it says in the Bible: *God alone will give a different heart, and he will give us a new spirit?*[11] Even the prophet David did not first purify his heart; the first thing he did was pray for the purification of his heart: *A pure heart create in me, O God,*[12] he cried. "Mortify your fleshly desires through continence." Even this is impossible to do with-out prayer. For example, the apostle Paul first prayed three times to avert and vanquish temptation and said: *With my mind I am a slave to the law of God, but with my flesh I am a slave to the law of sin.*[13] Can a prayer made without the appropriate preparation be insulting for God? Of all the prayers depicted in the Bible it is evident that they were offered for purification from sins; a preliminary purification from sins did not precede the prayer.... The prayer of Manasseh is witness to this.

After comparing all this with the Bible, I realized that the ser-mon was entirely without sound foundation and was spoken from inexperience. Everything in it was put head over heels or the reverse....Soothed by the Bible, I stopped thinking about what I had heard. I particularly regretted that I had heard nothing about what it means to pray unceasingly or how to do it. This thought kept an anxious hold on me....

Sunday of the Adoration of the Cross came, and I went to liturgy in the church of the Theological Academy. There a learned preacher was giving an instruction on the prayer of Jesus Christ on the cross, which serves as an example for our prayers. He based his remarks on the text: *Pray at all times in the spirit.*[14] When I heard this, I rejoiced, thinking that he would explain without fail what it meant to pray unceasingly and how this was done.

The preacher was shouting and shouting, all the while demonstrating the need for prayer in the spirit. "Not in mere verbiage ought prayer to consist," he said, "not in superficial petition, not in running to public doxologies in order to show off, not in a multiple recitation of prayers, and not in the duration of the hymnody but in the strength, in the attention, in the ardent zeal and the humble elevation of intellect and heart to God." In a word, prayer must primarily be offered in spirit; the human spirit with fervent outbursts and ardent desire must raise its own prayer. And such true prayer will penetrate the heavens in a moment. With a single heartfelt sigh filled with warmth, faith, and love it will reach the throne of God, it will be heard and will bear the desired fruit. True prayer of the spirit must be opposed above all to affected, ostentatious prayers carried on at length without the warmth of the heart, in imitation of the Pharisees. From this type of prayer Jesus Christ himself kept his disciples, saying: *In your prayer do not say empty words.*[15]

After hearing this through, I still had not satisfied my desire, and once again I was left in bewilderment. How does one pray unceasingly? I arrived home and with grief once again took up the Bible....I read and read, and I began to ponder: How can it be so? The preacher was explaining the text: *Pray in the spirit at all times in every prayer and supplication.*[16] But in his explanation not only did he not reveal how it is possible to pray *at all times,* that is, always, but he even censured prolonged prayers and advised short but ardent prayer. In this he contradicted himself. In the Bible too it says that we must pray always, constantly, and that we do not penetrate the heavens with short sighs! Here is how the prophets teach about this matter: *Draw near to your God always; remember your Lord forever; bear him ever in mind on all your paths,*[17] and not just in brief, ardent sighs. Indeed, it is impossible to fire up your own soul and heart, and the prophet David first sought to obtain this in prayer, saying: *Enkindle my entrails and my heart.*[18] In order to support his notion about the excellence of short, earnest prayer, the preacher cited the words of Jesus Christ, *Say nothing superfluous in your prayer,*[19] even though they were not spoken to condemn prolonged prayer but so that no one should offer many needless petitions concerning the necessities of life, in the manner of pagans. The Lord commanded not only prolonged prayer, but also prayer at all times, and he illustrated this in the parable—*that it is always fitting to pray and not grow weary....*[20] I verified all of this in the Bible, and since the sermons I heard did not satisfy my desire to learn how to pray without ceasing, I went off on my way....

I come to a certain town and inquire whether or not there are any instructive spiritual guides there. I hear that there is an archpriest, an esteemed old man, devout and strict; whenever he gives instructions, all the people come out of the church at the conclusion of the liturgy with fear and sighing. When I heard this, I rejoiced and impatiently awaited the next feast day in order to listen to so wise a teacher. Perhaps I will find in him some clarification of my perplexity about unceasing prayer.

On Sunday I went to the liturgy and purposely stood as close as possible to the sanctuary. Lo and behold, the archpriest came out to deliver his sermon. And what a sermon! To my good fortune he began his instruction with the following text: *Ask and it shall be given to you, seek and you shall find, knock and it shall be opened for you.*[21] When I heard this, I made the sign of the cross enthusiastically and listened with rapt attention. After many arguments demonstrating the necessity of prayer he began to indicate the methods and means by which prayer can be pleasing to God and practicable:

"The Lord spoke this example to illustrate commendable prayer: *Knock and it shall be opened for you;* and they knock not with words but with deeds. Thus we too must knock on the door of divine mercy; we must knock not with words alone but also with deeds. You will derive no benefit at all, though you prayed day and night but did not do works of piety, works of faith, works of love toward your neighbor, works of charity and works of rejecting everything sinful. What benefit will you have from prayer if you go to church less often than to the tavern? The church is a house of prayer; it is God's house, where the Lord himself resides. Consider this: if you intend personally to ask for something from the king, will you not need to come to his court often in order to gain access to him? What benefit will you have from prayer if you waste your money dishonorably on your passions, on luxury and household furnishings, but when you come to church to pray you light no candle before an icon, are stingy, and regret putting more out for the church or giving to the maintenance of the clergy and the poor? But scripture says: *By prayers and almsgiving sins are wiped clean.*[22] Without these works of piety, without these Christian virtues and love, you will not be able to knock on the door of divine mercy, and your prayer will be only a vain and empty howl, offending God's ear...."

At the conclusion of the sermon I started thinking. How did he put it? That there is no use in praying night and day if you do not do any works of piety? But is this not a work of piety—to pray day and night? If day and night were spent in prayer, there would not be any time left over for works of wickedness. And the same is said in the Bible: *Will the Lord not hear those who cry out to him day and night?*[23] "Prayer will not be heard without the casting off of sins," he said, but what other than frequent, customary prayer favors the defeat of sin? "Prayer will not be heard without works of faith, works of charity"—but how is it that the prayer of the haughty Pharisee was heard and that the prayer of the drowning Peter, who lacked faith, yielded fruit? "Prayer will not be heard without frequent attendance in church"—it is clear, I thought, that in saying this the preacher forgot what the holy prophet David said: *In all places of his dominion, bless the Lord, O my soul;*[24] and what the holy archdeacon Stephen said: *The Lord does not dwell in temples made with human hands.*[25]

In order to be convinced that what he said does not happen in that order, I opened the Bible and read in the book of the prophet Isaiah (chapter 55) the following exhortation: (First of all) *seek the Lord, and when you find him, call upon him.*... (followed by) *when he draws near to you,* (then) *let the wicked man forsake his ways and let him return to the Lord and he will be shown mercy, because the Lord will abundantly pardon your sins.* [26] Here I recognized a completely opposite series of steps. First of all, you must seek the Lord and call upon him in prayer. Then, when on account of this he draws near to your soul, you must endeavor to leave behind the works of sin, with his help, and return to the Lord, that is, to the fulfilling of his commands.

After hearing all these public sermons without receiving any understanding of how to pray unceasingly, I stopped listening to them and made up my mind, with the help of God, to search for an experienced and knowledgeable interlocutor whose conversation might explain unceasing prayer to me, something I adamantly sought to know.

I wandered from place to place for a long time, all the while reading the Bible and inquiring if there was a spiritual guide or God-fearing commentator somewhere. Finally some people told me that a nobleman had been living in a certain village for a long time and was saving himself. They said that he had a chapel in his house and did not go out anywhere. He spent his time praying to God and continually reading edifying books. When I heard this, I didn't walk, I ran to that village, and once I got there I sought out the landowner.

"What have you come to me for?" he asked.

"I have heard that you are a devout and reasonable man and so I beg you, for the sake of God, to explain to me what the words of the apostle *pray unceasingly* mean and how it is possible to pray unceasingly. I have long desired to find this out but I am completely unable to understand it."

The gentleman grew silent for a moment, looked at me intently and said:

"Unceasing interior prayer is the uninterrupted striving of the human spirit toward attentiveness in the divine center. In order to learn this sweet exercise you must bend the power of your will toward it and frequently ask the Lord to teach you how to pray unceasingly."

"I do not understand your words," I said. "I beg you to explain them to me more clearly."

"This is too lofty for you," he replied. "You will not understand. But if you pray as you know how, this very prayer will itself reveal to you how it can be unceasing. Everything takes its own time...."

After saying this he gave orders to feed me. He then gave me something for the road and sent me on my way. Again I walked. I thought and thought, I read and read the Bible, I reflected on what the gentleman had told me, but I could not understand anything. I so wanted to understand that I could not sleep at night. I traveled about two hundred kilometers[27] and entered a large provincial town. I noticed a monastery there. After putting up in an inn, I heard that the monastery had a kindly superior who was devout and hospitable toward pilgrims. I went to see him and he welcomed me gladly, bade me take a seat, and began to spread a table for me.

"Holy father," I said, "I have no need of food, but I do want you to give me spiritual instruction on how I may be saved."

"If you live uprightly and pray to God you will be holy."

"The fact of the matter is, I do not know how to pray unceasingly and I cannot even understand what unceasing prayer means. I beg you, father, explain this to me."

"I don't know how to make it clearer for you, dear brother.... Hmm, just a minute. I have a little book; it's explained there," and he brought out Bishop Dmitry's *Spiritual Training of the Inner Person*. "Read this page here...."

I started to read the following passage: "In Sacred Scripture it is customary to call an act that is performed often unceasing, that is, continually (always) performed; this is clearly the case—the *priests go continually into the first tent*,[28] that is, often or throughout the day, at the prescribed hours. In the same way too, prayer, which is often performed, is reckoned as being performed unceasingly."

"Now then, do you understand what it means to pray unceasingly?"

"I do not know how to make 'often' and 'unceasingly' agree as though they were one and the same thing. But, if you please, a few lines lower, look at what the same bishop writes: 'The words of the apostle *pray unceasingly* must be understood to refer to prayer performed by the intellect; for the intellect can always be fixed upon God and pray to him unceasingly.' Explain to me how the intellect can always be fixed upon God, not be distracted, and pray unceasingly. The bishop must have known the method."

"This is very difficult to grasp unless God himself provides assistance," said the superior.

I spent the night in his house and in the morning I thanked him for his affectionate hospitality. Then I set out further, not knowing myself where to, and I grieved over my lack of comprehension. For consolation I would read the Bible every moment. Thus I walked for about five days along the main road. Finally, toward evening a certain old man, who from appearances looked like a cleric, caught up with me. To my question he said that he was a monk of the great habit[29] from the hermitage, which was about ten kilometers off the main road, and he invited me to drop in to their hermitage. "We welcome pilgrims; they rest and eat together with the devout in the guest house." For some reason I was unwilling to go there, and I replied to his invitation in this way:

"My peace does not depend on lodgings but on spiritual instruction, and I am not chasing after food. I have lots of dried crusts in my pouch."

"But what kind of instruction are you searching for, and what are you perplexed about? Come along, dear brother, come along to our place; we have some experienced elders who are able to give spiritual nourishment and set you on the right path in the light of the Word of God and the discourses of the holy fathers."

"Here's how it is, father. Approximately one year ago, while I was at the liturgy, I heard during the reading of the epistle this commandment: *Pray unceasingly*. Since I was unable to understand this, I began to read the Bible and there too in many places I found the divine precept that it was necessary to pray unceasingly—always, at all times, in every place, not only when a person is busy working, not only when a person keeps vigil, but even in one's sleep....*I am sleeping but my heart is awake.*[30] This greatly astonished me and I could not understand how it was possible to accomplish. Powerful desire and curiosity were aroused in me to learn what this meant and what methods might be appropriate; day and night my mind was restless. After this I began going from church to church, listening to sermons on prayer. But no matter how many sermons I listened to, not a single one of them imparted any instructions on how to pray unceasingly. The only thing that was said concerned preparation for prayer through works of faith, through ascetic feats, and the virtues whose literal accomplishment is beyond the powers of a sinful person. All of this only frightened me and led to despondency; it did not teach me how to pray unceasingly or what such prayer meant. I read the Bible often and I checked what I had heard against what I was reading, but even here I did not find the desired knowledge. The only thing I saw was that what was being said in the sermons was not how it was expressed in the Bible; in fact, everything seemed to be the wrong way round. And so I have remained bewildered and troubled until now."

The elder made the sign of the cross and began to speak:

"I give thanks to God, dear brother, for this irresistible attraction to a knowledge of unceasing interior prayer which he has revealed in you. Recognize in this a divine calling and set your mind at ease. Be assured that up until this moment you were being put to a test consisting in the assent of your will to the voice of God and the opening of your understanding. It is not by the wisdom of this world nor by superficial inquisitiveness that the celestial light of unceasing interior prayer is reached, but, on the contrary, *by poverty of spirit and practical experience* it is found in mysterious simplicity. Hence, it is not at all surprising that you were unable to hear anything about the essential act of prayer and grasp the science of how to reach the unfailing activity of the latter. And to tell the truth, although many preach about prayer and there is much instruction about it from different writers, inasmuch as all their discourses are based for the greater part on speculation and the imaginings of the natural intellect and not on practical experience, they teach more about the properties than about the essence of the subject itself, and they do not understand the inner logic of the spirit. One person eloquently discusses the necessity of prayer; a second talks about its power and beneficial nature; a third speaks of the attendant means leading to the perfection of prayer, that is, that diligence, attentiveness, warmth of heart, purity of thought, reconciliation with one's enemies, humility, contrition, and the like are absolutely necessary for prayer. But *what in fact prayer is and how one may learn to pray*—even though these are questions of the first importance, very rarely among preachers of today can one find thorough explanations of them. Since they are more difficult to understand than all their above-mentioned discourses, they demand a mystical and practical knowledge, and not a merely scholastic learnedness. And what is even more regrettable is that this vain natural wisdom compels them to measure a divine act by human standards.

"In the matter of prayer many reason quite perversely. They think that preparatory means and ascetic feats will produce prayer and do not see that prayer gives rise to every act of asceticism and virtue, as you yourself have heard in their instructions. For this reason they even forbid one to attempt prayer, by prescribing heroic acts of virtue and victory over the passions as a preliminary step toward worthy prayer.

"In this case they wrongly conceive of the fruits or consequences of prayer as its methods and aids, thereby reducing the power of prayer to naught. This is completely against Sacred Scripture, for the holy apostle Paul gives a directive on prayer in words such as these: *I implore you first of all to make prayers.*[31] The first thing expressed in the apostle's directive on prayer here is that he places the work of prayer before all else. I implore you first of all to make prayers. Many good works are demanded of a Christian, but the work of prayer must be before all works because without it no other good work can be accomplished.... Without prayer it is impossible to find the path to the Lord, to understand

59

the truth, to crucify the flesh with its passions and desires, to illuminate the heart with the Light of Christ, and to be savingly united with God. None of this can be accomplished without preliminary frequent prayer. I say frequent because both perfection and righteousness of prayer are beyond our own capabilities, for, as even the holy apostle Paul says, *We do not know how or for what we pray*.[32] Consequently, only frequency and regularity are left to the portion of our ability as means to acquire prayerful purity, which is the mother of every spiritual blessing.... 'Possess the mother and she will produce a child for you,' says holy Isaac the Syrian. Learn first of all to obtain prayer and you will easily accomplish all the virtues. But those who have little practical experience and are unfamiliar with the mystical teachings of the holy fathers have no clear knowledge and little to say about it."

During this conversation we unwittingly had come up almost to the hermitage itself. In order not to let this wise elder slip away from me and the sooner to obtain what I desired, I hastened to say to him:

"Do me a favor, reverend father, and explain to me what unceasing interior prayer means and how it may be learned. I see that you know all about these things."

The elder lovingly accepted my request and invited me to his cell. "Come now and visit me, and I will give you a book of the holy fathers from which, with the help of God, you can understand and learn this type of prayer plainly and in detail."

We entered his cell and the elder began to say the following:

"The unceasing interior Jesus prayer is an uninterrupted, never dying invocation of the divine name Jesus Christ with the mind and the heart, all the while imagining his ongoing presence and asking for his pardon, during all occupations, in every place, at all times, even in sleep.... The prayer is expressed in the following words: *Lord Jesus Christ, Son of God, have mercy on me.* Those who acquire the habit of this invocation will experience great consolation and will always say this prayer. As a result they will be unable to live without the prayer, which of its own accord will speak itself in them. Now do you understand what unceasing prayer is?"

"I understand very well, father! For the sake of God teach me how to obtain it," I exclaimed with joy.

"We shall read about how to learn this prayer in the book called the *Philokalia*. It contains the complete and detailed science of unceasing interior prayer, expounded by twenty-five holy fathers.[33] So sublime and profitable is this book that it is revered as the chief and primary guide to the contemplative spiritual life and, as Saint Nikiphoros[34] expresses, 'it leads to salvation without labor and fasts.'"

"Is it then more sublime and holy than the Bible?" I asked.

"No, it is not more sublime nor is it holier than the Bible, but it does contain lucid explanations of what the Bible holds mystically and what cannot be easily grasped by our short-sighted mind. I will give you an example of this. The sun is the greatest, most brilliant, and most excellent luminary of the heavens, but you cannot contemplate it and examine it with the naked eye. You need a piece of treated artificial glass and although it is a million times smaller and duller than the sun, with the glass you can examine this magnificent emperor of the heavenly luminaries, admire it and attract its fiery rays. In the same way Sacred Scripture is a brilliant sun and the *Philokalia* is the necessary piece of glass which facilitates our access to that most sublime luminary. Listen now and I will read by what means unceasing interior prayer is to be learned."

The elder opened the *Philokalia*, searched for an instruction of Saint Symeon the New Theologian and began: "Sit in silence and alone. Bend your head. Close your eyes. Breathe ever more quietly. With the imagination look inside your heart. Carry your intellect, that is your thought, out of your head and into your heart. As you breathe say quietly with your lips or in your intellect alone: 'Lord Jesus Christ, Son of God, have mercy on me.'... Try to drive away your thoughts. Keep restful patience and repeat this process very frequently."

The elder then explained all of this to me, demonstrating it by example, and we read further from the *Philokalia* sayings of Saint Gregory of Sinai and venerable Saints Kallistos and Ignatios. For verification the elder showed me in various places in the Bible all that he read from the *Philokalia* and said: "Look here, this is where it is all drawn from." With delight I listened attentively to everything. I absorbed it with my memory and tried to remember everything in as much detail as possible. Thus we sat there the whole night through, and since we did not go to sleep we went to Orthros[35]....

The elder sent me away, giving me his blessing. He told me that while learning this prayer I should come to him with frank confession, for arbitrarily to take up the interior work of prayer without the verification of a guide would be improper and bring little success. As I stood in church I felt within myself a fervid eagerness to learn interior prayer as diligently as possible, and I asked God to help me in this regard.

Then I wondered how I would come to the elder for confession since it was forbidden to stay in the guest house more than three days and there were no living quarters around the hermitage. At length I heard that there was a village about four kilometers away and I went there to search out a place for myself. To my good fortune, God showed me a convenient setup. I took a job with a peasant all that summer to guard his kitchen garden and he let me live by myself in a thatched hut in the garden. Glory be to God! I had found a peaceful place and so I took up living there. I began to learn interior prayer following the method shown to me, and regularly visited the elder.

For a week I intently set about learning unceasing prayer in my solitude in the garden, exactly as the elder had explained to me. At first everything seemed to go quite well. Then I felt a heavy burden, laziness, boredom, overpowering sleep, and various thoughts closed in on me like a storm cloud. In distress I went to see the elder and I related to him my situation. He greeted me amiably and said:

"This, dear brother, is the war of the dark world against you. For this world there is nothing more dreadful in us than prayer of the heart. That is why it will attempt by every means to hinder you and turn you away from learning the prayer. But even the enemy acts only in accordance with God's will and permission, insofar as this is necessary for us. Obviously, you still need to be tested in regard to humility; therefore it is still too early for you to approach the lofty entrance of the heart with immoderate ardor, lest you fall into spiritual covetousness. I shall read to you an instruction concerning this from the *Philokalia*."

The elder looked for a teaching by Saint Nikiphoros the Monk and started to read: "If after you have labored a little while you are unable to enter the country of the heart as had been explained to you, do what I shall tell you, and with the help of God you will find what you are seeking. You know that the faculty for pronouncing words is located in the throat. By using this faculty, all the while suppressing your thoughts (you can if you wish), say without ceasing: *Lord Jesus Christ, Son of God, have mercy on me*. Force yourself to say this at all times. If you spend some time doing this, the heart's entrance will be opened to you without any doubt at all; this is proven by experience."[36]

"There, you hear what directions the holy fathers give in such a case," said the elder. "For this reason you must now accept the command with confidence—as often as possible say the Jesus prayer aloud. Here are some prayer beads for you. At the start say about three thousand prayers every day. Whether you are standing or sitting, whether you are walking or reclining, say without ceasing: *Lord Jesus Christ, Son of God, have mercy on me*. Say it neither loudly nor hurriedly. And without fail make the three thousand prayers faithfully each day, without adding or subtracting arbitrarily. God will assist you by this means even to attain the unceasing activity in the heart."

I received his instruction with gladness and went home. I began faithfully to fulfill this rule to the letter, just as the elder had instructed me. For about two days it was rather difficult for me but then it became so easy that when I did not say the prayers a sort of need to say the Jesus prayer made itself known. I began to pray it comfortably and easily, no longer with compulsion as had been the case before. I informed the elder about this and he ordered me to perform six thousand prayers daily. "Be calm," he said, "and as faithfully as possible try to accomplish the number of prayers commanded to you: God will work his mercy with you."

I spent the entire week in my solitary hut saying daily the six thousand Jesus prayers, not worrying about anything and not gazing at thoughts no matter how they assailed me. I just tried to carry out the elder's command exactly. And what happened? I became so accustomed to prayer that if for a brief period I should stop saying it, I felt that something was missing, that I had lost something. I would begin the prayer and again in that moment it became easy and gratifying. When I meet somebody I have no desire even to speak with them, and only want to be alone and say the prayer, so accustomed to it do I become in a week.

When he had not seen me for about ten days, the elder himself came to visit me. I reported to him my condition. After hearing me out, he said:

"You have now become accustomed to the prayer. See to it that you maintain and deepen this habit. Do not vainly waste your time, and with the help of God be resolved to perform twelve thousand prayers a day unfailingly. Keep to your solitude; rise early in the morning and go to bed late; and come to me for advice every two weeks."

I started acting as the elder had ordered me, and on the first day I barely managed to complete my canon of twelve-thousand prayers by late evening. The next day I accomplished this easily and with pleasure. As I repeated the prayer without ceasing, at first I felt a fatigue or a type of numbness of the tongue and some sort of constriction in the jaw, a pleasant and then light and fine pain in the roof of my mouth; further I felt a small pain in the thumb of my left hand with which I counted my beads, and an inflammation of the entire hand which extended right up to my elbow and produced a rather pleasant sensation. All of this somehow aroused me and compelled me to even greater practice of the prayer. Thus, for about five days I faithfully performed the twelve thousand prayers and together with the habit of prayer I received pleasure and delight.

One day early in the morning the prayer seemingly roused me from sleep. After waking up, I felt my lips twitching by themselves and my tongue was moving unceasingly. I wanted to control it but was unable to do so. I started to recite my morning prayers but my tongue said them clumsily, and my whole desire was struggling of its own accord to perform the Jesus prayer.

64

When I began the prayer, how easy and delightful it became. My tongue and mouth themselves, so it seemed, pronounced the words without any urging from me. I spent the whole day in joy, cut off as it were from everything else. It was like being in another world, and I easily completed the twelve thousand prayers in the early evening.

I very much wanted to say even more prayers but I dared not do more than the number prescribed by the elder. In this manner for the remaining days I continued to invoke the name of Jesus Christ with ease and attraction to it. Then I went to disclose these things to the elder and I told him everything in detail. After listening to me, he said:

"Glory be to God that the inclination and facility for prayer have been revealed to you. This is a natural thing that proceeds from frequent practice and ascetic feats, similar to a machine whose main wheel is given a push or some force after which it moves by itself for a long time; but in order to continue its motion, another wheel must be greased and given a slight push. Do you see with what excellent faculties the God who loves humankind has fitted even the sensual nature of humanity? Do you see what kinds of sensations can arise even outside of grace, not just in a purified sensuality but in a sinful soul, as you yourself have already experienced? But how excellent, enthralling, and delightful it is when God is pleased to reveal the gift of self-activating spiritual prayer and to cleanse the soul of its passions. This condition is indescribable and the revelation of this prayerful mystery is a *foretaste of celestial sweetness on earth*. Those who seek the Lord in the simplicity of an abundantly loving heart are considered worthy of this.... I now permit you: say as many prayers as you wish and as much as possible. Try to devote the whole time of your vigil to the prayer and invoke without number the name of Jesus Christ, entrusting yourself humbly to the will of God. Expect assistance from him, believing that he will not abandon you and will guide you on the right path."

After receiving this instruction I spent the whole summer vocally reciting the Jesus prayer without ceasing and I was very peaceful. I often dreamed in my sleep that I was saying the prayer. During the day, if I happened to meet anyone, all without exception were as dear to me as if they were my relatives, though I did not concern myself with them. My very thoughts completely calmed down by themselves and I thought about nothing at all except the prayer. My mind tended to listen to it and from time to time my heart began of its own accord to sense a warmth and a certain pleasure. When I happened to go to church, the lengthy service seemed short and no longer wore down my strength as before. My solitary hut seemed to me a magnificent palace. And I did not know how to thank God for sending me, great sinner that I am, so salutary an elder and instructor.

But not for long would I benefit from the instructions of my dear elder and guide, so full of divine wisdom. At the end of the summer he passed away. With tears I said farewell to him, thanking him for the fatherly teaching he had given wretched me, and as a blessing I asked to have as my own the prayer beads with which he always prayed.

Thus I was left alone. Finally even the summer passed and the kitchen garden was harvested. I had no place to live; the peasant settled accounts with me, and gave me two rubles for my guard duty and filled my pouch with dried crusts for the road. Again I went wandering from one place to the next, but I no longer walked with difficulties as before. The invocation of the name of Jesus Christ cheered me on the way, and all people treated me rather well; it seemed as if they all loved me. One day I started to think about what I ought to do with the money I had received for watching the kitchen garden. "What good is it to me?" I thought. "But hold on! I no longer have an elder; there is no one to teach me. Let me buy the *Philokalia* for myself and learn about interior prayer from it."

I blessed myself with the sign of the cross and went off with the prayer. I came to a provincial town and began to ask for the *Philokalia* from shop to shop. I found it in one shop but they were asking three rubles for it there, and I had only two. I haggled with him, but the merchant would not yield at all, and finally he said: "Look, go to that church and ask the church warden there. He has an old copy of the book; maybe he'll let you have it for two rubles."

I went and for the two rubles I in fact bought that copy of the *Philokalia*, all worn and old. I was happy to have acquired it somehow. I sewed a cloth cover for it and put it in my breast pocket with my Bible. So now I walk and continually say the Jesus prayer, which is more precious and sweeter to me than anything on earth. I sometimes walk seventy or more kilometers a day and I do not feel that I am walking; I only feel that I am saying the prayer. When a powerful cold chills me to the bone, I begin all the more intensely to say the prayer—and soon I am warmed all over. If hunger begins to overwhelm me, I begin invoking all the more often the name of Jesus Christ and I forget that I wanted to eat. When I become ill, when rheumatism begins in my back and legs, I pay attention to the prayer and no longer feel the pain. If someone insults or injures me, I only recall how sweet is the Jesus prayer, and then and there both insult and anger pass and I forget everything. I have become like some sort of half-conscious person; I have no worries about anything; nothing occupies me. I would not look at any vain thing and would rather be alone. Only by habit do I wish for one thing, to say the prayer without ceasing; and when I am occupied with it, I am very happy. Who knows what is happening with me?

Of course all of this is only sensual or, as the late elder would say, natural and artificial from force of habit, but owing to my unworthiness and stupidity I dare not proceed too quickly to an exploration of spiritual prayer within my heart. So I await the hour of God's will, trusting in the prayers of my late elder.

Even though I have not attained unceasing, self-activating spiritual prayer in the heart, still, glory be to God, I now clearly understand what the expression means that I heard in the Epistle: *Pray unceasingly*.[37]

6 November 1859

The Pilgrim's Tale
On the occasion of his second meeting,
13 December 1859

All who fear the Lord, come, and I will tell you
how much he has done for my soul.[1]

*F*or a long time I wandered through various places with the
Jesus prayer as my traveling companion. It encouraged and
consoled me on all my paths, in all my encounters and in every
situation. I began to feel at last that it would be better if I stopped
in one place somewhere so as to be alone more conveniently and
to study the *Philokalia*. Although I read a little from it when I
took shelter for the night or rested during the day, still I strongly desired to apply myself to it more seriously and, with faith, to
draw from it true instruction for the salvation of my soul by
means of the prayer of the heart. In spite of this desire of mine,
however, I was unable to hire myself out anywhere for heavy
labor because I have suffered a total lack of control over my left
arm since my childhood. Being thus unable to have a permanent
shelter, I went to Siberia to visit the relics of Bishop Innokenty
of Irkutsk.[2] My intention was that walking the woods and steppes
of Siberia would be quieter and consequently more conducive to
prayer and reading.

So off I went and I continually repeated the prayer aloud.
In no great length of time I felt that the prayer somehow was
beginning to move into my heart by itself. That is, it seemed that
as it beat normally my heart began to form the words of the
prayer inside itself with every heartbeat; for example, at the first

beat, Lord; at the second, Jesus; at the third, Christ; and so on. I stopped saying the prayer vocally and began to listen carefully to my heart speaking. So too I seemed to be looking into my heart with my eyes, and I remembered how my late elder used to explain this to me. Then I began to sense such agreeable pain in my heart and such love for Jesus Christ in my thoughts that it seemed that if I were to catch sight of him somewhere I would throw myself at his feet and not let him out of my arms, sweetly kissing and tearfully thanking him because on account of his Name he bestows such consolation on his unworthy and sinful creature in accordance with his mercy and love. Furthermore, a kind of blessed warming arose in my heart, and this warmth spread throughout my breast. This experience in particular led me to an assiduous reading of the *Philokalia* in order to verify my feelings, but equally to study a further lesson on the interior prayer of the heart. Without such verification I was afraid of succumbing to its charm, or of taking natural movements for ones of grace and becoming puffed up because I had acquired this prayer so rapidly. I had heard such a warning from my late elder. For this reason I walked more by night and I spent the days for the most part sitting under trees in the forest and reading the *Philokalia*....

Oh, how many new things, how many wise and hitherto unknown things did my reading reveal! In practicing them I tasted such sweetness the likes of which until then I had not even been able to imagine. It is true that when I was reading, certain passages were beyond the grasp of my dull mind, but they were made clear to me by the effects of the prayer of the heart. In addition, I now and then saw my late elder in my dreams and he explained many things to me and above all inclined my witless soul toward humility.

For almost two summer months I was blissfully happy, traveling mostly through the woods and along country roads. If I came into a village, I would ask for a bag of dried crusts and a handful of salt; I would fill my bark flask with water and then go on walking about one hundred kilometers.

Whether on account of the sins of my accursed soul, or because trials are necessary in the spiritual life, or for the sake of better instruction and experience, temptations were in the offing for me at the end of the forest. Indeed, I walked out onto the main road and was overtaken at twilight by two men whose heads gave them away as soldiers. They began demanding money from me. When I answered that I did not have even a kopeck, they did not believe me and shouted insolently: "You're lying! Pilgrims collect lots of money!" "Why bother talking with him," one of them said and he struck me on the head with a cudgel so that I lost consciousness. I don't know how long I lay there unconscious, but when I came to, I realized that I was lying at the edge of the forest near the road, all rumpled. I no longer had my pouch, only the cut cords from which it used to hang. Glory be to God that they did not take my passport, which I kept in my old rag of a cap in case I needed to show it quickly upon request. When I stood up I began to weep bitterly not so much because of my aching head as for my missing books: the Bible and the *Philokalia* were in the stolen bag. I did not stop grieving and crying day or night. Where is it now, the Bible which I read since childhood and which I always had with me? Where is my *Philokalia*, from which I drew both instruction and consolation? Unhappy me, I had lost the first and last treasure of my life without having had my fill of it. It were better had they killed me outright than for me to live without my spiritual nourishment. I can never get them back again!

For two days I could barely drag my feet, exhausted from this misfortune, and on the third day, strained to the breaking point, I dropped under a bush and fell asleep. I dreamt that I was in the hermitage, and in my elder's cell I bemoaned my misfortune. The elder comforted me and said:

"This is a lesson for you on indifference toward earthly things, so that you may more easily advance toward heaven. It has been allowed to happen to you so that you do not fall into spiritual voluptuousness. God wants Christians to renounce their own will, desire, and every predilection completely and to surrender themselves entirely to his divine will. He arranges

70

every event for the benefit and salvation of the individual, *for he wills that all men and women be saved.*[3] Thus, take courage and believe that *with the testing the Lord will also provide the way out.*[4] And soon you will be consoled much more than you now are grieving."

At these words I woke up and I felt increased vitality and my soul seemed full of light and peace. "Let the Lord's will be done," I said and making the sign of the cross I stood up and went on my way. The prayer once again began to function in my heart as before and for three days I traveled in peace.

Suddenly on the road I came upon a convoy of convicts being led under escort. As I came up alongside of them I saw the two men who had robbed me, and since they were walking in the outside file, I fell at their feet and earnestly begged them to tell me where my books were. At first they paid no attention to me but then one of them said:

"If you give us something, we'll tell you where they are. Give us a ruble."

I assured them that I would give it to them even if I had to beg the ruble from someone for the sake of Christ. "Here, if you wish, take my passport as a pledge."

They said that my books were being transported in a wagon following the prisoners with the rest of the booty they were found with.

"How can I get them back?"

"Ask the captain who is escorting them." I rushed to the captain and explained everything to him in detail. He asked me:

"Can you really read the Bible?"

"Not only can I read it all," I answered, "but I can even write. You will see an inscription in the Bible that this book is mine. And in my passport the same name is given."

The captain said: "These men are swindlers and runaway soldiers who have been living in an earthen hut and plundering many people. Yesterday they were caught by a clever coachman whose carriage and three [horses] they wanted to steal. I'll return your books to you if they are there. Why don't you come with us to the night camp? It's not far, about four kilometers, and then we won't have to stop the convoy for your sake."

71

I gladly walked beside the captain's riding horse and struck up a conversation with him. I noticed that he was a good and honest fellow and no longer young. He asked me who I was, where I came from, and where I was going. I answered all his questions with complete honesty. And so we went, right on to the night-camp station house. Finding my books, he returned them to me and said: "Where will you go, now that it is nightfall? Spend the night here in my anteroom." And so I did. When I got the books, I was so happy that I did not know how to thank God; I pressed the books to my breast and held them there until my hands grew stiff. Tears poured from my eyes out of joy and my heart beat sweetly with delight. The captain watched me and said: "It is clear that you love reading the Bible." I was so overjoyed that I could not give him any answer; I just wept. He continued: "I too, brother, read the Gospel carefully," at which point he unbuttoned his full-dress uniform and took out a small Gospel printed in Kiev and bound in silver. "Sit down there; I will tell you how this came about and serve me supper!"

We sat at table and the captain began his tale. "Ever since I was a young man I have served in the army, not in a garrison but in the field. The superior officers liked me for being a conscientious second lieutenant. But I was young then and so were my friends. Unfortunately, I took up drinking, and toward the end it developed into a sickness. When I don't drink, I'm a conscientious officer; but once I start up, I'm six weeks flat on my back. My fellow officers put up with me for a long time. Finally, on account of the rudeness and quarreling committed when I was drunk, they reduced me to the ranks for three years and transferred me to a garrison. If I didn't improve myself and stop drinking they threatened me with an even harsher punishment. In this hapless state, try as I might to control myself and no matter how often I submitted myself to a cure, I still was entirely unable to throw off my passion. For this reason they planned to transfer me to a convict labor gang. When I learned about this, I didn't know what to do with myself. One day I was sitting in the barracks lost in reverie. Suddenly some monk came in with a book to collect alms for the church. Anyone who could give did so. Approaching me he asked:

'Why are you so sad?'

"Striking up a conversation with him, I recounted my troubles to him. The monk sympathized with my situation and said:

'Exactly the same thing happened to my brother, and here is what helped him. His spiritual father gave him a copy of the Gospels with strict orders to read a chapter of the Gospels without delay should he feel the desire for wine; if he desired it again, he should read the next chapter. My brother began to do this and in a short period of time his desire for wine disappeared and now it has been fifteen years since he has taken a single drop of alcohol to his mouth. If you do the same thing, you'll see how it helps. I have a copy of the Gospels. Do let me bring it to you.'

"After hearing him out I said to him: 'How can your Gospel help me when none of my efforts and no medicinal means were able to control me?' I said this because I had never read the Gospel.

'Don't say that,' objected the monk. 'I assure you that it will be of use.'

"The next day the monk actually brought me this very copy of the Gospels. I opened it, looked it over, began to read and said: 'I can't take it. I don't understand anything in it. And I'm not accustomed to reading church script.' The monk continued to assure me, arguing that in the very words of the Gospel there was a gracious power, for what was written in it was what God himself had said. 'There is no need to understand, only read it diligently. One of the saints said: "If you do not understand the Word of God, the demons do understand what you are reading and they tremble." Your passion for drinking is certainly the result of the demons' provocation. I'll tell you another saying. Saint John Chrysostom writes that even the very chamber in which a copy of the Gospels is kept terrifies the spirits of darkness and is an unsuitable point of assault for their crafty schemes.'

"I gave the monk something, though what it was escapes me, took the copy of the Gospels from him and placed it in my little trunk with my other things. And then I forgot about it. A little while later, the time came for me to begin drinking again. I was dying for a drink and I quickly unlocked the little trunk to get

73

some money and run to the tavern. But as soon as I opened the lid the first thing that struck my eyes was the Gospel book, and I vividly recalled everything that the monk had told me. I unwrapped the copy and began reading the first chapter of Matthew. Although I read it through to the end I understood precisely nothing and I wondered: the monk said that the book contained God's exact words, but there were only names in the chapter. Okay, I said, let's read another chapter. I did so and it was more understandable. Let's read the third chapter. As soon as I started it, a bell sounded in the barracks—everyone had to go to their bunk. As a result it was impossible to get beyond the gates, and so I stayed put. When I got up the next morning, set on going for a drink, I thought: What if I read a chapter from the Gospel? I read one and did not understand it. Again I began craving a drink. I started reading again and it became easier. This encouraged me, so that every time I felt the urge for a drink I began reading a chapter from the Gospel. The further I read, the easier everything was; finally when I had finished all four evangelists the desire for drinking completely went away and I developed a loathing for it. And so, for exactly twenty years I have not had a drop of alcohol. Everyone was amazed at how much I had changed. After three years passed I was once again inducted into the officers' rank and then into the following ranks, and finally I was made a commanding officer. I married; I lucked out on a good wife. We have made a fortune and, glory be to God, we go on living life. We help the poor as we are able and welcome pilgrims. My son is already an officer and a good fellow to boot.

"Listen! Since the day I was cured of alcoholism I swore an oath that I would read the Gospels every day for the rest of my life, one entire Evangelist in twenty-four hours without letting any obstacle stand in the way. And even now this is what I do. If a lot of work arises from my duties and I am extremely worn out, I have my wife or my son read the whole Gospel to me in the evening after I have gone to bed. And so I fulfill my rule without omission. In gratitude and to the glory of God I bound this copy of the Gospels in pure silver and carry it in my breast pocket always."

I listened with delight to the captain's words and then said to him:

"I too have seen a similar case. At the factory in our village there was a certain craftsman who was very skilled at his job, a good and dear fellow; unfortunately he too used to indulge in drinking bouts, and rather often for that matter. A certain God-fearing individual advised him whenever he desired to drink wine to say thirty-three Jesus prayers in honor of the Most Holy Trinity and in keeping with the thirty-three years of Jesus Christ's earthly life. The craftsman obeyed. He began to carry this out and soon quit drinking altogether. And what is more! Three years later he entered a monastery."

"Which is greater?" asked the captain. "The Jesus prayer or the Gospel?"

"The Gospel and the Jesus prayer are one and the same thing," I replied. "For the divine name of Jesus Christ contains in itself all Gospel truths. The holy fathers say that the Jesus prayer is an abridgment of the entire Gospel."

At last we prayed. The captain started to read the Gospel according to Mark, from the beginning, and I listened and said the prayer in my heart. At the second hour after midnight the captain finished the Gospel and we parted for rest. In keeping with my habit, I rose early in the morning. Everyone was still sleeping. As soon as it started to get light, I flung myself into reading my beloved *Philokalia*. With such joy did I open it! It was as if I were seeing my own father who had been in a distant land, or a friend risen from the dead! I kissed it and thanked God for having returned it to me. Unhesitatingly I began to read "The Discourse on Innermost Activity" by Theoliptos of Philadelphia[5] in the second part of the *Philokalia*. The instruction surprised me, for he proposed that one and the same individual could perform three different things at one and the same time. "While seated in the refectory," he says, "give food to your body, reading to your ears, and prayer to your mind." But the recollection of yesterday evening expertly and in fact solved the meaning for me. Here too the mystery was revealed to me that the mind and the heart are not one and the same thing. When the captain got up, I went out to thank him for his kindness and to take my leave of him. He poured me a cup of tea, gave me a ruble, and bid me farewell. And so I set out on my path, rejoicing.

After traveling about a kilometer, I recalled that I had promised the soldiers a ruble, which I unexpectedly now had. Should I give it to them or not? One thought said: "They beat you and robbed you, and in any case they will not be able to make use of it since they are under arrest." But another thought brought forth something different: "Remember what is written in the Bible: *If your enemy is hungry, feed him.*⁶ And Christ himself said: *Love your enemies.... If someone wants your tunic, give him your cloak as well.*⁷ Convinced by this I turned back. Just as I approached the station all the convicts were being brought out to be driven on to the next station. I ran up to them quickly, shoved my ruble into their hands and said: "Repent and pray. Jesus Christ loves all people. He will not abandon you." I parted from them and went to the other side on my own way.

After walking some fifty kilometers on the main road I took it into my head to return to the country road for greater solitude and more convenient reading. I walked a long time through forests and dales, and rarely did I come upon villages anywhere. Sometimes I spent almost the entire day in the woods, diligently reading the *Philokalia.* I drew much and marvelous knowledge from it, and my heart burned hot for union with God by means of interior prayer, which I was struggling to learn under the guidance and verification of the *Philokalia.* At the same time it pained me that I still had not found a haven where I might peacefully devote myself to continual reading. At the time I was reading my Bible too and I felt that I was beginning to understand it more clearly. It was not as before, when a great deal of it appeared incomprehensible to me and often left me bewildered. Since the holy fathers say that the *Philokalia* is the key for opening the mysteries of Sacred Scripture, under its guidance I began partly to understand the hidden meaning of God's Word. I was beginning to have an inkling about such things as "the interior secret person of the heart,"⁸ "true prayer," and "worship in the spirit,"⁹ "the kingdom is within us,"¹⁰ "the Spirit intercedes for us with inexpressible groanings"¹¹ *come before me,*[12] *abide in me,*[13] *give me your heart*[14] and *to put on Christ,*[15] "the betrothal of the Spirit in our hearts,"[16] "the cry from the heart *Abba, Father!*"[17] and others besides. When I began to pray with my heart with all this in mind, everything surrounding me took on a delightful form: the trees, the grass, the birds, the earth, the air, and the light. All things seemed to be saying to me that they existed for humanity's sake, that they were testifying to God's love for humankind, that they all were praying and singing the glory of God. And I understood from this what the *Philokalia* calls *the knowledge of the speech of all creatures,* and I saw here how it was possible to converse with God's creation.

I wandered thus for a long time. In the end I found myself in such a forsaken place that for three days I didn't come upon a single village. My bread crusts were all gone and I became very low in spirits at the thought that I might die of hunger. As soon as I began to pray with my heart, my low spirits passed. I set all my hope in the will of God and became cheerful and at peace. After walking for some time along a road that skirted an immense forest, I caught sight of a watchdog running out of the forest ahead of me. I beckoned it and it approached and started to fawn about me. I rejoiced and thought: here is another mercy of God! There is undoubtedly a flock grazing in this forest, and of course this tame dog is the shepherd's, or perhaps a hunter is hunting here. Whichever it is I can at least beg for some bread if nothing else, because it's already another entire day since I ate something. Or at least I can ask where the nearest settlement is. After running around me and seeing that it would get nothing from me, the dog ran back into the forest along the same narrow path by which it had come out onto the road. I followed it. Walking on for about twenty-five meters[18] I saw through the trees that the dog had gone off into a burrow, from which it peered out and began to bark. And there from behind a thick tree came a skinny and pale middle-aged peasant. He asked me how I had come to this spot and I asked him why he was there. We began to chat amiably. The peasant invited me into his earthen hut. He explained that he was a forester and was guarding this forest, which had been sold for felling. He set bread and salt before me and we continued our conversation.

"I envy your being able to live so comfortably away from other human beings, not like me—knocking about from one place to the next and pushing my way through all sorts of people," I said.

"If you so desire, then please, you too can stay here," he answered. "Look. Not far from here is the former watchman's old earthen hut. It may indeed have tumbled down, but for the summer you can still live there. You have a passport, you'll have some bread with me; they bring some to me every week from our village. And there is even a tiny brook (he pointed with his hand) that never runs dry. I myself, brother, have been eating nothing but bread and drinking only water for ten years now, never anything else at all, never. But here's the situation. In the fall when the peasants are slaving away, about two hundred laborers will arrive here and fell this whole forest. Then, there'll be nothing for me here, and they won't let you stay here either."

When I heard this I was so overjoyed that I fell down at his feet. I did not know how to thank God for his exceeding kindness toward me. What I had fretted over and desired I now unexpectedly received. There were still about four months before late autumn and until then I could avail myself of the silence and peacefulness so amenable to an attentive reading of the *Philokalia*; I could study and acquire the unceasing prayer of the heart. So, with heartfelt joy I stayed until fall in the hut he had shown me. I talked some more with this brother who had welcomed me, and he began telling me about his life and his ideas.

"I had a good position in our village," he said. "I had my own workshop where I dyed red calico and canvas. I lived comfortably enough though not without sin. I cheated many in my business; I swore falsely, was abusive, got drunk, and brawled. There was in our village an old cleric who owned a really old book about the Last Judgment. He used to make the rounds of the Orthodox and read from it, and for this he was given money. He even came to my place. Give him about ten kopecks and bring him a glass of wine and he would read from evening until cock crow! And so I would sit at my work listening, and he would read about the kinds of torments waiting for us in hell, how the living would be changed and the dead raised, how God would sit in judgment, how the angels would sound their trumpets and what kind of fire, pitch, and worm would devour sinners. One day as I was listening to this I got scared and thought: 'What if the torments do not pass me by! Hold on! I'll get down to saving my soul. Perhaps I can pray away my sins.' I thought and thought and closed my trade business and sold my house. Since I was alone, I became a forester with the provision that my village commune give me bread and clothing and some wax candles for my devotions. So, I have been living here for more than ten years. I only eat once a day and all I eat is bread and water; every night I get up at the first cock crow and do prostrations to the ground until dawn. When I pray, I light seven candles in front of the icons. During the day, when I make my rounds in the forest, I wear chains weighing thirty-two kilograms[19] against my bare skin. I don't use foul language; I don't drink wine anymore; and I don't fight with anyone. I've had nothing to do with women and girls all my life. At first I rather liked living this way, but toward the end persistent thoughts assailed me—God only knows if you can pray away your sins, but this kind of life is hard. Is what is written in that little book really the truth? So-and-so died more than a hundred years ago and not even his ashes are left. Who really knows if there is a hell or not? Nobody has ever come back from that world. It seems that when people die and rot they vanish without a trace. Perhaps the priests and superiors themselves wrote that little book to frighten us idiots into living more modestly. And so we live on the earth toiling away and take comfort in nothing. But if in that world there is nothing, then what do we have from it? Isn't it better to take it easy here on earth and live happily? I wrestle with these thoughts," he continued, "and I'm afraid that I'll take up my former trade again!"

On hearing this I felt sorry for him and wondered to myself: "They say that certain scholars and intellectuals are free-thinkers and believe in nothing. But here one of our own simple peasants contemplates such unbelief. It is clear that the dark world is permitted to have access to everyone, and it perhaps assaults the simple even more easily. I must become wiser and fortify myself against the soul's enemy with the Word of God as much as possible."

In order to help this brother and do all I could to sustain his belief, I reached for my *Philokalia* in my sack, found chapter 109 by Saint Hesychios, and read it aloud. I explained to him that to abstain from sins merely out of fear of torments was of no avail and did not lead to victory. I told him that it was impossible for the soul to be liberated from the sins of many years by any means other than custody of the mind and purity of the heart.

"And since all of this is acquired by means of interior prayer," I added, "if anyone begins to perform saving feats of asceticism not only out of fear of the torments of hell, but even out of a desire for the kingdom of heaven, this too the holy fathers call the act of a hireling. They say that the fear of torment is the path of a slave, and the desire for reward in the kingdom is the path of a hireling. The Lord wishes us to come to him on the path of a son, that is, out of love and zeal for him, to conduct ourselves honorably and to take delight in saving union with him in soul and heart. No matter how much you wear yourself out, no matter what physical returns for your labors and ascetic feats you wish, if you do not always keep God in your mind and the unceasing Jesus prayer in your heart, you will never find respite from thoughts and you will always be easily inclined to sin at the slightest opportunity. Make an effort, brother, to say the Jesus prayer without ceasing. You are surely able to do so with ease in this solitude, and soon you will see the benefits of it: the godless thoughts will not come; faith and love for Jesus Christ will be revealed to you. You will know how the dead are raised, and the Last Judgment will be shown to you as it truly is. But in your heart will be such lightness and joy from the prayer that you will marvel, and you will be bored and discountenanced no more by your wholesome way of life."

Furthermore I explained to him as I could how to begin and how to continue the Jesus prayer without ceasing, how the Word of God commanded it and what the holy fathers taught about it. He declared his agreement with this and seemed more peaceful. After this I took my leave of him and locked myself in the old earthen hut that he had shown me.

My God! What tranquillity, what joy and what rapture I felt as soon as I crossed the threshold of that cave, or to put it better, that grave. It seemed to me like a magnificent imperial palace filled with every comfort and diversion. With joyous tears I thanked God and reflected: "Well now, with such peace and quiet you'll have to devote yourself intently to your task and ask the Lord to make you understand." So I began, first of all, to read the entire *Philokalia* in order, from beginning to end, with great attentiveness. In a short time I had read through the whole work and saw what wisdom, sanctity, and depth it contained. But because it dealt with prayer and other subjects using various exhortations of the holy fathers, I could not understand everything. Nor could I bring together into a whole what I wanted to know about interior prayer in particular, so that I could draw from this a method for learning the unceasing, self-activating prayer of the heart. Yet this was exactly what I wanted, in keeping with the divine command: *Be zealous for the greater gifts; do not quench the Spirit.*[20]

I thought and thought how to do it. My mind and understanding were insufficient, and there was no one who could explain things. I began to read the same thing again, hoping that the Lord would somehow make me understand. After this I did nothing for entire days except pray without ceasing, not stopping my prayer even for the briefest moment. My thoughts calmed down and I fell asleep. And there I dreamed that I was in the cell of my deceased elder, who was explaining the *Philokalia* to me. He said:

"This holy book is filled with great wisdom. It is a mysterious treasury of the meaning of God's hidden judgments. It is not accessible in every place and to everyone; however, it contains the kinds of precepts appropriate to the needs of each inquirer, wise precepts for the wise and simple precepts for the simple. For this reason you simple folk ought not to read it in the order by which the books of the fathers are arranged, one after the other. This is a theological arrangement. The uneducated person who wishes to learn interior prayer from the *Philokalia* must read it in the following order: first, read the book by Nikiphoros the Monk,[21] in part 2; second, the second book by Gregory of Sinai,[22] except for the brief chapters; third, Symeon the New Theologian's 'On the Three Modes of Prayer,'[23] and 'A Discourse on Faith'; fourth,

81

the book by Kallistos and Ignatios.[24] These fathers' works contain the full explanation, directions, and doctrine concerning the interior prayer of the heart. Anyone can understand them. If, however, you desire an even clearer instruction on prayer, look in part 4 for the 'Abbreviated Description of the Mode of Prayer' by his holiness Kallistos, patriarch of Constantinople."

I dreamt that I was holding the *Philokalia* in my hands and started searching for the indicated instructions, but I was not able to find them quickly at all. The elder turned a few pages himself and said: "There it is! I'll mark it for you." He picked up a piece of charcoal from the ground and drew a black line alongside the article.

I listened attentively to everything that the elder said and tried to remember it as firmly and with as much detail as possible. I woke up and since day had still not dawned I lay there and memorized all that I had seen and what the elder had said to me in my dream. Finally, I began to reflect: "God knows if the soul of the deceased elder appeared to me or if my own thoughts contrived it all, for I often think a lot about the *Philokalia* and the elder." In this bewildered state I got up, for day was already breaking. And what do you know! On the stone that takes the place of a table in my hut, I see the *Philokalia* opened to the very spot the elder had shown me, underlined with charcoal. The piece of charcoal lay next to the stone, exactly as I had dreamt it. This startled me, for I firmly recall that the book was not there in the evening—it was tucked in by my side at the head of the bed. Likewise I am certain that beforehand there were no marks of any kind at the place in question. This circumstance convinced me of the truth of my dream and that my elder of blessed memory enjoyed God's favor. So I took it upon myself to read the *Philokalia* in exactly the same order that the elder indicated. I read it once and I read the same thing a second time. The reading enkindled in my soul the desire and zeal to experience in fact everything that I had read. I understood as plain as day what interior prayer meant, how to attain it and what comes of it, how it delights the soul and heart, and how to discern whether or not this sweetness is from God, from nature or whether it is a deception.

SECOND MEETING

First of all I set about searching for the place of the heart in keeping with the instructions of Symeon the New Theologian. I closed my eyes and gazed into my heart with my mind, that is, with my imagination, desiring to visualize it in the left half of the chest, and I listened attentively to its beating. I occupied myself like this initially for half an hour several times a day. At first I perceived nothing but darkness. Then, in a short while I began to picture my heart and identify its movements. Later still in unison with the heart's rhythm I began to bring into it and draw out of it the Jesus prayer, following the instructions of Saint Gregory of Sinai and of Kallistos and Ignatios. That is, when I inhaled I visualized with my mind's eye the words *Lord Jesus Christ* in my heart, and when I exhaled, the words *have mercy on me*. At first I did this for one or two hours at a time; then as time went on I practiced it all the more frequently until in the end I was spending almost the entire day in this exercise. When something burdensome weighed me down, or when sloth or doubt befell me, I immediately began to read those passages in the *Philokalia* that give instructions on the work of the heart, and my inclination and zeal for prayer returned once again. After about three weeks I started to feel a pain in my heart and then a most pleasant warmth, consolation, and calm. This so stirred me and made me all the more eager to practice the prayer with diligence that all my thoughts were occupied by it and I felt great joy. From this time on I began to feel various and periodical sensations in my heart and mind. At times it was as if something delightful was boiling in my heart; at other times there was such lightness, freedom, and comfort in it that I was completely transformed and carried off into ecstasy. Sometimes I felt love for Jesus Christ and all of God's creation. Sometimes sweet tears of thanksgiving flowed on their own to the Lord for the mercy he showed me, a wretched sinner. Sometimes my hitherto foolish understanding became so clear that I easily understood and contemplated things I previously was unable even to think up. Sometimes the heart's sweet warmth spilled over my entire being and I tenderly felt the omnipresent Godhead by me. I sensed within myself the greatest happiness from invoking the name of Jesus Christ, and I realized what he meant when he said: *The kingdom of God is within you.*[25] By experiencing these and similar sweet consolations I observed that the fruits of the prayer of the heart are made manifest in three ways: in the spirit, in the feelings, and in revelations.

For example, in the spirit there is the sweetness of divine love, interior rest, rapture of the mind, purity of thought, and sweet recollection of God. In the feelings one senses a pleasant warming of the heart, the filling of all one's members with sweetness, a joyful bubbling in the heart, lightness, courage, pleasantness of life, and insensitivity to pain and sorrow. In revelations there is the illumination of the intellect, understanding of the Sacred Scriptures, knowledge of the speech of created things, renunciation of vanities, knowledge of the sweetness of the inner life, and confidence in the nearness of God and his love for us.

I spent about five months in solitude devoted to prayer and the enjoyment of these sensations. I grew so accustomed to the prayer of the heart that I practiced it without ceasing. In the end I felt that the prayer arose and was uttered in my mind and heart by itself, without any effort on my part. Not only in a watchful state but also in my sleep the prayer carried on in precisely the same way. Nothing interrupted it or stopped it for the briefest moment, no matter what I was doing. My soul thanked the Lord and my heart melted away in unceasing gladness.

The time came for the forest to be cleared; people started to throng, and I had to abandon my silent dwelling-place. After thanking the forester, I prayed and kissed the plot of ground where God had granted unworthy me to live. I took the pouch with my books and left. I wandered for quite some time from place to place until I ended up in Irkutsk. The self-activating prayer of the heart was my consolation and joy on the way. At every encounter and in every situation, wherever I was, whatever I did, and however I occupied myself, the prayer never stopped delighting me. It hindered nothing and was not diminished by anything. If I work at something and the prayer acts in my heart of its own accord, the task goes all the more quickly; and if I listen to something attentively or am reading, even then the prayer does not cease. It seems that at one and the same time I feel the one and the other thing, precisely as if I were split in two or as if I had two souls in one body. My God! How mysterious we humans are. *May your works be exalted, O Lord; with wisdom you have made them all!* [26]

I encountered many strange events and incidents on my journey, and if I were to tell them all I would not be finished in twenty-four hours. For example, once during the winter, toward evening, I was walking alone through the forest to spend the night in a village that came into view about two kilometers ahead. Suddenly a huge wolf came upon me and jumped at me. I had in my hands my elder's wooden prayer beads, as I always did. I warded the wolf off with them, but what do you think happened? They were snatched out of my hands and somehow got wrapped around the wolf's neck. The wolf lunged away from me. As he bounded through a blackthorn bush growing nearby, his hind legs became entangled in the bush and he got fastened by the beads to the bough of a dead tree. There he hung. He began to struggle, but it was hard for him to get free because the beads tightened around his neck. I made the sign of the cross with faith and approached with the intention of releasing the wolf a little, mostly because I thought that if he tore through the beads and ran off with them I would lose my precious prayer beads. I came forward and barely had taken hold of the beads when the wolf ripped them and ran away without a trace. So I gave thanks to God and remembered my blessed elder. I reached the village safely and went to an inn to ask for a night's lodgings.

I entered the building. Two people were seated at a table in the front corner. One was an old man and the other was a stout middle-aged fellow; from their appearance they seemed not to be commoners. They were drinking tea. I asked the peasant who was with their horses who they were. "The old man is a teacher at the elementary school," he told me, "and the other one is a scrivener from the Court of the Land. Both of them are nobles. I am taking them to the fair, which is about twenty kilometers from here."

After sitting for a bit, I asked an old woman for a needle and thread; then I went to the lamp and began sewing my torn prayer beads. The scrivener saw this and said:

"It looks as if you really got into making prostrations! Did you tear your beads?"

"I didn't tear them, a wolf did."

"What, do wolves pray now?" said the scrivener, who burst out laughing. I told them the whole affair in detail and how precious these prayer beads were to me. The scrivener laughed again and started speaking.

"You holier-than-thou types see miracles everywhere! But what's holy about this? You simply hurled something at the wolf, he took fright and ran off. Dogs and wolves are afraid of things thrown at them. No wonder he got caught in the woods. Does this happen so seldom in the world that everyone has to believe it's a miracle?"

The teacher began a conversation with him after listening to this:

"Don't jump to conclusions like that, sir. You're unfamiliar with the subject matter. As for me, I see in this peasant's narration the mystery of nature which is both sensory and spiritual."

"How's that?" asked the scrivener.

"Well, you see, although you do not have a higher education, you of course would have learned the short *Sacred History of Old and New Testaments*, published in question-and-answer form for elementary schools. You remember that when Adam, the first created human being, was in the holy state of innocence, all living creatures and wild animals obeyed him; they approached him with fear and he called them by name. The elder, whose beads these are, was a holy man. But what does holiness mean? Nothing other than the restoration of the innocent state of the first human to a sinner through ascetical acts. When the soul is sanctified, the body too is sanctified. The prayer beads were always in the hands of the sanctified one. Thus it follows that through the contact of his hands and his breathing on them a holy power was imparted to them, the power of the innocent state of the first human. That is the mystery of spiritual nature. All animals down to the present day naturally sense this power, and they sense it by means of smell, for the nose of wild animals and other creatures is the most important instrument of the senses. That is the mystery of sensory nature...."

"You scholars go on about powers and wisdom, but we put it simply: when you pour a glass of vodka and you have enough, there's your power!" said the scrivener and then he went for the cupboard.

"That is your business," said the teacher, "but I beg you to leave scientific learning to us."

I liked the way the teacher spoke, so I went over to him and said: "Dare I tell you, good sir, something more about my elder?" I explained to him how the elder appeared to me in a dream, took[27] the charcoal, and underlined passages in the *Philokalia*. The teacher listened to everything with attention, but the clerk, lying against the counter, growled:

"It's true what they say: those who read the Bible too much go crazy. That's the way it is! What kind of wood goblin will come and mark your books for you in the night? You simply let the book fall on the floor yourself in your sleep and it got smudged in soot. There's your miracle for you! Oh these old foxes! I've seen lots of your kind, brother!"

After he muttered this, the scrivener turned to the wall and fell asleep. When I noticed this, I turned to the teacher and said: "Look, if you like, I'll show you the book itself, where it is properly underlined and not smudged with soot." I pulled the *Philokalia* out of my bag and showed him, saying:

"This higher wisdom amazes me, how a bodiless soul could pick up a piece of charcoal and write with it."

The teacher looked at the paragraph and began to speak: "This too is a mystery of the spirits. I will explain it to you. You see, when spirits appear in bodily shape to a living human being, they gather up and put together for themselves a vital body made out of air and luminous matter. When they are finished appearing, they return what they borrowed to those elements out of which the composite of their body was drawn. And since air possesses elasticity, a power to contract and expand, so too the soul, which is cloaked in it, is able to pick up anything, to act and to write. But what kind of book do you have? Give it here so I can look at it."

He opened it to "A Sermon and Discourse" of Symeon the New Theologian. "This must be a theological book. I have never seen it before."

"Good sir, this book consists almost entirely of teaching on the interior prayer of the heart in the name of Jesus Christ, disclosed in every detail by twenty-five holy fathers."

The teacher said, "I know about interior prayer."

I prostrated myself at his feet and begged: "Do me a favor and tell me something about interior prayer."

"Well, in the New Testament it is said that human beings and the whole creation, unwillingly subject to vanity, naturally sigh, yearn, and desire to enter into the freedom of the children of God, and this sighing of creation, this innate yearning of souls is interior prayer. There is nothing to learn about it; it is in everyone and everything."

"But how do we find, uncover, and sense it in our heart? How can we be conscious of it and welcome it with our will? How do we get to the point where the prayer clearly acts, pleases, enlightens, and saves us?" I asked.

"I do not recall whether or not there is anything written about this in theological treatises," replied the teacher.

"It's all written here in this book," I said. The teacher took out a pencil and wrote down the title of the *Philokalia* and then said, "I'll have this book sent from Tobolsk without fail and I'll examine it."

And so we parted. When I left, I thanked God for the conversation with the teacher and I prayed that the Lord might dispose the scrivener to read the *Philokalia*, even if only once, so that he might come to understand and be saved. After this, while I was continuing my journey in the joy and nourishment of the uninterrupted prayer of the heart, yet another remarkable event happened to me. It took place one springtime as I was passing by a certain village. By chance I stopped at a priest's house. He was a good person who lived alone. I spent three days with him. After watching me for that length of time he said:

"Stay with me and I'll offer you some pay. I need someone conscientious. You have seen that I am having a new stone church built near the old wooden one. I have been unable to find a trust-worthy person to supervise the laborers and sit in the chapel to collect offerings for the construction. I see that you would be capable of this and that, given your inclinations, living there would suit you just fine. You could sit alone in the chapel and pray to God; there is a small private room for the church warden. Please stay, at least for the summer until the church is finished."

Although I offered lengthy excuses, the priest's persuasive begging made me agree, and I stayed from summer until autumn. I took up living in the chapel. At first I found it peaceful and amenable for saying my prayers, even though many people would come and go, especially on feast days: some to pray, others to yawn, and still others to swipe something from the collection plate. And since I read from time to time the Holy Bible or the *Philokalia*, some of the visitors struck up a conversation with me; others asked me to read something for them.

After a while I noticed that a certain peasant girl came to the chapel often and prayed for hours to God. Overhearing her mumbling I recognized that she was reciting some sort of strange prayers, and that others were completely garbled. I asked who had taught them to her. She said that it was her mother and added that her mother was a church-going woman whereas her father was one of the priestless Old Ritualists. Feeling sorry for her, I advised her to recite her prayers correctly in keeping with the tradition of Holy Church, and then I explained to her the *Our Father* and the *Rejoice, Theotokos Virgin*. At the end I said, "You would do well to say the Jesus prayer as often as possible; it, more than all other prayers, brings access to God and you will gain salvation for your soul through it." The girl listened attentively to my advice and began to act accordingly in her simplicity. And what do you think? After a brief while she declared to me that she had grown so accustomed to the Jesus prayer that she felt drawn to devote her-self to it continually, if it were possible. She went on to say that when she prayed she had a pleasant sensation and, upon finish-ing, joy and the desire to pray once more. I rejoiced at this and advised her to continue her prayer in the name of Jesus Christ all the more.

The end of summer was drawing near. Many of the visitors to the chapel began coming to me not only for reading and words of advice but also with various everyday worries, and even to learn about tracking down things they had mislaid or lost. It was clear that some of them took me for a sorcerer. Finally, even the girl I was talking about came to me in distress for advice about what she ought to do. Her father was intending to marry her off against her will to an Old Ritualist of the same priestless community, and a simple peasant would perform the marriage.

"What kind of lawful marriage is that?" she exclaimed. "It's just the same as fornication. I want to run away, and I'll go to the first place I see."

"But where would you run away to? They would find you anyway. In the present age you cannot completely hide yourself anywhere without documents; the police will search everywhere for you. It is better for you to pray all the more earnestly to God that he might wreck your father's plan by his own designs and preserve your soul from sin and heresy."

Still more time passed and I made up my mind to leave the chapel and continue my former journey. I visited the priest and told him. "Father, you know about my frame of mind. I need quiet to practice prayer, but it is very distracting and harmful for me here. I have fulfilled your request and spent the summer, but now release me and bless me for my solitary journey."

The priest was unwilling to release me and he began coaxing me to stay. "What prevents you from praying here? You have no other task but to sit in the chapel, and you have bread already made for you. Please, pray there both day and night. My brother, live with God! You fit this place. You don't prattle nonsense with the parishioners; in fact, you bring in an income for the church of God and you collect it faithfully. This is more pleasing in God's sight than is your solitary prayer. What is there for you in solitude? It is more pleasant to pray with people. God created us not so that we would know only ourselves but so that people would help each other and lead one another to salvation as each one is able. Look at the saints and universal doctors. Day and night they interceded and took pains for the church, and they preached everywhere. They did not sit in their solitude and hide themselves from people."

"God gives to each person, father, the proper gift. There have been many preachers and there have been many hermits. Those who found within themselves any sort of inclination toward any goal obeyed their inclination and said that it was God who pointed out their path of salvation. But what reason can you give me for this: many of the saints had the rank of bishop, superior, and priest, and they fled into solitary desert places so that they would not be disturbed and harmed in the midst of others? Saint Isaac the Syrian ran away from his episcopal pasture for this reason; so too did Saint Athanasios of Athos abandon his multitudinous monastery precisely because those places were full of temptations for them and because they truly believed the voice of Jesus Christ: *For what will it profit them if they gain the whole world but forfeit their life?*"[28]

"But they were saints, surely," the priest said.

"If saints were on their guard lest they be harmed by associating with men and women," I said, "what else remains for a powerless sinner to do?"

In the end I took leave of the good priest and he lovingly blessed me for my journey. Having traveled about ten kilometers I stopped to the spend the night in a hamlet. In the overnight lodgings I saw a desperately sick peasant and advised those with him to have him receive the sacred mysteries of Christ. They concurred and toward morning sent for the priest from their village parish. I waited so that I might reverence the Holy Gifts and pray before this great mystery. I went out into the street, sat on an embankment, and waited to meet the priest. All of a sudden the girl who used to pray in the chapel came running out of the backyard.

"How did you end up here?" I asked.

"We were to have the betrothal ceremony yesterday, to that Old Ritualist, so I ran away." At this she fell to my feet and said: "Do me a favor: take me with you and bring me away to some monastery. I do not want to marry. I will live in the monastery and say the Jesus prayer. They will listen to you there and take me in."

"I beg your pardon!" I said. "Where am I to take you? I do not know of a single monastery for women in this area. And how can I go with you if you do not have a passport? For one thing, no place will take you in and it's impossible to hide yourself anywhere nowadays. You'll be caught and sent back to your own village and in addition you will be punished for vagrancy. It is better for you to go home and pray to God. But if you do not want to get married, then pretend that you have some sort of illness. This is called saving pretense. That is what the holy mother of Saint Clement did and so did venerable Macrina, who saved herself in a men's monastery. Many others have done the same thing."

Then, as we were sitting there talking things over, we saw four peasants come galloping at full stride along the road, and they rode right up to us. They seized the girl and put her in a cart. One of the peasants set out with her. The other three bound my hands and drove me back to the village where I had spent the summer. To all of my attempts to explain myself they only shouted: "We'll teach you to seduce girls, you hypocrite!" Toward evening they brought me to the village court, fastened my feet in irons, and put me in the jail until morning while they made ready for the trial. The priest found out that I was in jail. He came to visit me, brought me something for dinner, and consoled me. He said that he would intercede for me and tell them, as a spiritual father, that I was not the type of person they thought I was. After sitting with me for a while, he left.

Later in the evening the magistrate was traveling to some other place through the village and he stopped at the deputy's. The villagers told him what had happened. He ordered an assembly and had me brought to the courtroom. We went in, stood, and waited. Then the magistrate arrived, already lit up. Wearing his service cap he sat at the table and shouted:

"Fellows! See here!"

"We see, sir." The whole gathering answered in one voice.

"What do you see?"

"He is the one we see."

"Hey, you beasts, listen up!"

"We're listening, sir."

"I have examined the case. Hey, Epifan! This girl, your daughter, she took nothing from your house?"

"Nothing, sir."

"Was she caught doing foolish things with that dimwit?"

"No, sir."

"Then here is how I will decide and judge the case. You can help your daughter yourself by pinning her tail so she won't run away like a bitch. As for that fellow, tomorrow we'll give him a thrashing, drive him out of the village, and tell him in no uncertain terms never to set foot here again. And that's that."

After saying this, the magistrate started to get down from the table, but he staggered and fell. They let him sleep but took me back to jail. Early in the morning two men came, the village police chief and an assistant; they flogged me and released me. I went and thanked God that he had found me worthy to suffer for his name. This consoled me and intensified the unceasing prayer of the heart. None of these events grieved me in the slightest; it was as though they had happened to someone else and I merely watched them. Even when they were flogging me I had the strength to endure it. The prayer that delighted my heart did not permit me to notice anything else. After traveling for about four kilometers, I met the girl's mother coming from the market with her purchases. When she caught sight of me she said: "Our groom has called off the marriage. You see, he got angry with Akulka because she ran away from him." Then she gave me some bread and a pie, and I went further on my way. The weather was dry and I had no desire to spend the night in some hamlet. In the evening I spied two fenced-in hayricks in the woods, and I spread myself out underneath them to spend the night.

When I had fallen asleep I dreamed that I was walking along a road and reading the chapters of Anthony the Great from the *Philokalia*. Suddenly my elder caught up to me and said: "Don't read there! Here, read in this spot." He pointed to chapter 35 of John of Karpathos,[29] in which the following is written: "Sometimes the one teaching submits to ignominy and endures temptation for the sake of those drawing spiritual benefit from him." Then he pointed to chapter 41, where it says: "Those who make the most

zealous use of prayer will be taken prisoner by frightful and fero-
cious temptations." Then he spoke:

"Be vigilant in spirit and do not grow weary! Remember what
the apostle said: *The one who is in you is greater than the one who is in
the world.*[30] You now know through experience that no testing is permitted beyond an individual's strength, but *with the testing God will
also provide the way out.*[31] Reliance on this divine help strengthened
and guided the holy ascetics to ardor and zeal, for they not only
spent their whole life in unceasing prayer themselves, but out of
love they instructed and revealed this to others too, as opportunity and time permitted. About this, Saint Gregory of Thessaloniki[32]
said: 'Not only should we ourselves pray unceasingly in the name
of Jesus Christ, in keeping with the divine command, but we must
also teach and reveal this to others, to everyone in general—to
monks and seculars, to the wise and the simple, to men and
women and children—and we must arouse in everyone zeal for
unceasing prayer.' Similarly, Kallistos Antelikudis[33] says that mental activity concerning the Lord, that is, interior prayer, contemplative knowledge, and methods for raising the soul on high
should not be retained only in our own mind; we must rather take
notes and pass these things on in writing and exposition for common use and because of love. Indeed, the word of God speaks of
this, that *a brother helped by a brother is like a strong and lofty city.*[34]
However, in this case, it is of utmost necessity to flee vainglory and
to take care lest the seed of divine teaching be sown to the wind."

I woke up and felt great joy in my heart and strength in my
soul, and I went further on my journey. Quite some time after
this there was yet another event. If you please, I will tell it.

One day, namely, 24 March, I felt an insurmountable desire to
receive the Holy Mysteries of Christ on the morrow, that is, on the
day dedicated to the commemoration of the holy Annunciation of
the most pure Mother of God. I inquired whether or not the
church was far away. They told me it was thirty kilometers distant,
and so for the remainder of the day and through the night I walked
in order to get there for Orthros. The weather was most foul,
alternating between rain and snow, and then came a strong wind
and the cold. On my way I had to cross a small stream, and no

sooner had I stepped into the middle of it than the ice gave way under my feet and I was plunged in water up to my waist. Soaking wet, I arrived at Orthros. I held out even through the Divine Liturgy, and God made me worthy to receive communion. In order to spend the day in tranquillity, without hindrance to spiritual joy, I got permission from the church sexton to remain in the guardhouse until morning. The whole day I experienced ineffable joy and sweetness of the heart. I lay in the bunk over the stove in that unheated guard hut as though I were resting in the bosom of Abraham.

The prayer was forcefully active. Love for the Lord Jesus Christ and the Mother of God swirled like delightful waves in my heart and seemed to immerse my soul in consoling rapture. At night I suddenly felt a powerful aching in my legs and then I recalled that they were damp. Disregarding this I began all the more diligently to pay heed to my heart with prayer and I no longer felt the pain. In the morning I wanted to rise but I saw that I was unable even to stir my legs a little, for they were paralyzed and limp, like lashes. The sexton dragged me violently out of the bunk, so I sat there for two days without moving. The third day the sexton began to chase me out of the guardhouse, saying: "If you die here, just imagine the fuss over you." Somehow I managed to crawl out on my hands and so I lay on the church porch. I was there for about two days. The people who passed me by paid not the slightest bit of attention to me nor my requests. Finally, some peasant fellow approached me, sat down, and began a conversation. Among other things he said:

"What will you give me? I will cure you; I had exactly the same thing myself and I know a remedy for it."

"I have nothing to give you," I answered.

"And what is in your bag there?"

"Some crusts of bread and some books."

"What if you work for me just for one summer, if I cure you?"

"I can't even do that. As you can see, I have the use of only one arm, the other has withered almost completely away."

"Then what do you know how to do?"

"The only thing I can do is read and write."

"Hmm. Write can you? Well, teach my little boy, my dear little son, to write. He knows how to read a little bit, but I would like him to be able to write. But instructors charge too much—twenty rubles for the training."

I agreed to this, and he and the sexton dragged me out and settled me in the peasant's backyard, in an old empty bathhouse. Then he began to cure me. From the fields, the roads, and refuse pits he picked up nearly a bushel of various rotted bones, from birds and all sorts of creatures. He washed them thoroughly and broke them into small pieces with a stone. Then he placed them in a large earthenware pot, covered it with a lid that had a slit in it, and overturned it into an empty pot embedded in the ground. He smeared a thick layer of clay all over the top of the pot and after surrounding it with a pile of wood, he burned it for over twenty-four hours. As he piled on more wood, he said: "We'll get some tar from the bones." The next day he dug the pot out of the ground. Through the slit in the jar and into the pot had dripped about a pint of thick, reddish, oily liquid, pungent like fresh raw meat. The bones, however, which in the jar had been all black and rotten, were now so white and clean and translucent that they seemed to be mother of pearl or even pearl itself. I rubbed my legs with this liquid five times a day. And what do think? Two days later I felt that I could move my toes a little. On the third day I was able to bend and unbend my legs and on the fifth day I stood on them and walked about the yard with a cane. In a word, after a week my legs had become as strong as before. I thanked God for this and thought to myself: "What divine wisdom there is in creation! Dry, putrid bones, almost entirely turned into earth, preserve in themselves such vital force, color, smell, and power of acting on living bodies; it is as though they communicate life to dead bodies. This is a pledge of the future resurrection of the body. How I would like to show this to that forester with whom I lived, in view of his doubts about the general resurrection."

Having recovered in this fashion, I began to teach the boy. Instead of the usual writing samples, I wrote down the Jesus prayer and made him copy it, showing him how to space out the words nicely. Teaching him was restful for me because during the day he waited on a steward and came to me for studying only when the steward was sleeping, that is, from dawn until the late church services. The boy caught on quickly and soon began to write things in an orderly fashion. When the steward saw him writing, he asked: "Who is teaching you?" The boy said that it was a one-armed pilgrim who lived in his family's bathhouse. The inquisitive steward came to get a look at me and found me reading from the *Philokalia*. Striking up a conversation with me, he asked:

"What are you reading?" I showed him the book.

"Oh, that's the *Philokalia*," he said. "I used to see that book at our Catholic priest's when I was living in Wilno. I was told, however, that it contains some sort of strange tricks. Yes, yes, a science for prayer, written down by Greek monks, similar to the way fanatics in India and Bukhara sit and puff themselves up, wanting to experience a tickling in their heart. In their stupidity they consider this natural sensation to be prayer, as though given to them by God. If you get up and say the *Our Father* as Christ taught, then you're right for the whole day, instead of rhyming off the same thing without interruption. That is how you'll go crazy, if you'll pardon me, and you'll harm your heart as well."

"Dear sir, do not think so about this holy book. Simple Greek monks did not write it, but the ancient, great, and most holy men whom even your church honors, such as Anthony the Great, Makarios the Great, Mark the Ascetic, John Chrysostom, and others. And the Indian and Bukharan monks adopted the method of the heart for interior prayer from them; only they spoiled it and perverted it themselves, as my own elder has told me. In the *Philokalia*, however, all the instructions about the practice of the prayer of the heart are drawn from the Word of God—from the Holy Bible. Just as Jesus Christ, who instructed us to say the *Our Father*, commanded unceasing prayer as well, when he said: *Seek me with all your heart*;[35] *abide in me as I abide in you*;[36] *pray without ceasing*;[37] *everyone who calls on the name of the Lord shall be saved*.[38] But the holy fathers, by introducing the witness of the holy king David in the Psalter, *Taste and see that the Lord is good*,[39] explain it in this way: the Christian must search by every means and acquire delight in prayer and search for consolation in it without ceasing, and not simply say the *Our Father* once a day.... Here, I'll read for you how these holy fathers censure those who do not try to gain and learn the sweet prayer of the heart. They write that such people commit a sin in three ways. First, such people show themselves to contradict the divinely inspired scriptures. Second, they do not suppose that there is a higher and more perfect state for the soul, and are satisfied with external acts of virtue; they cannot have a hunger and thirst for righteousness and so are deprived of blessedness and happiness in the Lord. Third, by thinking about themselves on the basis of their external virtues they frequently fall into deception or pride and thereby make vain their salvation."

"You are reading something lofty there," said the steward. "Where are we lay folk to be in pursuit of it?"

"Here, I'll read you something simpler, about how even good people who live in the world have learned unceasing prayer." I found the saying of Symeon the New Theologian concerning the youth, George, and began to read it. This pleased the steward and he said to me:

"Let me have that book to read. I'll examine it now and then in my spare time."

"I'll give it to you for twenty-four hours, but for no longer, because I read it every day and I cannot live without it."

"Well, at least copy out for me what you just now read and I'll pay you."

"I do not need payment. I shall copy it for love if only God will grant you zeal for prayer."

I immediately wrote down with pleasure the sermon that I had read aloud. He read it to his wife and it pleased them both. They began to send for me time and again, and I would go to their home often with the *Philokalia* and read there, while they listened to me as they drank their tea.

Once they let me stay for dinner. The steward's wife, a kindly old lady, sat with us and was eating some grilled fish when she inadvertently choked on a bone. No matter how we tried to help her, we could not dislodge the bone. She felt a sharp pain in her throat and after about two hours went to lie down. Then they sent for the doctor who was thirty kilometers away. I excused myself and went home, it being evening already. During the night, in a light sleep, I heard the voice of my elder, but I saw no one. The voice said to me: "Your master cured you but there you are, unable to help the steward's wife? God has instructed us to share our neighbors' suffering."

"I would gladly help but with what? I do not know any remedies."

"Well, here is what you are to do. From the very beginning of her life she has had an aversion to lamp oil. Not only can she not use it, she is even unable to bear the odor without feeling nauseous. So, give her a spoonful of the oil to drink. It will make her vomit and the bone will be disgorged; the wound which the bone scratched in her throat will be coated with the oil, and she will recover."

"And how will I give her the oil if she has an aversion to it? She won't drink it."

"You are to order the steward to hold her by the head and then pour it into her mouth all at once, with force if necessary."

After I woke up I immediately went to the steward and related to him all of this in detail. He, however, said: "What will your oil do now? Look at her: she is already wheezing and delirious, and her neck is all swollen. Yes, please, let's try; oil is a harmless medicine, though it won't do any good either."

He poured some lamp oil into a wineglass and somehow we gave it to her to swallow. Straight away she began violently heaving and the bone was quickly thrown up with some blood. She calmed down and fell into a deep sleep.

In the morning I came to call on her and saw that she was sitting up and drinking tea. Both she and her husband were amazed[40] at the healing and even more so that I had been told in my dream that she did not like oil, for no one but the two of them knew this. Then the doctor arrived and the steward's wife told him what had happened to her, and I told him how the peasant had healed my legs. The doctor heard our stories and said: "Neither the one nor the other case is surprising; in both instances the very power of nature itself was at work. Nonetheless

I'll write it down for memory's sake." He took out a pencil and made a note in his little book.

After this the word spread quickly throughout the neighborhood that I was a prophet, doctor, and sorcerer. People started coming to me without interruption from all parts with their various affairs and circumstances; they brought me gifts and started honoring me and indulged my needs. After a week I took stock of this and, fearing that I might fall into vainglory and pride, and be injured by the distraction, I left the place secretly at night. Thus once again I set out on my solitary journey, and I felt such lightness as if a mountain had been taken off my shoulders. The prayer consoled me more and more so that sometimes my heart bubbled up out of measureless love for the Lord Jesus Christ, and from this sweet bubbling it was as if consoling streams spilled over throughout my entire being. The memory of Jesus Christ was so imprinted on my mind that, when I reflected on the events of the Gospel, I saw them as if they were before my eyes. I was moved and wept for joy. Sometimes I felt such gladness in my heart that I was unable even to relate it. It happened that for three days running I did not enter into human habitations and in my ecstasy I felt as if I were the only person on earth—alone, a wretched sinner, before the merciful God who loves humankind. This solitude comforted me and when I was alone the prayerful sweetness was much more tangible than when I was in a crowd.

Finally I reached Irkutsk. Prostrating myself before the holy relics of Bishop Innokenty, I began to ponder: "Where now am I to go?" I had no desire to live here for long, for the town was populous. Reflecting on this, I walked along a street. A local merchant met me, stopped me, and started talking:

"Are you a pilgrim? Why don't you come to my house? I welcome all pilgrims." I went with him to his opulent home. He asked me what kind of person I was and I told him my situation.

"Well, you'd be better to make a pilgrimage to old Jerusalem! There are holy places there, the likes of which are nowhere else!"

"I would gladly go there," I replied, "but I do not have the wherewithal for it. I can get to the sea over dry land, but as for crossing the sea—I have nothing with which to pay for the trip. That takes a lot of money."

The merchant said, "If you wish I will offer you the means. Last year I already sent one pilgrim there from among our townsfolk."

I fell at his feet, but he continued: "Listen! I will give you a letter to my own son in Odessa. He lives there and has a trading business with Constantinople. He also has ships that sail there. He will gladly transport you to Constantinople, and there he will order his managers to book passage for you on a ship to Jerusalem. He'll pay for it, since it doesn't cost very much."

When I heard this I rejoiced and thanked my benefactor many times for his kindness. Even more did I thank God for showing me his exceeding fatherly love and concern for me, a wretched sinner who has done nothing good for himself or for other people, and like a freeloader has devoured the bread of strangers in my idleness.

I was the guest of this beneficent merchant for three days. He wrote a letter about me to his son as he had promised and here I am now on my way to Odessa with the intention of reaching the holy city of Jerusalem itself; but I do not know whether or not the Lord will permit me to venerate his life-bringing tomb.

The Pilgrim's Tale
On the occasion of his third and farewell meeting, 20 December 1859

"*H*ere I am actually on the road to Jerusalem. I have come to say farewell and to give thanks for the Christian love shown me, an unworthy sinner."

"I have heard a great deal from you about your travels, and I would be interested to learn about your origins and life prior to your pilgrimage."

"Right from my birth my life has been all such a mess. I was born in a village in Orel province. After father and mother died, the two of us were left alone—my older brother and I. He was ten and I was two years old. So our grandfather took us into his home to provide for us. He was a well-to-do old man and honest. He kept an inn on the main road and because of his goodness many travelers put up there. We began to live with him. My brother was a playful lad and used to run all over the village, whereas I mostly hung around my grandfather. On feast days we would go with him to church and at home he often read the Bible, in fact, the very one I have with me. My brother grew up and ruined himself: he took to drinking. I was already seven years old when, one day, I was lying with my brother on the stove and he pushed me off. I injured my left arm and even now I have no use of it; it is all withered away.

"When my grandfather saw that I would be unsuited for work on the land, he began to teach me reading and writing. But since we had no ABC-book he taught me using this same Bible:

he pointed out the A's and made me form words and recognize the letters. And so in some sort of way, I do not understand how, over the course of time I learned how to read by repeating after him. Finally, when grandfather became hard of seeing he often made me read the Bible while he listened and corrected me.... A scrivener from the local administration frequently stayed at our inn and he wrote beautifully. I would watch him and loved how he wrote. So, following his example, I too began to form words. He instructed me, would give me paper and ink, and sharpened my quill. Thus I too learned to write. Grandfather was glad about this and urged me on: 'God has now disclosed to you reading and writing. You'll become a somebody, so thank the Lord for this and pray often.' We attended all the services at church and prayed very frequently at home. While grandfather and grandmother made prostrations or knelt, they had me read the psalm *Have mercy on me God.*[1]

"Finally, when I was seventeen, my grandmother died. Grandfather said to me: 'Now we have no mistress of the house, but how can we make do without a woman? Your older brother has worn himself out; I want to find you a wife.' I objected on the grounds that I was a cripple, but grandfather insisted and had me married: they chose a decent and good young woman, twenty years of age. A year passed and my grandfather became sick unto death. He summoned me and started to bid me farewell, saying: 'My house and the entire inheritance are yours. Live according to your conscience; do not deceive anyone; and pray all the more so to God. Everything comes from him. Do not hope in anything but God. Go to church, read the Bible, and remember me and the old lady. The money is yours too, a thousand rubles. Take care not to spend it to no purpose, but don't be miserly either. Give to the poor and to God's church.' Then he died and I buried him. My brother grew envious because the house and property were given to me alone. He became angry with me, and the enemy helped him to such an extent that he even intended to kill me. Finally, this is what he did. At night while we were sleeping and when there was not a single guest, he broke into the pantry where the money was kept, removed it from the chest, and set fire to the pantry. We became aware of it only when the whole house and compound had caught fire, and we were scarcely able to jump through a window, wearing only our nightclothes. The Bible lay under our head and we took it with us. As we watched our house burn, we said to each other: 'Glory be to God, at least the Bible was spared; there is something to comfort us in our grief.' All our possessions were destroyed in the fire and my brother left us without a trace. Only after he started drinking and bragging did we learn that he took the money and set the house on fire. We were left naked and barefoot, utterly destitute.

"In debt we somehow put up a little hut and began living as cotters. My wife was skilled with her hands; she was a master at weaving, spinning, and sewing. She took in work from people and sewed day and night and fed me. Because I had only one useful hand, I couldn't even braid bast shoes. She would braid or sew and I would sit beside her and read the Bible. She listened and sometimes she even burst into tears. When I asked her, 'What are you crying about?', she answered that she was moved to tears because everything was written so well in the Bible. We remembered grandfather's injunction: we prayed regularly; every morning we read the Akathist of the Mother of God,[2] and at night both of us performed a thousand prostrations so as not to be tempted. In this way we lived peacefully for two years. What is surprising in all this is that although we had no idea about the interior prayer done in one's heart and had never even heard about it, but prayed only simply with the tongue and like dimwits turning somersaults, made prostrations without knowing why, still the desire for prayer was there and the long, external prayer done without understanding did not appear difficult but was performed with pleasure. Clearly, one teacher spoke the truth when he said that there is a secret prayer inside a person and that he himself does not know how it is produced of its own accord invisibly in the soul nor how it inspires to prayer whoever has the knowledge and ability. Two years of our lives passed by in this way when my wife suddenly took ill with a high fever. After receiving communion, she passed away on the ninth day.

"I was left entirely alone. I was unable to do anything, and I had to beg for alms, but I was embarrassed to beg for alms. Besides, such sadness on account of my wife beset me that I did not know where I might end up. If I went into our hut and saw her clothes or some little frock, I would howl and fall down senseless! Since I could no longer bear my anguish living at home, I sold the hut for twenty rubles. Whatever clothes[3] of mine or my wife's were there, I distributed them all among the poor.

"Because of my crippled arm I was issued a permanent discharge passport, and I immediately picked up my beloved Bible and went where my eyes pointed me. After I departed, I wondered 'Where shall I go now? First off, I'll go to Kiev and pray to the Servants of God and ask them for help in my pain.' As soon as I had made up my mind about this, I felt relieved and I reached Kiev comforted. Since then I have been wandering non-stop from place to place for fourteen years;[4] I have made the rounds of many churches and monasteries, and more and more now I wander about the steppes and the forests. I do not know if the Lord will favor me to reach holy Jerusalem. If it is God's will, it will be time to rest my sinful bones there."

"And just how old are you?"

"Thirty-three."

"Well, dear brother, you have attained the measure of the stature of Christ."[5]

The Pilgrim's Tale
On the occasion of a fourth
and unexpected meeting

It is good for me to cleave to God, to place the hope of my
salvation in the Lord.[1]

*T*he Russian proverb is correct: man proposes, but God disposes. I supposed that right now I would be on my way to
the holy city of Jerusalem, but it has turned out otherwise. An
utterly unforeseen circumstance kept me for three more days in
the same place. I could not bear not coming to you in order to
inform you about this and to receive advice for my decision concerning the situation that came about entirely unexpectedly in
the following manner.

After taking my leave of everyone, I set out on my journey
with God's help. I only got as far as the outskirts of town when I
saw a familiar person standing at the gate of the last house. He
once had been like me, a pilgrim, and I had not seen him for three
years. We greeted each other and he asked me where I was going.
I replied: "If it pleases God, I'm hoping to go to old Jerusalem!"

"Glory be to God!" he joined in. "There's a good fellow
traveler for you here!"

"God be with you and with him," I said, "but you must
know that in keeping with my own ways I never travel with com-
panions. I am used to wandering always alone."

"Yes, but listen here! I know that you will like this traveling
companion; you'll both get along just fine. Look here, the father

of the master of this house, where I have been hired as a laborer, is also going to old Jerusalem, because of a vow. You'll have a merry time with him. He is a local townsman, a good old man, stone-deaf to boot. It doesn't matter how you shout, he can't hear a thing. If you need to ask him about something, you'll have to write it down for him on paper and then he'll reply. He won't bother you on the journey; he will say nothing. Even at home he grows more and more silent. But you will be essential for him on the road, and here's why. His son is giving him a horse to take as far as Odessa, where he is to sell it. Although the old man wants to go on foot, the horse will go with him too because of his luggage and some presents for the Lord's tomb. And you can put your knapsack there as well. Now just think. How can we send someone old and deaf on such a lengthy journey alone with a horse? We have been searching and searching for an escort but they all ask a lot of money, and it is dangerous to send him off with an unknown individual, since he will have both money and belongings with him. Agree to it, brother, really, it will be all right. Set your mind to it[2] for the glory of God and for love of your neighbor. I'll vouch for you to the owners and they will be beside themselves for joy. They are good people and love me very much. I have been working for them now for two years."

After talking at the gate, he brought me into the landowner's house and when I saw that they must be honest people, I agreed to their proposal. So now we are intending to set out on our journey on the third day of the feast of Christ's nativity, if God so wills, after Holy Liturgy. Such are the unexpected events one meets with on life's path. But[3] all the while God and his Holy Providence govern our deeds and intentions, as it is written: *Both the willing and the doing are God's work.*[4]

"I am sincerely glad, dearest brother, that the Lord has arranged for me to see you so soon and unexpectedly. And since you are now free, I shall keep you for a bit more time with love and you shall tell me more about the instructive encounters you have had on your lengthy pilgrimage. I have listened to all your other accounts with pleasure and attentiveness."

107

FOURTH MEETING

There was much that was both good and bad. It would take a long time to recount everything, and besides, I have already forgotten many things because I tried especially to remember only what guided and aroused my lazy soul to prayer. All the rest I rarely called to mind; or, to say it better, I tried to forget what happened, in keeping with the instruction of the holy apostle Paul: *I strive toward the honor of the sublime vocation, forgetting what is behind and pressing onward to what lies ahead.*[5] My late elder of blessed memory used to say that obstacles to the prayer of the heart attack from two sides, from the left and from the right. That is, if the enemy does not succeed in turning us away from prayer by means of vain thoughts and sinful imaginings, he will bring to mind edifying memories or introduce beautiful thoughts, by some such means, but only in order to distract us from prayer, which he finds insufferable. This is known as right-handed theft, by which the soul, disdaining conversation with God, turns toward satisfying conversation with itself or with creatures. For this reason my elder begged me not to welcome even the most beautiful thoughts during prayer, and if I happened to notice, as the day passed, that I was spending more time in edifying reflections and conversation than in essential, free-of-images prayer of the heart, I was to deem this too to be intemperance or self-interested spiritual avarice. This is especially true for novices, whose time spent in prayer must exceed by a significant amount the time that is spent practicing the other works of a devout life.

Still one cannot forget everything! Other things have so engraved themselves on my memory that, even though I haven't thought of them for a long time, I can recall them vividly. Take, for example, the few days God arranged for me to spend with a certain pious family in the following manner.

I was wandering about Tobolsk province when I happened to pass through a certain district town. I had very few crusts of bread remaining and so I entered one house in order to beg for some bread for the road. The owner said to me: "Glory be to God! You have arrived at the very moment that my wife is taking some loaves out of the oven. Here are some warm loaves. Pray to God for us." After thanking them I began putting the bread into my pouch when the mistress saw me and said: "What a flimsy bag. It's all worn through. I'll change it for you." She gave me a nice firm bag. I thanked them from my soul and went on further. At the entrance to a grocer's I asked for a little salt, and the shopkeeper poured me a little bag full. I rejoiced in spirit and thanked God for showing such good people to unworthy me. There you are, I thought, no worries about food for the week. I'll be full and content. *Bless the Lord, O my soul!*[6]

Having walked about five kilometers from that town I saw on the same road a small village and a small wooden church that was nonetheless nicely decorated on the outside and painted. As I passed by it, I felt like making a prostration to the temple of God and, after entering the church porch I prayed a little while. On the side, in a meadow, two little ones about five or six years old were playing. I thought they must be the parish priest's children, although they were well dressed. Having entertained this thought, I moved on. I hadn't managed to get ten paces from the church when I heard a shout after me: "Dear little beggar, dear little beggar, stop!" It was the two little ones I had seen, a boy and a girl, who were shouting and running after me. I stopped and when they caught up to me they took me by the hand.

"Come to our mommy. She loves beggars."

"I am not a beggar," I said, "but a traveler."

"Then why do you have a bag?"

"This is my bread for the road."

"No. You must come. Mommy will give you money for the road."

"And just where is your mommy?" I asked.

"There behind the church, behind that little grove."

They brought me into a beautiful garden in the middle of which I saw a large manor house. We went into the mansion itself. How clean and orderly it was there! Then the lady of the house came running toward us. "Welcome! From where has God sent you to us? Sit down, do sit down, dear one," and she took my pouch, laid it on a table, and made me sit in a comfortable padded chair. "Wouldn't you like something to eat and a little tea? Will you be needing anything?"

"I most humbly thank you," I replied. "I have a whole bag full of food. And although I do drink tea, since I am a peasant man I am not accustomed to it. Your zeal and kindly manner are more precious to me than any fare. I shall pray to God that he bless you for your Gospel-inspired love of strangers."

As I said this, I sensed a powerful urge to turn inward. The prayer began bubbling up warmly in my heart and I would need peace and quiet in order to give free rein to this self-igniting flame of prayer and to conceal from these people the outward signs of prayer such as tears, sighing, and unusual movements of the face and mouth. So I stood up and said:

"Please pardon me, good lady! It is time for me to go. May the Lord Jesus Christ be with you and your dear little children!"

"Oh no! God preserve you from leaving! I won't allow it. My husband will be coming from town this evening. He serves there as a judge in the district court. How glad he will be to see you. He considers every pilgrim to be a messenger of God. If you go away he will be deeply hurt not to have seen you. Besides, tomorrow is Sunday. You shall pray with us at the liturgy, and we will dine together on what God has sent. Every holiday we have up to thirty poor sisters and brothers of Christ as guests. But why have you not told me anything about yourself? Where are you from and where does your journey take you? Talk with me a little while. I love to hear the spiritual conversations of God-pleasing people. Children! Children! Take the stranger's pouch and bring it into the icon-room. He will spend the night there."

When I heard these words I was amazed and wondered: "Am I talking with a human being or am I having some sort of apparition?" So I stayed to wait for the master of the house. I briefly recounted my travels and said that I was going to Irkutsk.

"Well isn't that opportune," said the lady. "You will undoubtedly be going through Tobolsk, and my mother lives there as a nun in the convent. She already wears the great habit. We will give you a letter and she will receive you. Many come to her for spiritual advice. And, by the way, you can bring her this little book of Saint John Climacus that we ordered for her from Moscow at her request. How fine this will be."

110

Finally the time for dinner drew near and we sat down at table. Four more ladies came and started to eat with us. After the first course one of the visiting ladies got up, made a bow to the icon, and then bowed to us. She went and brought the second course and then sat down again. Then another lady likewise went for the third course. Seeing this I started to speak to the mistress of the house.

"May I be so bold as to ask, good lady. Are these women your relatives?"

"Yes, they are sisters to me. This one is the cook; this one the coachman's wife; this one is the chatelaine; and this one is my chambermaid. All of them are married. In my whole house I do not have a single unmarried woman."

When I heard this I was even more astounded, and I thanked God for showing me such God-pleasing people. I sensed the powerful movement of prayer in my heart; thus, in order to be alone all the more quickly and not impede the prayer, I rose from table and told the lady of the house: "You need to rest after dinner, but I shall go for a stroll in the garden, for I am used to walking."

"No, I do not rest after dinner," she said. "I shall go to the garden with you and you will tell me something instructive. If you go off alone, the children will give you no peace. As soon as they see you they will not leave you for a minute, so much do they love the poor sisters and brothers of Christ and pilgrims."

There was nothing for me to do, and we went. Upon entering the garden, so that I might more conveniently preserve my silence and not speak, I prostrated myself at the lady's feet and said: "I beg you, good lady, in the name of God, tell me, have you been living such a godly life for long and how did you achieve this piety?"

"If you please, I will tell you everything. You see, my mother is the great-granddaughter of Bishop Ioasaf, whose reliquiae are on display in Belgorod. We had a large house in town, a wing of which was rented to an impoverished noble. He died after a while, but his wife was left pregnant. She herself died giving birth. The infant was left a poor orphan, without father or mother. Out of

111

pity my mother took charge of his upbringing, and a year later I was born. We grew up together and learned from the same tutors and governesses, and got as used to each other as though we were brother and sister. Sometime later my own father passed away and my mother, abandoning town life, moved with us to her property in this village. When we had come of age, mom married me to her foundling son, handed this very village over to us and after building a cell for herself, found a place in the monastery. As she gave us her parental blessing she also instructed us to live in a Christian manner, to pray to God and above all to strive to fulfill the chief commandment of God, which is to love one's neighbors, to feed and assist the poor brothers and sisters of Christ in simplicity and meekness, to raise children in the fear of God, and to treat our servants as if they were our sisters and brothers. We have been living here in solitude in this manner for ten years now, trying to fulfill our dear mother's instruction as we are able. We have a hospice for beggars, and right now there are more than ten lame and sick people living there. If you wish, we will visit them tomorrow."

At the end of this tale I asked, "Where is that book of Saint John Climacus that you wanted to send to your mother?"

"Let's go inside and I'll find it for you."

We had only just sat down to read when the lord of the manor came in. Catching sight of me, he gave me a warm hug and we kissed each other as friends in the Christian manner. He led me into his chamber, saying, "My dearest brother, let us go into my office. Bless my cell. I think that she (pointing to the lady of the manor) has quite bored you. As soon as she sees some pilgrim, man or woman, or a sick person, she is happy to stay with them day and night. That is how it has been in her family since time immemorial."

We went into his office. What a lot of books! What beautiful icons! A full-sized Life-giving Cross with the Gospels lying next to it. I prayed and then said: "My good sir, you have here God's own paradise. There is the Lord Jesus Christ himself, his most pure Mother, and his holy saints. And these (pointing to the books) are their divine, living, and unfading words and instructions. I think that you often enjoy heavenly conversation with them."

"Yes," he answered. "I confess that I am an avid reader."

"What kind of books do you have here?" I asked.

"I have many spiritual books," was the reply. "There is the complete yearly cycle of the menology,[7] the works of John Chrysostom, Basil the Great, many theology and philosophy books, as well as many books of sermons of more recent illustrious preachers. My library cost me about five thousand rubles."

"You wouldn't happen to have something on prayer, would you?"

"Here is the most recent book on prayer, the work of a certain priest from St. Petersburg."

The lord of the manor got for me an exposition on the Lord's Prayer, *Our Father*, and we began to read it with pleasure. A little while later the lady joined us, bringing tea, and the children dragged in a basket, all silver-plated, full of biscuits like little pies the likes of which I have never tasted in my life. The man took the book from me and gave it to his wife. "We'll get her to read it," he said. "She reads beautifully. And we'll fortify ourselves with tea." She began to read and we listened. As I listened to the reading I paid attention to the prayer arising in my heart. The further the reading went the more the prayer developed and delighted me. Suddenly I saw something flash quickly in the air before my eyes, perhaps my deceased elder. I started and so as to hide this I said, "Excuse me, I dozed off a little!" Then and there I felt as if my elder's spirit penetrated my own[8] or set it alight. I sensed some sort of light in my mind and a multitude of thoughts about prayer. I was just crossing myself and setting my will to drive off these thoughts when the lady came to the end of the book and her husband asked me if I had liked the reading. Our conversation began again.

"I liked it very much," I answered. "The *Our Father* is the loftiest and most precious of all the written prayers that we Christians have, for the Lord Jesus Christ himself taught it to us. The interpretation of the prayer that has just been read is very good, only it is for the most part all directed toward Christian activity; however, in my reading of the holy fathers I have come across a speculative, mystical explanation of the prayer."

"In which of the fathers did you read this?"

"Well, in Maximos the Confessor, for example, and in Peter of Damaskos, from the *Philokalia*."

"Please tell it to us if you remember it."

"All right. The beginning of the prayer, *Our Father who art in heaven*, is explained as a call to Christian love toward our neighbors as children of the one Father. This is quite correct, but the holy fathers explain it further and more spiritually. They say that in this utterance it is necessary to lift the mind to heaven to the heavenly Father and to recall our obligation to place ourselves every moment in the presence of God and to walk before God. *Hallowed be thy name* is explained as the zeal not to pronounce the divine name without reverence or in a false oath; in a word, that his holy name should be pronounced in a holy manner, and not used in vain. The mystical interpreters see here plainly a petition concerning the interior prayer of the heart, that is, that God's most holy name should be imprinted on the heart and be sanctified through self-activating prayer. It should hallow all the feelings and powers of the soul. *May his kingdom come* into our hearts refers to interior peace, quiet, and spiritual joy. Likewise well explained is that we must understand the words *give us today our daily bread* as a petition concerning the requirements necessary for our physical life, not for excess but only what is necessary and sufficient to help our neighbors. Maximos the Confessor, however, understands the words 'daily bread' to mean food for the soul and the bread of heaven, that is, zeal for reading the Word of God, Holy Communion in the Body and Blood of Christ, union of the soul with God, contemplation, and unceasing prayer of the heart."

"Ah! This is a great work indeed. It is almost impossible for those living in the world to attain to interior prayer!" exclaimed the master of the house. "It's all we can manage, with the Lord's help, to say our normal prayers without sloth."

"My good sir, do not think like that. If this were impossible and insurmountably difficult, God would not have commanded

114

everyone to do it. His strength is made perfect in weakness.[9] Experienced as they are, the holy fathers suggest methods that make the path leading to the prayer of the heart easier. Of course, for those who renounce the world they recommend special lofty methods, but even for the laity they likewise prescribe suitable methods that truly lead to the acquisition of interior prayer."

"Nowhere have I come across anything like that in my reading," he said.

"Allow me, if you will, to read from my copy of the *Philokalia*."

I picked up my *Philokalia* and found the article by Peter of Damaskos, part 3, page 48, and I began to read: "It is more necessary to learn to call on the name of God than it is to breathe—at all times, in every place, and in every occupation. The apostle writes *pray unceasingly*; that is, he teaches us to have the remembrance of God at all times, in every place, and in every kind of circumstance. If you are doing anything you must have in your memory the Creator of all things; if you see light, remember the One who has bestowed this on you; if you see the sky, the sea, and all things that are found in them, marvel and glorify the One who created them; if you put some article of clothing on yourself, recall whose gift this is and thank the One who provides for your life. To say it briefly, let every action be for you a reason for remembering and glorifying God. In this way you will be praying unceasingly, and because of this your soul will always be glad!"[10]

"There, you can see how this method for acquiring unceasing prayer is convenient, easy, and accessible to anyone who has some amount of human feeling!"

They were extraordinarily pleased by this. The master of the house embraced me rapturously and thanked me. He examined the *Philokalia* and said, "I must buy a copy of that book without fail. I'll get it right away in St. Petersburg. And now, for a reminder, I'll copy out the passage that you have just read. Dictate it to me."

Then and there he wrote it out beautifully. Then he exclaimed, "My God! Why I even have an icon of Saint Peter of Damaskos!" He picked up a frame, put what he had written under the glass, and hung it below the icon. "There," he said, "the living word of

God's saint below his image will often remind me to put his saving advice into practice."

After this we went to supper. What reverent silence and quiet there was throughout the meal! After finishing supper all of us, adults and children, prayed at length. They compelled me to read the Akathist in honor of Jesus Most Sweet. When I finished, their servants went to bed but we three remained in the dining room. Then the mistress of the house brought me a white shirt and stockings. I bowed down at her feet and said, "I will not take the stockings, dear woman. I have never worn stockings in my life. We are accustomed to wrap our feet in cloth inside our shoes."[11]

She hurried off and brought back her old caftan of thin cloth and cut it into two foot-wrappings. "Look," the master of the house said. "The poor fellow's footgear is almost completely worn out," and he brought his new large shoes, which he wore over his top boots. Then he said, "Go into that room, there is no one there, and change your underwear." I went and got undressed and put on the underwear, and then came back out to them. They sat me on a chair and began to put shoes on my feet. The master started to wrap my feet with the cloth strips and the mistress started putting on the shoes. At first I was reluctant to yield to them, but they ordered me to sit down and said, "Sit down and be quiet. Christ washed his disciples' feet." There was nothing for me to do and I started to cry. They too began weeping.

Afterwards the mistress left for the bedchambers to sleep with the children, but the master and I went into a pavilion in the garden. For a long time we did not fall asleep, but lay there talking. He then set about to speak to me formally:

"Tell me, for God's sake, in all truth and by your conscience, who are you? Perhaps you are of good birth and are only assuming the guise of a fool for Christ. You read and write well and you speak correctly and are able to discuss things. This doesn't go with a peasant upbringing."

"I have told my background to both you and your wife with complete honesty and a pure heart, and I never thought to lie or deceive you. And why should I? What I say to you is not my own but what I heard from my own elder who was full of divine wis-

116

dom, and what I read with attentiveness in the holy fathers. But more than all this, interior prayer gives light to my ignorance. I did not acquire this prayer by myself; rather the mercy of God and my elder's instruction have come to dwell in my heart. Anyone can do all that. You need only to sink deeply into your heart in ever-increasing silence and invoke more and more the enlightening name of Jesus Christ, and at once you will sense an inner light. You will understand everything; you will see even some of the mysteries of the kingdom of God in this light. This is already a profound and illuminating mystery—when individuals recognize their ability to go deep within themselves, to see themselves from the inside, to take delight in self-knowledge, to take pity on themselves and to weep sweetly over their own fall and their depraved will.

"To reason and talk with people sensibly is not a very difficult matter, and it is possible for anyone because the mind and heart precede human learning and wisdom. If there is a mind, it is possible to refine it, either by study or some skill, but if there is no intellect, then no kind of wise teaching and no form of training will help. The fact of the matter is that we are distant from ourselves and have little desire to get near to ourselves. We all run away so as not to meet ourselves; we exchange truth for trinkets and we think: 'I would gladly devote myself to spiritual things or prayer, but there is no time. The troubles and cares of life leave no time for such an undertaking.' Yet what is more important and necessary? The salvation and eternal life of the soul or the transitory life of the body on which we spend so much effort, more than cattle on perishable food? It is this that I spoke about, and it leads people either to prudence or foolishness."

"Forgive me, dear brother," he said. "I asked you this not out of mere curiosity but out of good nature and Christian sympathy for you. And also because two years ago I saw an example that gave rise to my question for you. You see, a certain beggar came to our house with the passport of a retired soldier. He was old and decrepit, so poor that he was practically naked and barefooted. He spoke little and as simply as if he were an ordinary peasant. We brought him to the hospice and for about five days he was seriously ill. For that reason we moved him into this pavilion and calmed him. My wife and I began to nurse him and treat his illness. Finally he began visibly to approach death. We prepared him by calling for our priest, who heard his confession, gave him communion, and anointed him. On the eve of his death he got up and requested from me a sheet of paper and a pen. He asked me to close the door and let no one in until he had written his testament for his son. This he asked me to send to his son at an address in St. Petersburg after his death. I was dumbfounded when I saw how he wrote, not only with beautiful and well-trained handwriting but even his composition was excellent, correct, and very delicate. In fact, I'll read his testament to you tomorrow, I have a copy of it. All of this set me wondering and aroused my curiosity to ask him about his background and life. After first having me solemnly swear not to reveal anything to anyone until after his death, he gave a beautiful account of his whole life, to the glory of God.

"'I was Prince X,' he said. 'I owned a very large fortune and led the most splendid, luxurious, and dissipated life. My wife died and I lived with my son, who served happily in the Guards. One day, as I was getting ready to go to a ball at the residence of a very important personage, I was exceedingly angered by my valet. Unable to control my flaring temper, I struck him severely on the head and ordered him sent away to his village. This was in the evening, and the next morning the valet was dead from inflammation in his head. But I got away with it, and though I regretted my rashness I quickly forgot about it. Then six weeks passed and the dead valet began appearing to me, at first in my sleep. He disturbed me every night, repeating incessantly, "Unscrupulous man! You are my murderer!" Then I began to see him as I woke up and when I was fully awake. The more time passed, the more often he would appear to me, and then he disturbed me almost without interruption. Finally I started to see with him other dead men whom I had brutally offended and the women whom I had seduced. All of them reproached me without interruption and gave me no rest, so that I could not sleep; I could neither eat nor drink nor do anything else. I grew completely exhausted and my skin stuck to my bones. All the efforts of skilled physicians were of no avail at all. I went to be treated in foreign lands, but after

118

undergoing treatments for half a year I obtained not the slightest relief, and the excruciating apparitions recurred with ever-increasing severity. I was brought back scarcely alive and I experienced in full measure the terrors of hell's torments in my soul even before its separation from my body. I was convinced that hell existed and I knew full well what it meant. In this excruciating state I recognized my own lawless actions. I repented and made my confession. I gave freedom to all those serving in my household and swore an oath to myself that for my entire life I would afflict myself with all manner of ascetic labors and disguise myself as a beggar so that, because of my lawlessness, I would be the most humble servant for the lowliest class. No sooner did I firmly come to this decision than the apparitions that had been plaguing me ceased. I felt such joy and sweetness and peace with God that I cannot fully describe it. So here too I knew through experience what paradise means and in what manner the kingdom of God opens wide inside our hearts. I soon completely regained my health, fulfilled my intention, and departed from my homeland in secret with the passport of a retired soldier. And it is now already fifteen years that I have been wandering all over Siberia. Sometimes I hired myself out to peasants for any work within my powers; sometimes I would find sustenance with the name of Christ. Ah, in the midst of all these privations what blessedness, happiness, and peace of mind I have tasted! Only someone who has been transported out of the torments of hell into the paradise of God by the mercy of the Intercessor can fully understand this.' After he recounted this, he handed me his testament to forward to his son, and the next day he passed away.

"I have here a copy of his testament in a little pouch lying near my Bible. If you would like to read it, I'll bring it out right away. Here, if you please."

FOURTH MEETING

Reading the Testament
**In the name of the God who is glorified in Trinity,
the Father and the Son and the Holy Spirit.**

My most beloved son!

You have not seen your father for fifteen years now. But in his obscurity he has garnered information about you from time to time, and nourished a paternal love for you that urges him to send you these words before his death. May they be for you a lesson for life. You know how I suffered for my carelessness and inattentive life. You do not know, however, how blissfully happy I was on my pilgrimage, enjoying the fruits of repentance. I die at peace in the house of your benefactor and mine, for the good deeds poured out on the father must touch the sensitive heart of a grateful son. Render to him my gratitude as you are able. Leaving with you my parental blessing I adjure you to remember God and guard your conscience, to be prudent, good and sober-minded, and to treat your subordinates as benevolently and politely as possible. Do not despise beggars and pilgrims, recalling that even your dying father found tranquillity and peace for his tormented soul only in a life of begging and pilgrimage. Invoking the grace of God upon you, I close my eyes in peace in the hope of eternal life through the mercy of the One who intercedes for humankind, the Lord Jesus Christ.

Your father X

Thus I and the good gentleman lay there talking, and I asked him a question.

"I think, good sir, that your hospice must cause you cares and anxieties, am I right? To be sure many of our brother and sister pilgrims wander because they have nothing to do or because they are lazy, and some even steal on the road, as I have happened to see."

"There have not been many such cases," he answered. "For the most part it is real pilgrims who happen along. We shower even greater kindness on the rogues and keep them with us. After living among our good beggar brothers and sisters in Christ, they often amend themselves and leave the hospice humble and meek people. For not long ago there was an example of this. A local townsman became so depraved that everyone resolutely drove him away from their doors with canes and no one would give him a crust of bread. He was a drunken, violent, and quarrelsome man and in addition he used to steal. In this state he came to us starving and asked for some bread and wine. He was particularly eager for the wine. We welcomed him warmly and said, 'Live with us, and we will give you as much wine as you want, but only on this condition, that after you have quenched your thirst, you will lie down straight away and go to sleep. If you cause the slightest trouble or become unruly, not only will we drive you away and never receive you here again, but I will make a report to the district police officer or the governor to have you sent off to a penal settlement as a suspected vagrant.' He agreed to this and remained with us. For a week or more he really did drink a lot, as much as he wanted. But always, in keeping with his promise and owing to his attachment to wine, he would lie down to sleep or go out into the garden and lie down there and keep quiet so as not to be deprived of the wine. When he sobered up the hospice residents persuaded him to get control of himself, even if at the start he did so only a little at a time. He gradually began drinking less and less. And finally after about three months he became a temperate person and now he has become employed somewhere and no longer eats the bread of strangers. He came by to thank me the day before yesterday."

What wisdom is made perfect under the guidance of love, I thought and exclaimed, "Blessed be God who reveals his mercy in the sheepfold under your protection!"

After our conversation the master and I dropped off to sleep for about an hour and a half. We heard the bells for Orthros, made ourselves ready, and went to the church. Although we only just entered the church, the lady and her children had been there for some time already. The Divine Liturgy began immediately after Orthros. The man and one of his little boys and I stood in the sanctuary while the woman and her little girl stood by a window looking into the sanctuary so that they could see the elevation of the

Holy Gifts. My God, how they prayed on their knees, what tears of joy they shed! So radiant did their faces become that I, too, joyfully cried my eyes out as I gazed on them.

At the end of the service, the lord and lady, the priest, the servants, and all the beggars went to the dinner table, and there were about forty beggars. Cripples, invalids, children—everyone sat down at the same table. And such peacefulness and silence! Plucking up my courage, I said to the lord in a low voice, "You know, in monasteries they read the *Lives of the Saints* during meals, and you could do the same here. You have the complete cycle of readings."

The lord turned to his wife and said, "Indeed, Masha, let's introduce that custom! It will be most edifying. I'll read at the first meal, then you at the next, father at the next meal, and after that the rest of our sisters and brothers who know how to read, in turn."

The priest, eating, began to talk. "I love to listen, but as for reading, well, with all due respect I have absolutely no free time. I run back home and don't know which way to turn, what with all the troubles and cares I have. First one thing, then another has to be done. A bunch of kids, and animals galore! The whole day long is spent in useless things; I don't even have time for reading and study! And as for what I learned in the seminary, well I've long since forgotten it all."

I shuddered as I listened to this, but the lord, sitting next to me, took my hand and said, "Father is saying this out of humility. He is always belittling himself, but he is really the most kindly man and leads a God-pleasing life. He has been a widower for twenty years and is bringing up a whole family of grandchildren. And besides this, he holds services quite often."

At these words the following assertion of Nikitas Stithatos[12] from the *Philokalia* entered my mind: "The nature of things is betrayed by the inner disposition of the soul, that is, people reach conclusions about others based on what they themselves are."[13] And further on he says, "The person who has attained true prayer and love does not differentiate things. Such a person does not distinguish the righteous from the sinner but loves everyone equally and does not condemn them, just as God causes the sun to shine and the rain to fall on both the righteous and the unrighteous." Silence returned.

Across from me sat a totally blind beggar from the hospice. The lord was looking after him by cutting up some fish, giving him a spoon, and pouring him some soup. Looking intently at him I noticed that this beggar had his mouth wide open and his tongue moved without stopping and as if it were trembling. I wondered if this fellow were not one of those who pray, and I continued to observe him.

At the conclusion of the meal an old woman became giddy; she groaned loudly and was taken ill. The lord and lady led her away to their bedroom and laid her in their bed. The lady of the house stayed behind to tend to her; the priest went to bring the reserved sacrament just in case; and the lord ordered his carriage hitched up and then he set off to town at a gallop to fetch a doctor. We all went our own way. I went to the hospice to talk with the blind beggar, but even more because I felt what seemed to be the voice of prayer. The need for prayerful outpourings was strong, but I had not had any solitude or quiet for forty-eight hours. In my heart it felt as if some sort of flood was struggling to burst forth and stream through all my limbs, but as I held it back, an intense though comforting pain in my heart resulted that demanded silent privacy and satisfaction in prayer. I came to realize why true practitioners of self-activating prayer flee from people and hide themselves in obscurity. I likewise understood why Saint Hesychios[14] called even the most spiritual and useful conversation empty talk if it was immoderate, just as Saint Ephrem the Syrian says: "Good speech is silver (like unto silver), but silence is pure gold." Reflecting on all of this I came to the hospice. There everyone was resting after dinner. I climbed up into the garret, calmed down, rested and prayed. When the beggars got up, I found the blind man and led him out into the kitchen garden. We sat down alone and began to talk.

"Tell me, for the sake of God, and for my spiritual benefit, do you say the Jesus prayer?"

"I have been saying it without ceasing for quite some time."

"What do you feel from this?"

"Only this, that I cannot be without prayer either day or night."

"By what means did God reveal this practice to you? Tell me, dear brother."

"You see, I'm a local, one of the guild; I earned my bread with tailoring jobs, and traveled around other provinces too, from village to village, sewing peasant clothes. I happened to live for a long time in one village with a peasant, in exchange for sewing clothes for his family. On a feast day I spied three books on the icon case and I asked, "Who of you reads?"

"No one," they told me. "These books were left to us by an uncle. He could read and write."

"Picking up one of the books I opened it at random and read the words, as I now recall, 'Unceasing prayer means always to invoke the Name of God—whether one is talking, or sitting, or walking, or working, or eating, or doing any other thing. In every place and at all times one must invoke the Name of God.' After reading this I began to think that I could easily do it, so I started to whisper the prayer while I sewed, and I liked it. Those who were living with me took notice and said in jest, 'Are you a wizard or what? What are you always whispering?' In order to conceal this I stopped moving my lips and began to say the prayer only with my tongue. Finally I grew so accustomed to saying the prayer that my tongue produces it by itself day and night, and it gives me pleasure. I went about like this for a long time and then suddenly I became completely blind. Almost everyone in our family gradually goes blind. Because I am so poor, you see, our commune sent me to an almshouse located in the provincial capital of Tobolsk. I am on my way there now, but these gentlefolk have held me up because they want to give me a cart as far as Tobolsk."

"And what was the title of the book you were reading? It wasn't the *Philokalia*, was it?"

"To tell you the truth, I don't know. I didn't even look at the title page."

I took out my copy of the *Philokalia*, searched in part 4 for the words of Patriarch Kallistos,[15] which the blind man had told me from memory, and began to read them.

"Why that's it," said the blind man. "Read some more, brother. How really good it is!"

When I reached the lines where it is said, "it is necessary to pray with the heart," he began storming me with questions—what does that mean and how is it done? I said that the whole doctrine of the prayer of the heart is precisely set forth in this book, the *Philokalia*. He begged me with enthusiasm to read him everything.

"This is what we will do," I said. "When were you planning to set out for Tobolsk?"

"Why, right away," he answered.

"Very well then. I too am thinking about taking to the road tomorrow. We shall go together and I will read you everything that pertains to the prayer of the heart. I will show you a method for finding the place of your heart and entering it."

"And what about the cart?" he asked.

"Heh, what do you want with a cart! Or don't you know that Tobolsk is only one hundred and fifty kilometers from here? We'll get there slowly, the two of us alone. You know how good it will be to walk and it will be more convenient for talking and reading about the prayer."

So we agreed. In the evening the lord himself came to invite us all to supper. After supper I disclosed to him that the blind man and I would be taking to the road and that we would not need a cart because it would be easier to read the *Philokalia*. The lord said, "I too liked the *Philokalia* very much. I have already written a letter and put together some money so that tomorrow when I go to court I can send it to St. Petersburg and have a copy sent to me by the first post."

So the next morning we set off on our way, giving abundant thanks to these gentlefolk for their exemplary love and kindness. Both of them accompanied us for about a kilometer from their dwelling and we said our good-byes. The blind man and I went on, covering the distance little by little—about ten or fifteen kilometers a day. We spent all the rest of the time sitting in lonely woods reading the *Philokalia*. I read for him everything about the prayer of the heart in the order that my deceased elder had shown me. That is, I began with the books of Nikiphoros the Monk, Gregory of Sinai, and so on. How avidly and attentively he would listen! And what pleasure and delight it brought him! He then started to pose me such questions about prayer that my mind was insufficient to solve them. After we read through the *Philokalia*, he began earnestly begging me to give him practical examples of the method by which to find the heart with the mind, how to introduce the divine name of Jesus Christ into the heart, and how to pray interiorly with the heart with sweetness. I thus began to give an account.

"Now, you do not see anything, but you can surely imagine with your mind and picture to yourself the things that you used to see before, that is, a person or some object or one of your own limbs, for example, a hand or foot. Can you imagine it as though you were looking at it, and can you turn your eyes and fix them on it, even though they are blind?"

"Yes, I can," replied the blind man.

"Well then, form an image of your heart in precisely the same way; direct your eyes toward it as though you were looking at it. Listen attentively with your mind to its beating and how it pounds, one beat after another. The holy fathers call this 'bringing the mind out of one's head down into one's heart.' When you have mastered this, begin to fit the words of the prayer to every beat of the heart, all the while looking at it. Thus, with the first beat, say or think 'Lord'; with the second, 'Jesus'; with the third, 'Christ'; with the fourth, 'have mercy'; and with the fifth, 'on me.' Repeat this over and over again. It will be easy for you since you already have a basis and preparation for the prayer of the heart. Then, once you are used to this, begin to bring the whole Jesus prayer in and out of your heart in harmony with your breathing, as the fathers teach. That is, as you inhale say or imagine 'Lord Jesus Christ,' and as you exhale, 'have mercy on me.' Devote yourself to this as often and as much as you can and you will quickly feel a very pleasant pain in your heart; then warmth and ardor will come. With the help of God you will attain the self-activating, delightful, interior prayer of the heart. Only at this stage beware of any ideas in the mind and any type of visions that appear. Do

126

not accept any imaginings whatsoever, for the holy fathers sternly command us to keep our interior prayer free of images, lest we fall into temptation."

The blind man listened attentively to all of this and studiously set to work, following the method I showed him. Particularly when we stopped for the night, he spent lengthy periods in prayer. After about five days he began to feel intense warmth and ineffable pleasure in his heart, and then a great desire to devote himself unceasingly to this prayer, which was uncovering in him a love for Jesus Christ. Finally, from time to time, he began to see light, although he observed no objects or things in it. Then, when he entered his heart, it seemed to him as though the strong flame of a lighted candle blazed sweetly inside his heart and, rushing out through his throat, illuminated him. In this flame he was able to see even distant objects, as indeed happened on one occasion.

We were walking through a forest and he was silent, sunk in prayer. Suddenly he said to me, "What a pity! The church is already burning! There, the belfry has fallen." I said to him, "Stop imagining empty things! You are being tempted. You must turn aside all thoughts as quickly as possible. How can you possibly see what is happening in the town? We are nineteen kilometers from it!" He obeyed and continued to pray in silence. Toward evening we arrived in the town and I saw with my own eyes several burnt houses and a fallen belfry, which had been built with ties of timber. Some people were milling about wondering how the fallen belfry had not crushed anyone. The way I put things together, this whole misfortune occurred at the very same time as the blind man was telling me about it. He then began to speak to me about it.

"You said that this vision of mine was vain, but there you are. How can I not thank and love the Lord Jesus Christ who reveals his grace even to sinners and to the blind and foolish! And I thank you too for teaching me the activity of the heart."

"If you want to love Jesus Christ—love, and if you want to give thanks—thank him, for his grace is everywhere, in a pure heart and in a sinful heart as well. *No one can say the name of Jesus Christ except by the Holy Spirit*,[16] according to the Word of God; therefore, the grace of the Holy Spirit is already present in anyone who pronounces the divine name in any way whatsoever. But beware of taking every oracular vision for immediate revelations of grace, because they frequently occur even naturally in the order of things. The human soul is relatively boundless. It can see in the dark and something quite remote as if it happened close by. Only we do not give free rein to this spiritual ability and we suppress it either with the bonds of our corpulent body or with the confusion of our thoughts and our scattered intentions. But when we concentrate within ourselves, when we divert our attention away from all that surrounds us and become refined in our mind, then the soul enters into its proper domain and operates on the highest level. It is thus a natural thing.

"I heard my deceased elder say that even people who do not pray, but who either have the ability or are sick, see light streaming from every article in the darkest of rooms; they distinguish objects, sense their double, and penetrate the thoughts of other people. But what proceeds directly from the grace of God in the prayer of the heart gives so much delight that no tongue is able to express it. It cannot be matched by any material thing; it is even beyond compare. Everything perceptible is base in comparison with the sweet sensations of grace in the heart."

My blind companion listened eagerly to this and became even more humble. The prayer grew more and more in his heart and delighted him beyond words. I rejoiced at this with all my soul and fervently thanked God for granting me to see so blessed a servant of his.

We finally reached Tobolsk. I took him to the almshouse and left him there. After affectionately bidding him farewell, I went further on my way. For about a month I walked along without hurrying and deeply felt how edifying and instructive good, living examples are. I read the *Philokalia* often and verified everything that I said to the blind man of prayer. His instructive example kindled in me fervor, gratitude, and love for the Lord Jesus. The prayer of the heart caused me so much delight that I supposed there was no one on earth happier than I. I was at a loss to think how there could be a greater and better delight in the kingdom of heaven. Not only did I feel this inside my soul, but also everything external presented itself to me in ravishing guise. Everything drew me to love and give thanks to God. People, trees, plants, animals— all of them were to me like kinsfolk, on all of them I found the imprint of the name of Jesus Christ. I sometimes felt such lightness that I seemed to have no body and was not walking but rather floating joyously through the air. Sometimes I entered completely within myself and clearly saw all my internal organs, and I marveled profoundly at the most wise composition of the human body. Sometimes I felt such gladness that I thought I had been made tsar. In the midst of such consolations I wished that God would let me die as soon as possible so that I might be poured out in thankfulness at his footstool in the world of spirits.

Perhaps I took immoderate delight in these sensations? Or was the divine will permitting me this extravagance? For some time I had felt a sort of trembling and even fear in my heart. Would I again have some misfortunes or disasters, as happened after meeting that girl to whom I taught the Jesus prayer in the chapel? Thoughts loomed over me like a storm cloud and I recalled the words of Saint John of Karpathos, who said that the master will often submit to dishonor and suffer disasters and temptations for the sake of those who profited spiritually from him. Fighting against these thoughts, I redoubled my prayer, which completely dispelled them. Thus encouraged, I thought "May God's will be done. I am ready to suffer whatever the Lord Jesus Christ will send me on account of my wickedness and my arrogant disposition." And those to whom I not long ago revealed the secret of entry into the heart and interior prayer had been made ready immediately by the mysterious teaching of God even before my meeting with them. Calmed by this, I once again went on my way with consolation and prayer, and I rejoiced even more than before. For two days it rained and the road became so muddy that I was hardly able to pull my feet out of the mire. I was walking across the steppe, and for fifteen kilometers or so I came across not a single settlement. Finally, toward evening I saw a solitary house right by the road. I was glad indeed and thought, "Well now, here I'll ask to rest and spend the night, and tomorrow morning, God willing, perhaps the weather will be a bit better." As I approached, I saw a tipsy old man in a soldier's greatcoat, seated on the mound of earth in front of the house. I made a bow and said, "Would it be possible to ask someone if I might spend the night here?"

"Who else but me can let you!" shouted the old man. "I'm in charge here! This is a post station and I'm the postmaster!"

"Won't you let me stay the night then, good sir?"

"Do you have a passport; Show me a valid document now!"

I gave him my passport, he took it in his hand and then asked again: "Where is your passport?"

"In your hands," I replied.

"Well, let's go inside." The postmaster put on his spectacles, read the passport through and said, "All right, the document is valid! Stay the night! I'm a good man, you'll see. Look, I'll even offer you a glass."

"I have never been a drinker," I replied.

"I don't give a damn. At least have supper with us."

They sat at table, he and the cook, a young woman who also had been drinking more than enough and they sat me down with them. During the meal they quarreled, reproached each other, and finally they scuffled. The postmaster went off into the passage to sleep in a storeroom while the cook began to tidy up and wash the cups and spoons. She continued to heap abuse on the old man.

Taking a seat I could see that she would not calm down soon, so I said: "Good woman, where might I sleep. I am very tired from the journey."

"I'll make a bed for you, sir."

She placed a bench against the one under the front window, spread a felt mat over them, and laid out a pillow. I lay down and closed my eyes, as though I were sleeping. The cook gadded about for a long time yet, and finally she tidied up. And then what? She lit a fire, lay down beside me, and began caressing me. Suddenly I had strong feelings of lust and I didn't know what to do. I began to awaken the prayer but it stayed put and wouldn't run. And it would only be a minute before my ruinous fall.... Suddenly the whole window above us, the frames, panes of glass, and fragments of the jambs, was smashed to smithereens and came showering down on us with a frightening thunder and shudder. Outside the window a groan and very powerful roar rang out. I was scared to death and I shoved the woman away from me so hard that she flew onto the middle of the floor, and the whole house shook. I jumped up and fell on my knees, crying out to God and thinking that the earth had yawned beneath me to swallow me, a transgressor. Then I saw two post drivers carrying a man into the house, so completely covered in blood that his face could not be seen. This horrified me still more. He was a military courier who had been galloping to change horses here. His driver, failing to negotiate the turn through the gates, broke in the window with the pole, and as there was a mound in front of the house, the carriage overturned and the courier fell out. He cut his head badly on a sharpened stake that strengthened the mound. The courier demanded some water and wine. He washed the wound himself, bathed it with wine and drank a glass. Then he shouted, "Horses!" Standing near him I said, "Good sir, how can you ride with pain like that?" "A military courier has no time to be sore," he replied and then galloped off.

The men dragged the woman, unconscious, over to the stove in the corner and covered her with a bast mat. "This fit of hers is caused by fear," they said. "She'll sleep it off!" The postmaster took a drink for his bad head and then went back to sleep again. I was left alone. My God! What a situation I was in! Despondency and grief tormented me, and pity too lest the woman should die in so wretched a state. For there were few signs of life in her except for her infrequent and heavy breathing. I began to pray and ask for mercy from the Lord. I laid my elder's prayer beads on the suffering woman's head and started to invoke the name of Jesus Christ. The woman soon got up and began to pace from corner to corner, like a madcap. Finally she went out of the house. As I was praying I felt my strength weaken and I dropped off to sleep a little before the light. Then I heard a voice as though inside of me say: "You faint-hearted man! Learn to recognize the ways of divine providence in human affairs. How many miracles, how many instructive lessons you can observe in present events. Take heart and trust in the omnipresent divine love of our Lord Jesus Christ! Read more closely the seventh and twelfth chapters of Gregory of Sinai and be consoled."

As soon as I woke up I got my *Philokalia*, found the indicated chapters, and read the following in them: "Those who are defeated against their will because of weakness shall be forgiven right away by the One who knows our intentions and human hearts. If temptation occurs, it is for experience and the crown, for assistance comes quickly from the God who permits it, and by these things our models are known."[17] How this revived me! From that moment on I was firmly convinced that everything that happens in life proceeds through providence and everything is brought to a useful end. Thus, in the morning, after taking leave of the postmaster, I got under way. I walked and sent my prayer aloft with faith, hope, and thanksgiving to the Father of mercies and all consolation, who did not let me perish in my sins!

I'll tell you yet another circumstance relating to the above case. About six years after this happened, I was passing by a women's convent and I went into the church to pray. The hospitable hegumenissa[18] invited me into her room after the liturgy and had tea served. All of a sudden some guests came to see her unexpectedly and she went off with them, leaving me with the nuns, her cell servants. The humble nun who was pouring tea piqued my curiosity to ask: "Have you been in this monastery long, mother?"

"Five years," she answered. "I was suffering madness when they brought me here, but God has shown me his favor in this place. Mother hegumenissa took me into her own cell and tonsured me."

"What caused your madness?" I asked.

"Fright. I was working in a station house and one night as I slept a horse broke in the window. I took fright and went out of my mind. For the whole year my relatives took me from one holy place to the next, but it was only here that I was healed."

When I heard this, I got the point and couldn't get out of there fast enough. After I left, I rejoiced in my soul and glorified God, who wisely orders all things for the good.

Many other things happened besides. If I wanted to tell them all in order, I wouldn't be finished talking even after three days and nights. Though perhaps I can tell one more thing.

On a clear summer day I saw a cemetery near the road, or what is known as a *pogost*, that is, a church and a few houses for the clergy. The bells were ringing for liturgy and I made my way there. Some people from the surrounding area were going there too, but others had taken a seat on the grass before reaching the church, and when they saw me walking quickly, said to me: "Don't hurry. You'll have plenty of opportunity for standing once the service begins. Services take a long time. The priest is sick and such an awkward fellow."

The service did indeed go on for a very long time. The young but very thin and pale priest celebrated quite slowly, though very reverently and with feeling. At the end of the liturgy he delivered a beautiful, clear sermon "On the Means of Acquiring Love for God." At the very end of the service he came out and began to speak to the people. "I have just taught you love by my words; now I shall teach you love by my deeds. I invite those who wish to come now to my house for breakfast."

A few of the people followed him, including me. We went directly into the garden. Beneath a tree was a table, and all around it were long benches. A Gospel book lay on the table. The priest sat down, opened the Gospels, and began to read and explain so beautifully and lovingly that we all listened with attention and pleasure. Then tea was served, and some vodka and good appetizers were placed on the table. Everyone drank up and ate, but the priest turned to me and said:

"And you, brother, how come you didn't take a drink? Don't pay any notice to me. I don't drink anything, neither tea nor vodka. It's not because of temperance, but because I have been sick a long time and any strong drink does me harm." Then, turning to the people, he continued: "It is now a holiday and you have permission to be comforted with food. Have all of you had sufficient to eat and does anyone need anything?"

The people gave no reply, but humbly bowing to their pastor, they all went their separate ways. The priest left me to eat and I said to him during the meal, "How reverently and slowly you celebrate, father!"

"Yes," he replied. "Although my parishioners don't like it and they grumble, still there is nothing to be done, for I love to meditate on each word of the prayers and enjoy them. Then only do I say them aloud. But without that interior awareness and feeling, each spoken word is useless both to myself and to others. All that matters is in the inner life and attentive prayer."

"Yet how few people concern themselves with interior activity," I said.

"That is because they do not want to; they do not care about interior spiritual enlightenment," said the priest.

Once again I asked, "And how does one attain it? It seems to be very difficult."

"Not at all. In order to be spiritually enlightened and to become an attentive and introspective person, you should take some one text of Sacred Scripture and for as long as possible keep your whole attention and meditation on it alone, and the light of understanding will be revealed to you. In the same way you must proceed with prayer, if you wish it to be pure, right, and enjoyable. Choose some short prayer consisting of few but powerful words and repeat it over and over for a long time. You will feel a taste for prayer."

The priest's instruction pleased me a great deal. How practical and simple it was, yet at the same time profound and very wise. I mentally thanked God for showing me such a true pastor of his church. At the end of the meal, the priest said to me:

"You have a sleep after dinner and I'll busy myself with reading the Word of God and preparing for tomorrow's sermon."

So, I went out into the kitchen. There was no one there except one very old woman, who was sitting hunched over in a corner, coughing. I sat beneath a little window, took my *Philokalia* out of my bag, and began reading quietly to myself. Finally I cocked an ear and heard the old woman, who was sitting in the corner, whisper the Jesus prayer. I rejoiced to hear the most holy name of the Lord spoken so often. Then I began to speak to her.

"How good it is, mother, that you are always saying the Jesus prayer! It is a most Christian and wholesome action."

"Yes, good sir," she answered; "in my old age all I ask is the 'Lord have mercy.' "

"Have you been long accustomed to praying in this way?"

"Since my youth, dear father. And I couldn't exist without it, for the Jesus prayer delivered me from ruin and death."

"How's that? Please, tell me about it for the glory of God and in praise of the gracious power of the Jesus prayer."

I put the *Philokalia* away in my bag and sat closer to her. She began to tell her story.

"I was a young and pretty maiden. My parents had made arrangements for my marriage. The very day before the wedding, the groom came to visit and before he had taken even ten steps, he suddenly fell over and died without once gasping. I was so terrified by this that I renounced marriage once and for all time and made up my mind to live as a virgin, to visit holy places, and to pray to God. I was, however, afraid to embark alone on this journey lest wicked people bring disgrace upon me because of my youth. Then an old woman pilgrim whom I knew taught me to say the Jesus prayer unceasingly on the road, wherever I might go, and firmly to believe that in saying this prayer no misfortune whatsoever would occur on the way. I believed this. And exactly as she said, for about five years I journeyed safely, even to distant holy places. My parents gave me money for this. Once I was going to a certain town to venerate a miraculous icon, but the road was quite out-of-the-way and for many kilometers I had to go across the steppe and through coppices. But I sensed no danger, having confidence that the Jesus prayer which I was saying would not allow any misfortune to touch me. There I was, already approaching the town—it was within sight, about five or six kilometers away. I headed more directly, away from the road, along a path through a small copse. Suddenly a dispatch rider came galloping up to me from the road, got off his horse, stopped me, and began to ask me where I came from and where I was going. I answered. Then he started to make advances toward me repeatedly.

"Really now, what are you doing? Get away from me!"

"He pulled a blue bank note[19] out of his wallet and offered it to me. I rebuffed his offer and only wanted to run away from him.

Turning beet red he pulled out a large clasp-knife, which he wore attached to a watch chain, flicked it open and pointed with it to my chest, saying: 'I'm going to kill you right now!' I was scared to death and thought: 'Lord Jesus Christ! Even your prayer is of no avail here!' But he lashed his horse's reins around his waist and began to approach me. I began to cry out: 'Breadwinner! Be a good father, at least let me take off my dress. It is a new one and I want to wear it to church.' I had only just slipped it off and waved it across my head when the horse took fright, snorted, and bolted on all fours and dashed off. As for him, poor fellow, the horse pulled him by the reins at top speed across stumps[20] and shrubs. I regained consciousness but there was no more trace of him.

"There I gave many thanks to God for rescuing me, and I was convinced how powerful and preserving that Jesus prayer was. I walked for about two kilometers and found the wallet from which he had offered me the blue note. It still had various papers and his passport. So I arrived in the town and right at the gates there was a crowd of people and some police. The horse was tied up and shaking, all in a lather. The man was lying on the ground with a fractured head and all cut up by the knife that he dangled by a chain around his waist. The town governor arrived and questioned him. Then he let out a sigh: 'What to do? He doesn't know who he is or where he is from.' I approached and said: 'Isn't this his wallet? I picked it up not far from here on the road. Perhaps it fell out of his breast pocket.' The town governor took out the papers, but he returned the blue note and the old and greasy wallet to me and said: 'Thanks for making him known to us. (It turned out that he was a herdsman, trading in cattle and driving them to various provinces.) This is a windfall for you. For according to the law a third part of lost goods goes to the one who finds them.'

"So, I went on my way. I venerated the miraculous icon and returned home. And as I had already seen the power of the Jesus prayer over me, I became bold. I developed a strong desire to go to Jerusalem, but since my parents were not well off, I did not have enough money to go there and come back home. And I grieved over this. One day I was in a very pensive mood and I opened up my trunk to get a white shirt. And there I saw the wallet that the governor had given to me. I wondered why he had given me such an old and greasy thing, so I picked it up and threw it away. But then I took it into my head to rip it open. Maybe the old leather would be good for something. I started to slit it open and found sewn into a corner five hundred-ruble notes. I was so happy about this that I even started crying. With this money I went to Jerusalem, spent a year there, and came back home. Since that time I always say the prayer and am consoled. In my old age I became ill, and the local priest, in his kindness, took me in and provides for me."

Listening to this story with delight, I did not know how to thank God for that day, which had revealed to me so many edifying examples. Then, asking for the blessing of that good and reverent priest, I went on my way rejoicing.

Not so long ago, when I was coming here through Kazan province, I happened to learn yet again how the very power of prayer in the name of the Lord Jesus Christ is revealed clearly and vividly even in those who perform it unconsciously, and how frequency and duration of prayer are the reliable and shortest route to the acquisition of the blessed fruits of prayer. I once happened to spend the night in a Tatar settlement. When I came into the village I saw a carriage and a Russian coachman under the window of one of the huts. Filled with joy I took it into my head to ask for lodgings for the night there, thinking that at least I would spend the night among Christians. I went up to the coachman and asked him where he was going. He replied that his lord was traveling from Kazan to Crimea. At the same time I was talking with the coachman, the lord turned back the leather flap and looked out of the carriage. He hailed me and said, "I too am spending the night here, but I haven't gone into the hut because Tatar places are filthy. I made up my mind to remain in my carriage for the night." The lord then got out to stroll about. It was a fine evening and we struck up a conversation. Interspersed with many questions he told me some things about himself too.

"Until I was sixty-five years old I served as a captain of the first rank in the navy. As old age approached, an incurable disease befell me, gout. I retired from service and went to live, almost continually sick, on my wife's farm in Crimea. My wife was a flighty person with a dissipated nature, and a great cardplayer. She became bored living with a sick man. So she left me and went off to our daughter in Kazan, who by chance was married there to a civil servant. My wife fleeced me thoroughly and even took the house serfs with her, leaving behind only an eight-year-old boy, my godson. The boy, who was in my service, was a clever lad and did all my household chores: he tidied up my room, stoked the oven, cooked my gruel, and warmed up the samovar. Yet for all that he was extraordinarily playful and an incessantly mischievous boy, continually running about and making noise, shouting and playing and romping, and thus thoroughly disturbing me. Now, because I was sick and bored, I loved to read spiritual books all the time. I have a lovely book by Gregory Palamas on the Jesus prayer. I read it almost continually and even said the prayer now and then. My boy hindered me, and none of the threats or punishments restrained him from his pranks. Then I hit upon the following method. I made him sit on a bench in my room and ordered him to say the Jesus prayer unceasingly. At first he didn't like this idea, and he would avoid it in all sorts of ways, even at times falling silent. In order to reinforce my orders I put a birch rod beside me. When he was saying the prayer, I would read my book quietly or listen to him say the words. All he had to do was stop and I would show him the birch. Frightened, he would take up the prayer again. This was very soothing for me, and silence settled over my dwelling. After a while I noticed that I no longer needed the birch rod. The boy started to carry out my orders more willingly and diligently. Further, I observed a complete change in his character: he became placid and taciturn and made greater progress in his household tasks. I was happy about this and began to give him more freedom. Finally, what came of it? He grew so used to the prayer that he said it almost always and during every activity, without the slightest compulsion on my part at all. When I asked him about this, he answered that he had an irresistible desire to say the prayer all the time.

"What do you feel when you are praying?"

"Nothing, I only feel that it is nice when I am saying it."

"What do you mean by nice?"

"I don't know how to put it."

"Does it make you cheerful?"

"Yes, cheerful."

He was already twelve years old when war broke out in Crimea. I went away to my daughter in Kazan and took him with me. Here they lodged him in the kitchen with the other serfs, and this bored him very much. He complained to me that the serfs, playing and joking among themselves, would accost him and laugh at him, thereby preventing him from saying the prayer. Finally, after about three months, he came out to me and said: "I am going home. I am unbearably bored here and it is so noisy." I said to him: "How can you go such a distance all alone and in the winter? Wait and when I go I'll take you too." The next day my boy disappeared. We sent everywhere to look for him but we found him nowhere. Finally, I received a letter from Crimea from the servants left on our farm, saying that the boy had been found dead in my empty house on 4 April, the day after Easter. He was lying on the floor of my room, his hands folded devoutly on his breast, a peaked cap under his head, and he had on the very same thin frock-coat that he wore around the house and which he was wearing when he went away. They buried him there, in my garden.

"When I received this news I was extremely surprised. How had the boy reached the farm so quickly? He went away on 26 February and was found dead on 4 April. To cross around three thousand kilometers in one month—God help you to do it even with horses! He would have had to cover nearly a hundred kilometers a day, and in addition to this he was wearing thin clothing, had no passport, and not a kopeck of cash! Let's suppose that someone gave him a ride along the way; even then none of it could be without God's special providence and care for him. That boy of mine," said the lord, "tasted the fruit of prayer and I in my old age still haven't reached his measure."

After this I began to speak to the lord.

"Good sir, the lovely book of Gregory Palamas that you like to read—I know it myself, but it only deals with the oral Jesus prayer, for the most part. Why don't you read the book bearing the title *Philokalia*; there you will find the full and perfect study of how to attain to the spiritual Jesus prayer in your mind and heart and to taste its most sweet fruit."

I then showed him my *Philokalia*. I could see that he took my advice with pleasure, and he promised to procure a copy of the book for himself.

"Good heavens!" I reflected to myself. "What marvelous signs of God's power there are in the power of prayer! And how wise and instructive was what had happened to the boy. The birch rod taught him prayer and besides served as a means of consolation. Are these not the birch rods of God—our griefs and misfortunes encountered on the path of prayer? For what are we afraid of and put out of countenance by when the hand of our Heavenly Father shows them to us, a hand full of boundless love, and when these birch rods teach us to learn prayer more diligently and lead us to indescribable consolation?"

"Forgive me, for God's sake. I have been chattering away long enough. The holy fathers call even spiritual conversation idle talk if it lasts too long. It is time for me to go and call on my fellow traveler to Jerusalem. Pray for me, a wretched sinner, that the Lord in his great mercy will order our journey for the good."

"With all my soul I wish, beloved brother, that the abundantly loving grace of God may spread as a canopy over your path and accompany you as the angel Raphael went with Tobias!"

The End

23 December 1859.

This pilgrim was of medium build, with a body made lean by self-control and austere life. He had a handsome face, expressive eyes, and a broad and thick beard. He showed abundant love toward all and was affable with humility.

Appendix
Tales Five, Six, and Seven

The Pilgrim's Tale
On the occasion of the fifth meeting

A year had passed since my last rendezvous with the pilgrim, when finally a faint knock on the door and an entreating voice announced the arrival of that devout confrere to the heartfelt delight of the one who met him....

"Come in, beloved brother! Let us thank the Lord together, who has blessed your journey and return!"

"Glory and thanksgiving to the Most High Father of mercies for all that he ordains according to his foresight. For it is always beneficial for us, pilgrims and strangers in an alien land! Here I am, a sinner, who took his leave of you last year, again being honored through the mercy of God to see and hear your joyful welcome. And of course, you are expecting of me a detailed account of the holy city of God, Jerusalem, to which my soul was drawn and my unalterable purpose ranged. But what we wish for is not always fulfilled. That is what happened in my case, and it is not surprising. For why should I, wretched sinner that I am, be made worthy of setting foot in that hallowed land where the divine footsteps of the Lord Jesus Christ have left an imprint?

"You remember, good sir, that I set out from here last year with a companion, a deaf old man, and that I had a letter from an Irkutsk merchant for his son in Odessa asking him to send me to Jerusalem. Well, we reached Odessa safely in no time at all. My companion immediately booked passage on a ship for Constantinople and set sail. Staying behind I went to look for the son of the Irkutsk merchant, using the address on the letter. Although I soon found his apartment, to my surprise and sorrow I discovered

143

that my intended benefactor was no longer among the living. Three weeks had already passed since his burial after a short illness. Although this caused me much sadness, I pinned my hopes on the power of God. All the household servants were in mourning and the widow of the deceased, who was left with three small children, felt so despondent that she wept uncontrollably. Several times a day she collapsed and suffered torments. It seemed that she too would not live long because of her profound melancholy. Still, in the midst of all this, they received me kindly. She did not have the means, given the circumstances, to send me to Jerusalem but had me stay as a guest of the family for two weeks until the father of the deceased, in keeping with his promise, came to Odessa to make arrangements, settle accounts, and manage the business affairs of his orphaned family. And so I stayed....

"I spent a week there, then a month, and then another. But instead of coming, the merchant sent a letter informing them that because of his own circumstances he could not come. He advised them to dismiss the shop assistants and for all of them to come immediately to him in Irkutsk. When they began gathering things up and bustling about, I noticed that I was no longer of any interest to them; so, thanking them for their hospitality and taking leave of them, I set off again to wander about Russia....

"I thought and thought: Where shall I go now? Finally I settled on the idea of going first of all to Kiev, where I had not been for many years. So off I went.... Of course at first I bemoaned the fact that my desire to be in Jerusalem was unfulfilled, but I reflected that this too likely happened by divine providence, and I calmed myself with the hope that the Lord, who loves the human race, would take the intention for the deed and would not let my wretched journey be without edification and spiritual benefit.... That is indeed how it turned out, for I met the sort of people who revealed to me much that I did not know and who enlightened my dark soul for salvation. If I had not been directed on this path by necessity, I would not have met my spiritual benefactors. By day I walked with the prayer, and in the evening, after halting for the night, I read my *Philokalia* to fortify my soul in its struggle against the invisible enemies of salvation.

"Finally, having gone some seventy kilometers from Odessa, I came upon a strange and marvelous incident. A long train of about thirty wagons carrying goods was under way and I overtook them. The forward wagoner, who was heading the train, walked alongside of his horse, while the others went at some distance from him in a group. They had to go past a spring-fed pond in which broken spring ice was churning and drifting in the water along the edges of the pond with a frightening din. Suddenly the young lead wagoner halted his horse, and behind him the whole train of wagons had to halt too. All the wagoners ran toward him and saw that he had begun to take off his clothes. They asked him why he was undressing and the answer they received was that he had a burning desire to bathe in the pond. Some of the astonished wagoners started to make fun of him, others scolded him, calling him insane. The head, the brother of the by now naked wagoner, tried to block his path and shoved him to drive on. The other defended himself and was in no mind to obey. For a joke, some of the young wagoners started to fetch water out of the pond using the buckets with which they watered their horses and splashed it over the one who wanted to bathe, some on his head, others from behind. 'There you are,' they said, 'we'll give you a bath!' As soon as the water touched his body, he cried out: 'Ah, that feels good!' Then he sat on the ground. They continued to splash water on him, when he soon after lay down and then and there peacefully died. They all took fright, not understanding why this had happened. The older men hurried about and bemoaned the fact that they would have to inform the courts about this, while the rest of them concluded that he was fated at birth to die such a death.

"I stayed with them for about an hour and then went on further. About five kilometers from them I saw a village on the main road, and as I entered it I came across an old priest walking along a street. I took it into my head to tell him what I had seen and to hear what he had to say about it. The priest brought me into his house and after I related to him what I saw, I asked him to explain to me the cause of what had occurred."

"I am unable to tell you anything about this, dear brother, except perhaps that there are many miraculous and to our mind incomprehensible things in nature. This, I think, is arranged by God to show humanity more clearly how the rule and providence of God in nature can cause direct and unnatural changes to the laws of nature, in certain well-known cases.... I myself once happened to be witness to a similar event. Not far from our village there is a very deep and precipitous ravine. Although it is not wide, it is some twenty or so meters deep, and it is quite terrifying to look down at its dark bottom. A footbridge of sorts was built across it for pedestrians. A peasant from my parish, a family man of good behavior, suddenly for no reason felt an irresistible desire to throw himself from the footbridge into the gorge. For the entire week he fought against this idea and urge. Finally, no longer able to contain this powerful impulse, he got up early, went out hurriedly, and jumped into the gorge. Soon after, we heard his moaning and with difficulty we brought him out of the gorge. He had broken both legs. When asked the reason for his fall, he replied that even though he now felt severe pain, his soul was at peace. He stated that he yielded to an irresistible urge, which the whole week long had so stirred him up that he would have been ready to give up his life in order to satisfy the desire. He was treated for more than a year in the town hospital. I used to visit him and when I saw doctors around him, like you I often wanted to hear their explanation for this incident. With one voice the doctors told me that it was 'rage.' When I then asked them to explain to me using medical science what that might be and what causes its attacks, I learned nothing more from them, except that it was one of the secrets of nature still not uncovered by medicine. For my part I made the observation that if a person confronted by such a secret of nature were to turn to God in prayer and confided in good people, this so-called irresistible rage of yours would not achieve its purpose. Truly there is much in human life that we have no clear understanding of."

While we were talking it had grown dark and I stayed the night there. In the morning the village constable sent a police clerk to get permission from the priest to bury the deceased man in the cemetery and to say that in the autopsy the doctor found no signs of madness or *delirium tremens* in the dead man, but attributed his death to a sudden stroke.

"There you have it!" the priest said to me. "Even medicine could not determine the cause of his uncontrollable urge for the water."

Bidding farewell to the priest, I went on my way.

After traveling for a few days and growing rather fatigued, I came to a large commercial town called Belaia Tserkov. As it was getting on toward evening already, I began to look for a place to spend the night. In the bazaar itself I ran into a man who also looked like a traveler, for he was inquiring in the various stalls where the house of a certain resident was located. When he saw me he approached and said, "It seems that you too are a pilgrim, so let's go together and look for a local townsman by the name of Evreinov. He is a good Christian, keeps a prosperous inn, and loves to take in pilgrims. Look, I've got a note about him...." I gladly agreed and we soon hunted down his house. Although we did not find the owner himself at home, his wife, a goodly old woman, received us warmly and set aside an isolated private attic in the garret for us to rest in. After making ourselves comfortable, we rested for a while. The owner arrived and invited us to have supper with him. During the meal we found plenty to talk about. They wanted to know who we were and where we came from. Somehow or other the talk came around to his surname: Why was he called Evreinov[1]?

"I will tell you a remarkable incident concerning this," he replied and began his story. "You see, my father was a Jew, a native of the town of Shklov, and he was a bitter enemy of Christians. Ever since childhood he was preparing to be a rabbi and diligently mastered all the Jewish gossip in order to refute Christianity. One day he happened to be walking through a Christian cemetery and saw there a human skull. In both its jaws were some disfigured teeth. The skull must have been pulled out of a recently dug grave. In his bitterness he began to jeer at the skull. He spat on it, heaped abuse on it, and trampled it under foot. Not satisfied with this, he picked it up and stuck it on a stake, in the same way that people dress up stakes with the bones of animals to ward away birds of prey. After having lots of fun in this way he went home. The following night, just after he fell asleep, an unknown person appeared before him and violently upbraided him. 'How dare you swear at the mortal remains of my bones! I am a Christian, but you are Christ's enemy!' Several times every night this vision was repeated, depriving my father of both sleep and rest. Then the specter started to flash before him even during the daytime, and the echo of his reproving voice was heard. As time went on the vision recurred more and more often. Finally, beginning to feel depression, fear, and loss of strength, my father ran to see his rabbis, who even read prayers and exorcisms over him; however, not only did the vision not leave him alone, but it became even more frequent and aggressive. Since his situation by then became public, a certain Christian business acquaintance of his learned about it and began to counsel him to accept the Christian faith. He persuaded him that apart from this there were no other means by which he could be delivered from this perturbing apparition. Although the Jew was loath to do so, he nonetheless made this response: 'I would gladly do anything if only I were delivered from this tormenting and unbearable vision.' The Christian rejoiced at these words and talked him into sending a request to the local bishop for baptism and reception into the Christian church. The Jew wrote out the request, and still loath to do it, signed the paper. The very moment that the request was signed, the vision ceased and never again bothered him. He was extraordinarily happy at this and, having completely regained his composure, he felt such a burning and solid faith in Jesus Christ that he headed immediately to the bishop, told him what had transpired, and declared his heartfelt desire to be baptized. With zeal and success he quickly mastered the dogmas of the Christian faith and was baptized. He then went away to live in this town, married my mother, a good Christian woman, and led a devout and comfortable life. He was very generous to the poor, something he taught me as well, and before his death he left me his instructions about this and his blessing. And that is why I have the surname Evreinov!"

I listened to this story with reverence and humility and thought to myself, "Good heavens! How merciful our Lord Jesus

Christ is and how great is his love! By what diverse paths he draws sinners to himself and how wisely he turns insignificant events into a guide for great deeds! Who could have foreseen that the Jew's mischievous tricks with a dead bone would bring him to true knowledge of Jesus Christ and guide him to a devout life?"

At the end of supper we thanked God and our host, and went to our attic to rest. We did not want to go to sleep as yet, so my companion and I carried on with our conversation. He announced that he was a merchant from Mogilev and that he had spent two years in Bessarabia as a novice in one of the local monasteries there, but he had only a temporary passport. He was now going home in order to receive a permanent discharge from the merchant company so he could enter the monastic life. He praised the monasteries there, their rule and discipline and the strict life of many pious elders living there. He assured me that Bessarabian monasteries weighed against Russian ones were like heaven against earth. He urged me to go there too.

While we were engaged in this conversation, a third overnight guest joined us. He was a noncommissioned officer on a leave of absence for the time being, going home on furlough. We saw that he was weary from his trip. We said our prayers together and lay down to sleep. Rising early in the morning, we began to make everything ready for the journey. Just as we were about to go to thank the owner, we suddenly heard the bells ringing for Orthros. The merchant and I began to weigh what to do: "How can we leave after hearing the bells without going to God's church? It is best that we attend Orthros and pray in the holy temple, and then it will be more comforting for us to go." Thus we made up our minds, and we invited the officer to go with us. He, however, said to us: "Why pray in church when you're on the road, and what profit does God have from our being in church? Let's go home and say our prayers there! Go ahead, if you wish, but I am not coming. While you are standing through Orthros I will have gone about five kilometers ahead. Anyway, I want to be home as soon as possible...." To this the merchant said to him: "Take care, brother, not to guess at the future. Who knows how God will bring it to pass?"

Thus we went to church while the officer took to the road. After staying through Orthros (there was also an early liturgy), we returned to our attic to make ready our knapsacks when we saw that our hostess had brought a samovar. "Where are you off to? Look, have a cup of tea and eat dinner with us. We can't let you go hungry, can we?" So we stayed. We had been sitting around the samovar not even for half an hour when suddenly our noncommissioned officer came running in toward us, all out of breath.

"I have come to you in sorrow and in joy."

"What do you mean?" we asked him.

"Here's what I mean! When I said good-bye and set off, I took it into my head to drop into a pub, get change for a note, and to have a drink to make the trip easier. So I went in, changed my money, drank a glass, and hit the road like a bat out of hell. After about three kilometers I felt like counting the money that the publican had given me. I sat by the roadside, took out my wallet and counted the money. It was all there. Suddenly I noticed that my passport was missing. There were only some papers and the money. I was so scared that I nearly lost my head. Then it dawned on me. Of course, I dropped it when I was settling up in the pub. Well, back to the pub! I ran and ran, and again woe laid hold of me. What if it's not there? There would be trouble! When I arrived I asked the publican but he said, 'I haven't seen it.' Once again sorrow took hold of me. Well, I searched and poked around the places where I had been standing and hanging out. And what do you think? In my good fortune I found the passport. It was folded and lying on the floor among the straw and sweepings, completely trampled under foot in the dirt. Thank God! Was I ever glad! It was as if a mountain had fallen from my shoulders. Although it was filthy and coated with mud, enough to have my teeth knocked out over it, that doesn't matter. At least I can go home and back all in one piece. I came to tell you about it. And what's more, in my fear I've rubbed my foot so raw from running that I can't possibly walk on it. I came to ask for some salve to bandage on the wound."

"There you are, brother! This all happened to you because you wouldn't listen and come with us to pray," began the merchant. "You only wanted to get a long way ahead of us, but the opposite happened: here you are back with us, and lame to boot. I told you, didn't I, not to try to guess the future, and see! That's how it has turned out. It wasn't enough that you didn't go to church. You had to say things like 'What profit does God have that we pray?' That, brother, was bad.... Of course, God has no need of our sinful prayer; however, because of his love for us, he loves when we pray. And what is acceptable to God is not just the holy prayer that the Holy Spirit himself enables us to offer and stirs up within us, for God demands this of us when he commands *Abide in me and I in you* (John 15:4). But, precious in his sight is each seemingly small act done for his sake, every intention, impulse, and even every thought directed to his glory and to our salvation. For all of this the boundless mercy of God gives a generous reward. God's love renders boons a thousand times more than human action deserves. If you do something for God worth nothing but a mite, he will pay you back with a gold coin. If you but intend to go to the Father, he already comes out to meet you. You say with a short and dry phrase, 'Receive me, have mercy on me!' But he is already embracing you and kissing you. See what love our Heavenly Father has for us unworthy ones! And because of this love he rejoices over each of our saving gestures, however small.

"This is how it seems to you: what glory does the Lord have from this and what benefit for you if you pray a little and then are once again distracted, or if you do some good deed of little importance, for example, if you recite some such prayer, perform five or ten prostrations, sigh from the heart and call upon the name of Jesus Christ, or if you pay heed to some good thought, or if you settle down to read something spiritually helpful, or if you abstain from some type of food or bear a small injury in silence? To you, none of this seems to be enough for your complete salvation and looks like fruitless activity. Not at all! None of these little acts is done in vain. Each one will be taken into account by the all-seeing eye of God and receive a hundredfold in reward, not just in eternity but even here in this life. Saint John Chrysostom himself confirms this when he says, 'No good of any sort, no matter how

151

unimportant it may be, will be despised by the Righteous Judge. If sins are investigated in such detail that we shall give an answer for every word, every desire, and every thought, then how much more will good deeds be taken into account with the most particular detail, regardless of how small they are, and be imputed to us as merit before our abundantly loving Judge.'

"I will give you an example of this that I myself saw last year. In a Bessarabian monastery where I was staying there was an elder monk of good life. One day temptation beset him: he had a craving for dried fish. Since at that time it was impossible to get any in the monastery, he meant to go to the bazaar and buy some. He struggled with this thought for a long time and reasoned that a monk must be satisfied with the common food of the brothers and shun voluptuousness. Moreover, he reasoned that it was unseemly and sinful for a monk to walk about a bazaar in the midst of a crowd. The enemy's guile finally gained the upper hand of his reasoning. Yielding to his self-will, he made up his mind and went for the fish. After he had left the monastery and was walking along a street in town, he noticed that he did not have his prayer beads on his wrist and he started to wonder: 'How is it that I am going to war like a soldier without his sword? This is unseemly, and when lay people meet me they will condemn me and be caused to stumble, seeing a monk without his prayer beads.' He was about to turn around to get them; however, when he looked in his pocket he found them there. He pulled them out, made the sign of the cross, and wrapped them around his hand. Then he went on calmly. As he approached the bazaar he saw standing near the stalls a horse with a large cart-load of enormous vats. All of a sudden this horse was frightened by something. It bolted with all its might and stamped with its hooves. The horse bounded toward him, and, brushing against his shoulder, it knocked him to the ground, although it did not hurt him very much. Right on its heels, some two paces from him, the load tipped over and the wagon was smashed to smithereens. He got up quickly and was of course frightened, but at the same time he marveled at how God had saved his life. For if the load had fallen even one second earlier, he would have been smashed to pieces like the wagon. Thinking no further about it, he bought some fish, returned to the monastery, ate it and, after saying some prayers, lay down to sleep.

"In his light sleep there appeared before him a resplendent elder whom he did not know. He said: 'Listen. I am the protector of this monastery and want to teach you to understand and remember the lesson just given to you.... Look now: your feeble struggle against sensual pleasure and your laziness in the practice of self-knowledge and self-renunciation have given the enemy the means to assault you. He prepared for you that fatal event that exploded before your eyes. But your guardian angel foresaw this and inspired in you the thought to say a prayer, to remember your beads. When you heeded this suggestion, obeyed it, and put it into action, this is what saved you from death. Do you see God's love for humankind and his bountiful reward for even a slight turning toward him?' After saying this the phantom elder hurriedly left the cell, and the monk made a prostration at his feet. In so doing he woke up and realized that he was not on his pallet but was stretched out on bended knees at the threshold of the door. He thereupon recounted this vision, to the spiritual benefit of many people, myself among them.

"Truly boundless is God's love for us sinners! Is it not astounding that for so small an act, for pulling his prayer beads out of his pocket, wrapping them around his hand and calling on the divine name only once, for this very thing life was given to the man! And that on the scales of human destiny one brief minute spent invoking Jesus Christ should outweigh many hours wasted in laziness! In truth, here the tiny mite is rewarded with the gold coin! Do you see, brother, how powerful prayer is and how mighty the name of Jesus Christ when we invoke it! Saint John of Karpathos says in the *Philokalia* that when we call upon the name of Jesus Christ in the Jesus prayer and say 'have mercy on me, a sinner,' to every such petition the mysterious voice of God responds: 'Child, your sins are forgiven you.'... He goes on to say that in that hour when we are saying the prayer, we differ in no way from the saints, holy monks, and martyrs, for as St. John Chrysostom also says, 'prayer, although it is offered by us who abound in sins, immediately cleanses us.' (Sermon on prayer 23.) God's mercy toward us is

153

great, but we, sinful and remiss, do not want to give him even one small hour in thanksgiving, and we exchange the time of prayer, which is more important than all else, for our day-to-day troubles and cares, forgetting God and our duty! For this reason we frequently are exposed to misfortunes and calamities, but this too does the all-loving divine providence appoint for our instruction and for our returning to God."

When the merchant had finished his conversation with the officer, I said to him: "Well, esteemed sir, how you have delighted my sinful soul! I would even prostrate myself at your feet for this!"

When he heard this, he began talking with me: "It appears that you are a fan of spiritual tales, right? Wait a minute and I will read for you something similar to the one I just recounted. See, sinner that I am, I have a precious little book called *Agapy, or The Salvation of Sinners*. There are many wonderful events in it."

He pulled the book out of his pocket and began reading me a lovely tale about some pious man named Agathonikos, who from his childhood had been taught by his pious parents to say the prayer "Rejoice, Theotokos Virgin,"[2] before the icon of the Mother of God every day without fail. He carried this out each and every day. Then, when he reached adulthood, he began to live by himself and, much ado about the cares and troubles of life, he rarely said that prayer anymore. Finally he abandoned it altogether. One evening he welcomed a pilgrim into his home to spend the night. The pilgrim declared that he was a hermit from the Thebaid and had seen a vision telling him to go to Agathonikos and reproach him for having given up the prayer to the Mother of God. Agathonikos said the reason for this was that though he had been saying the prayer he had not seen any profit from it at all for many years. The hermit then said to him: "Remember, blind and ungrateful man, how many times the prayer helped you and delivered you from disaster! Remember how in your childhood you were miraculously saved from drowning in the river! Do you recall how an epidemic of contagious disease carried off many of your neighbors to the grave, yet you remained healthy? Do you recall when you were traveling with your friend how you both fell out of the carriage? He broke his leg but you suffered no injuries. Do you not know that one of your young acquaintances who used to be healthy is now incapacitated but you are healthy and feel no pain?" After reminding Agathonikos of many other instances, he finally said: "Be aware that all of these things were warded away from you by the protection of the Most Holy Theotokos because of that brief prayer with which you daily lifted your soul to union with God.... Take care that you continue to say it in the future. Do not stop praising the Empress of Heaven with this prayer, lest you be abandoned by her!"

At the end of the reading we were invited to dinner. After fortifying ourselves and thanking our host, we set out on our journey, each of us going our own separate way as we each saw fit.

After this I walked for about five days, comforted by the reminiscence of the stories that I had heard from the pious merchant in Belaia Tserkov. I was starting to near Kiev when all of a sudden for no reason at all I felt a kind of heaviness, weakening, and gloomy thoughts. Prayer came laboriously and a sort of sluggishness beset me. So, seeing a small woods and some thick shrubs along the roadside, I went there to sit somewhere under an out-of-the-way bush and read the *Philokalia* in order to revive my drooping soul and comfort my faintheartedness. Finding a quiet little spot, I began to read in part 4 of the *Philokalia* St. John Cassian the Roman on the eight thoughts.[3] After reading happily for about half an hour I was surprised to see a man about one hundred meters away from me in the depths of the forest. He was kneeling motionless. I rejoiced at this, thinking that he was of course praying to God, and I began reading once again. After reading for an hour or more, I again glimpsed that fellow and he was still kneeling there motionless. I became very moved by this and thought, "What pious servants of God there are in the world!" While I was reflecting on this, the man suddenly fell to the ground and lay there peacefully. This startled me, and, since I had not seen his face, for he was kneeling with his back toward me, curiosity took hold of me to go and see what kind of man this was. When I reached him I found him in a light sleep. He was a country lad of about twenty-five years old, clean-shaven and handsome, but pale, barefooted, wearing a peasant caftan

155

tied around the waist with a rope. He had nothing else with him, neither a satchel nor even a walking stick. Hearing the rustling of my approach he awoke and got up. I asked him who he was. He told me that he was a state peasant from Smolensk province on his way from Kiev.

"Where are traveling to now?" I asked.

"I don't know myself," he replied. "Wherever God will lead me."

"Have you been away from home for long?"

"Yes. It's already been five years."

"Where have you been living all this time?"

"I've been walking from one holy place to another, from monastery to monastery and from church to church. There is nothing for me at home. I am an orphan without kith or kin. And besides this, I have a lame foot. So I'm knocking about the whole wide world!"

"It appears that someone who fears God has taught you not simply to be a beggar but to visit holy places," I told him.

"Well, you see, ever since I was a boy I went around with the shepherds in our village, because I was an orphan," he answered, "and for about ten years everything was fine. Then one day, after driving the flock home, I didn't suspect that our village elder's very best ewe was not there. Our village elder was a wicked and inhumane person. When he came home in the evening and saw that his ewe was not there, he ran to me and began scolding and threatening me. He told me to go and look for the ewe and swore 'I'll beat the living daylights out of you and break your arms and legs.' Knowing how wicked he was, I went after the ewe, looking in all the places where I pastured the flock during the day. I searched and searched and searched way past midnight but there wasn't a trace of it anywhere. It was such a dark night, for it was already approaching the fall. Just as I found myself deep in the forest—and in our province the forests are impenetrable—a storm suddenly arose. It seemed as if all the trees were reeling! In the distance wolves started howling and I was struck with such fright that my hair stood on end. The farther I went the more terrifying it got, and I very nearly fainted from fright. Then and there I fell on my knees, made the sign of the cross, and said with all my might, 'Lord Jesus Christ, have mercy on me.' As soon as I said this I suddenly became so at ease that it was as if I had never been in any distress at all. All my fearfulness passed and in my heart I felt so good it was as if I had flown up to heaven.... I was glad about this and, well, I haven't stopped saying the prayer. I no longer recall if the storm lasted a long time or how the night went. The next thing I saw, it was already broad daylight and I was still kneeling on the same spot. I calmly stood up, and since I was not going to find the ewe, I went home. But all was well in my heart, and I was saying the prayer just as I wanted to. As soon as I entered the village, the village elder saw that I had not brought his ewe and he beat me until I was half dead. That's when he put this foot out of joint. After these blows I lay almost motionless for six weeks, and all I knew was that I said the prayer and it comforted me. Then I got a little bit better and began to go begging. Since being jostled about among people bored me, and also meant a good deal of sin, I went wandering from one holy place to another and through forests too. So it is that I have been wandering for five years now."

Listening to this I rejoiced in my soul that the Lord had made me worthy to see such a grace-filled individual. I asked him, "Do you continue to say this prayer even now?"

"I cannot live without it," he replied. "If I merely call to mind how fine I felt in those woods, it is as if someone pushes me to my knees and I begin to pray again.... I do not know if my sinful prayer is pleasing to God or not, for when I pray I sometimes feel great joy and, I really can't say from where, a lightness and cheerful calm. Sometimes I feel heaviness, boredom, and dejection. But in the face of all this I want to go on praying always until death."

"Don't be distraught, beloved brother. Everything that happens during prayer is pleasing to God and works for one's salvation. The holy fathers say: whether lightness or heaviness—all is well. No type of prayer, whether good or bad, is lost in the sight of God. Lightness, warmth, and sweetness show that God is rewarding and consoling a person for this feat, whereas heaviness, moroseness, and dryness indicate that God is purifying and strengthening the soul and saving it by means of this beneficial trial, making it ready with humility to savor the future gracious sweetness. Here, as proof of this I shall read to you from Saint John Climacus."

I searched for the article and read it to him. He heard it through with attention and delight and thanked me very much for it. Then we said our good-byes. He went into the very depths of the forest but I regained the road and continued my journey, thanking God for making me, a sinner, worthy to receive such edification.

The next day, with the help of God, I arrived in Kiev. My first and foremost desire was to fast a while, confess my sins, and receive the Holy Mysteries of Christ in that blessed place. For this reason I stopped rather close to the Holy Servants of God[4] in order more conveniently to enter God's temple. A good old cossack invited me into his hut, and since he lived alone, I had peace and quiet there for the duration of the week, during which I prepared myself for confession. I learned that some seven kilometers from Kiev, in the Kitaev hermitage, there was a confessor of ascetic life who was very wise and sensible. Whoever goes to him for confession arrives at a feeling of tender compassion and returns with his saving instruction and lightness in the soul. This made me very happy, and I immediately went to see him. I heard from him many wise instructions beneficial for the soul. One thing that particularly stuck in my mind and strongly worked on my sinful soul was the method for conquering sinful inclinations, fulfilling the commandments, and acquiring humility, which he clearly demonstrated on the foundation of the Sacred Scriptures and the practical teachings of the holy fathers. This method, which he considered to be the most powerful and at the same time accessible, almost unique for every individual, even the sick, entailed the unceasing articulation of mercy through the name of the Lord Jesus Christ. He gave me for a blessing a printed leaflet about this, which I read with spiritual benefit every time, and am aroused to carry out its instruction. Here, I have it with me. Would you like to read it?

FIFTH MEETING

An Instruction on the Jesus Prayer
by which grace takes up its abode and saves the soul.
The prayer is as follows:

Lord Jesus Christ, Son of God, have mercy on me, a sinner.
If any say the Jesus prayer, insisting on it, let them say this prayer
unceasingly, just as breath issues from the nostrils without ceasing.
In this way after some years the Holy Spirit shall come to dwell in
them; Christ, the Son of God, shall enter them; the Father shall
come to them. After entering them, the Holy Trinity will make its
abode there. The prayer will offer each one's heart in sacrifice, and
the heart will sacrifice the prayer. The heart shall cry out this
prayer unceasingly by day and by night, and that person will be
freed from all the enemy's snares for the sake of Christ Jesus, our
Lord, to Whom be glory with the Father and the All Holy Spirit
now and always and unto the ages of ages. (From *A Florilegium of
Abba Dorotheos,* chapter 31.)

After listening to everything with rapt attention, I tenderly
asked this holy father to hear my confession and admit me to the
Holy Mysteries of Christ. Thus, the next morning, after being
made worthy of Communion, I wanted to return to Kiev with this
grace-filled viaticum. This good father of mine, however, was
planning to go to the Lavra for two days, so he had me stay for
two days in his hermitage cell so that in its silence I could give
myself up to the prayer without hindrance. In fact, I spent both
days as if I were in heaven. By the prayers of my elder I, though
unworthy, enjoyed perfect calm. The Jesus prayer so delighted me
and welled up so easily in my heart that for those days I seemed
to forget about everything and about myself.

Finally the confessor returned and I asked for his instruction
and advice on where I now ought to continue my pilgrim way. He
blessed me in this fashion: "You must go to Pochaev and venerate
there the Wonderworking Footprint of the most holy Mother of
God,[5] and she will direct your feet into the way of peace." I took
his advice with faith and went to Pochaev three days later.

I traveled for about two hundred kilometers, though not
without annoyance, for the road passed through pubs and Jewish

159

villages and I seldom came across a Christian dwelling. On one farm I noticed a Russian Christian inn and, glad of it, I went there to spend the night and to ask for some bread for the road, for my crusts were coming to an end. I saw there the innkeeper, an old man, clearly well-off; and I learned that he and I were from the same province—Orel. As soon as I entered the room, his first question was, "What religion are you?" I answered that I was an Orthodox Christian.

"What orthodoxy you have!" he said with a grin. "For you, orthodoxy is only in your speech, but in your deeds you are a Muslim infidel. I know this faith of yours, brother! A learned parish priest once seduced me myself and led me into temptation. I converted to your church but after I spent half a year in it I went back to our community. Even to enter that church of yours means to be led astray! The readers mumble the liturgical books somehow and it's all with omissions and things no one can understand. The singers in the villages are no better than in a pub. The people stand there any old way, men together with women, and during the service they talk among themselves, fidget from one side to the other, and look around. They walk back and forth so much that they let no one pray in peace and quiet. What kind of divine service is that? It's nothing but a sin! But in our services everything can be understood; there are no omissions, the singing touches the heart, and the people stand there quietly, the men by themselves and the women by themselves. Everyone knows where and which bow to make following the law of the Holy Church. In other words, when you come to our church you sense that you have come to a divine service. But when you go into your church, you can't figure out where you've come to—to a temple or a bazaar!"

When I heard this I realized that this old man was a deep-rooted Old Ritualist,[6] but since he spoke plausibly I could not argue with him or convert him. I just thought to myself that it was impossible to bring the Old Ritualists back to the true church until church services are put right among us and until the clergy in particular set an example in this regard. The Old Ritualist knows nothing of the inner life, and relies on externals, whereas we neglect them.

And so I wanted to get away from there; and I had already gone out into the entrance hall when I unexpectedly saw through the open door of a private room a man who did not look like a Russian. He was lying on his bed reading a book. He motioned me to come over to him and asked who I was. I told him. Then he began to speak.

"Listen, dear fellow, won't you agree to look after me, a sick man, for a week or so, until with God's help I get better? I am a Greek, a monk from Athos, the Holy Mountain. I am in Russia to collect alms for my monastery. Well, as I was returning home I became ill, so ill that I am unable to walk from the pain in my legs. So I've rented these quarters here. Don't refuse me, servant of God! I will pay you."

"I have no need of payment of any kind. I shall look after you with pleasure, in any way I can, for the sake of the divine name."

And so I remained with him. I heard a great deal from him about the salvation of our souls. He told me about Athos, the Holy Mountain, about the great ascetics there, and about many hermits and recluses. He had a copy of the *Philokalia* in Greek and a book by Isaac the Syrian. We read together and checked the Slavic translation by Paisy Velichkovsky[7] against the original Greek. He exclaimed that it was impossible to translate more accurately and faithfully from the Greek than the *Philokalia* had been translated into Slavic by Paisy. I noticed that he prayed without ceasing and was experienced in the interior prayer of the heart (and he was often speaking Russian), so I questioned him on this matter. He willingly discussed a great deal concerning this and I listened attentively. I even wrote down many of his words. Here, for example, is how he explained to me about the excellence and greatness of the Jesus prayer:

"Even its very form shows the greatness of the Jesus prayer," he said, "for it consists of two parts. In the first of them, that is, *Lord Jesus Christ, Son of God*, it introduces the mind to the history of the life of Jesus Christ or, as the holy fathers put it, 'it abbreviates in itself the holy Gospel.' In the second part, that is, *have mercy on me a sinner*, it presents the history of our weakness and sinfulness. It is remarkable that the desire and petition of a poor, sinful, and humble soul cannot be expressed more wisely, more basically, and more distinctly than with these words, '*have mercy on me!*' No other phrase would be as satisfactory and full as this. For example, if one were to say: 'Forgive me! Put away my sins! Cleanse my faults, blot out my transgressions!' all of this would only have expressed a petition for deliverance from punishment, the result of servile fear and a remiss soul. But the phrase *have mercy on me* not merely expresses the desire to receive forgiveness, which is provoked by fear, but presents the sincere cry of a filial love hoping in the mercy of God and humbly acknowledging its own powerlessness to break the will and keep spiritual vigilance over the self. The cry for mercy is not only about the forgiveness of sins but also about the sending down of mercy, revealed in God's bestowal of the spirit of fortitude, a spirit that gives strength to resist temptations and to conquer the inclination to sin. It is similar to a poor debtor who asks a kindly creditor not only to forgive him his debt but also to give alms, thereby taking pity on his extreme poverty. This profound phrase, *have mercy on me*, conveys so to speak: 'Merciful Lord! Forgive me my sins and help me to correct my life. Open wide in my soul a keen effort to follow your commands. Show kindness by forgiving the sins I have committed and by the conversion of my dissolute mind, will, and heart toward you alone.'"

I spent around five days with this elder. Little by little his strength returned and his health improved. I found the time so edifying that I did not notice how quickly it flew by, for in that chamber, which was like being in silent seclusion, we devoted ourselves to absolutely nothing else but praying mystically, invoking the name of Jesus Christ, and discussing one single topic, namely, interior prayer.

One day a pilgrim visited us and he complained bitterly, grieved, and railed against the Jews, through whose settlements he was traveling and enduring from them unfriendliness and deceit. He was so bitter against them that he cursed them and even considered them unworthy to live on earth because of their obstinacy and unbelief. Finally he said that he had an invincible aversion toward them. When he heard this, this elder of mine began to make him listen to reason.

"You are wrong, my friend, so to rail against the Jews and curse them," he said. "They too are God's creatures, just as we are. You should pity them and pray for them, not curse them. Believe me, your loathing of them comes from your not being confirmed in the love of God and because you do not have interior peace. I will read you a passage about this from the holy fathers. Listen to what Mark the Monk[8] writes: 'The soul that is interiorly united with God is by reason of its surpassing joy like a mild and simple-hearted child and no longer condemns anyone, be they a pagan Greek, a Jew, or a sinner. It looks on everyone without distinction with a pure eye and rejoices equally over the whole world, and wishes that everyone, be they Greeks or Jews or pagans, praise the Lord.' And the Egyptian Makarios the Great[9] says that the inward contemplatives 'are overcome with so much love that, if it were possible, they would give a dwelling place in their womb to every human being, making no difference between evil and good.' There, dear brother, you hear how the holy fathers think, and for this reason I advise you, after you have laid aside your fury, to regard everyone as living under the providence of the all-knowing God, and when you meet with vexations, above all to accuse yourself of a lack of patience and humility."

A week or more finally passed. The elder recovered, and after I had thanked him from the bottom of my heart for all his blessed instructions, we said good-bye. He set off for home and I went the way I had planned.

I was now beginning to approach Pochaev. I had not yet gone a hundred kilometers when a soldier overtook me. We got into a conversation and I asked him where he was going. He told me that he was traveling to his homeland in Kamenets-Podolsk province. Walking about ten kilometers with him in silence, I noticed that he was sighing heavily, as if mourning something. He was quite gloomy. I asked him, "Why are you so sad?"

He drew close to me and said, "Good man! Since you have noticed my sorrow, if you solemnly swear and make a vow that you will inform no one, I will tell you everything about myself, for my death is near and I have no one to talk things over with."

I assured him as a Christian that I had no need whatsoever to tell his affairs to anyone and that in Christian love I would be glad to give him any advice I could. He began to tell his story.

"Well, you see, I was drafted into the army from the peasants. After serving for five years it became unbearably difficult for me, and I was often beaten for carelessness and drunkenness. I even took it into my head to run away. I have been a deserter for the last fifteen years. For about six years I roamed about and took cover wherever I could. I stole from storerooms and barns, led off horses, broke into shops. I earned my living by this all alone, but I palmed off the stolen goods to the various scoundrels I knew. The money I drank away; I led a debauched life and committed every sin except murder. And all of this went off fine. In the end I landed in jail for wandering without a passport, but when the chance came, I ran away from there too. Then unexpectedly I met a soldier who was going home to a distant province on permanent discharge. Since he was sick and could scarcely walk, he asked me to bring him as far as the next village so that he could more easily rent a room. And I took him there. The village police officer let us spend the night in a shed on some hay, and there we lay down. Waking up early in the morning I glanced over and my soldier friend was already dead. His body was completely stiff. I hastily felt around for his documents, that is, his discharge. When I found it, and a tidy sum of money too, I was out of that shed, through the backyards and into the woods as quickly as possible, while everyone was still sleeping....

"And so off I went. I read through his passport and saw that his age and distinguishing features were almost identical to my own. I rejoiced at this and went boldly to the distant Astrakhan province. There I started to become respectable and got a job with laborers. I joined up with an old tradesman who had his own house and traded in cattle. He was a loner and lived alone with his widow-daughter. After spending a year in his house I married that daughter of his. Then the old man died. We were unable to keep up the trading business; I started to drink again and so did my wife. In a year we went through everything left after the old man's death. Finally my wife took ill and died. I sold everything that was left, the house too, and I soon squandered that money as well. There was nothing to live on, nothing to eat. So I took up my former trade again, and I made a living by stealing even more boldly, for I had a passport. In this way I became debauched again for a year.

"For one long spell I had no success in stealing anything at all. I even took a scrawny old nag from a cotter and sold it for fifty kopecks to the knackers. I took the money, went into a tavern, and drank some wine. I got the idea to go a village where there was a wedding; since everyone would be sleeping after the banquet, it would be easier to steal whatever fell into my hands. As the sun had not completely set, I went into the woods to wait for darkness. I lay down there and fell into a deep sleep.

"I dreamed that I was standing in a vast and beautiful meadow. Suddenly a terrifying cloud began to move across the sky, and soon such a powerful clap of thunder resounded that the ground under me gaped open. It seemed as if someone had pushed me up to my shoulders into the ground, which then jammed against me on all sides. Only my head and arms remained on the outside. Then this terrible cloud seemed to descend to the ground and out of it stepped my grandfather, who had been dead for about twenty years. He was a devout man and spent about thirty years as the church elder in our village. With an angry and terrible face he approached me, and I began shaking out of fright. Looking around myself, I saw close by several heaps of things that I had stolen at various times. I grew even more frightened. My grandfather came up to me and, pointing to the first heap, said threateningly: 'What is this? Crush him!' Suddenly the earth on all sides began to press and squeeze me so hard that I, unable to bear the pain, the agony, and the exhaustion, moaned and cried out: 'Have mercy!' But the torture only continued....

"Then my grandfather pointed to another heap and said again, 'And what is this? Crush him even harder!' I felt such violent pain and agony that no torture on this earth could compare with it. Finally my grandfather led toward me that nag which I had stolen the day before and he shouted, 'And what is this? Crush him as hard as you can!' I was squeezed so agonizingly on all sides that I cannot even describe how cruel, terrible, and exhausting it was. It was exactly as if all my sinews were being pulled out of me. I was smothering with such frightful pain that it was impossible to bear. I felt that I must fall unconscious if this torture were to continue even a little longer. But the nag kicked and struck me on the cheek, cutting it open. The moment I felt the blow I woke up utterly horrified and I was shaking like a leaf. I looked around and saw that it was already daylight and the sun was rising. I grabbed at my cheek, and blood was flowing from it. And those parts of my body that had been in the earth had all become stiff, it seemed, and little bugs were crawling up and down them. In this state of fright I somehow just managed to stand up and make my way home. My cheek ached a long time. Look, you can still see the scar; it wasn't there before.

"After this vision, fear and dread often beset me, and as soon as I recall that torment which I dreamt, the agony and exhaustion begin again and so painfully that I do not know what to do with myself. What is more, this began to happen more often and finally I grew afraid of people and became ashamed, as if everyone had found out about my former knavery. Then, because of this melancholy I could not drink or eat or sleep, and I was as unsteady as a shadow. I thought about going to my regiment and owning up to everything—once I endured my punishment perhaps God would remit my sins—but I was afraid and lost courage because they would make me run the gauntlet. And so, losing patience, I wanted to hang myself. Then I had the idea that since I didn't have long to live anyway and would soon die because all my strength was gone, I would go and bid farewell to my homeland and die there. I have a nephew there. Well, I have been on my way there for half a year already and all the while sadness and fear torment me.... What do you think, good man, what am I to do? I really can't take much more."

After hearing all this I was astonished and I praised the wisdom and goodness of God, seeing how he converts sinners by different means. I said:

"Dear brother! During that time of fear and sadness you ought to have prayed to God. This is the chief remedy for all our troubles."

"That's completely out of the question," he said. "I thought that as soon as I began praying, God would destroy me."

"Rubbish, brother! It's the devil who puts these thoughts into your head. God is endlessly merciful. He shares the sinners' pain and speedily forgives those who repent. Surely you know the Jesus prayer, that is, *Lord Jesus Christ, Son of God, have mercy on me a sinner*. You must say it without ceasing."

"Why, of course I know that prayer! Even when I went out stealing, I sometimes recited it to be bolder."

"So look here now. God did not destroy you even when you said the prayer on your way to do wrong. Will he be your undoing when you begin to pray on the path of repentance? Now, do you see that these thoughts are from the enemy? Believe me, dear brother, if you say this prayer unceasingly, no matter what may happen in your thoughts, you will soon feel joy, your every fear and burden will pass and in the end you will be completely at peace. You will be a devout person and all your sinful passions will fall away. I assure you of this, for I have seen this many times in my experience."

After this I told him a few cases where the Jesus prayer had shown its wonder-working power over sinners. Finally I persuaded him to come with me to the Pochaev Mother of God, the refuge of sinners, before he went to his homeland, and there to make his confession and receive communion. My soldier friend listened to all of this attentively and, as I perceived, with joy. Thus he agreed to everything.

We went to Pochaev together on this condition, that neither of us was to say anything to the other, but was to pray the Jesus prayer without ceasing. We walked for a whole day without saying a word. The next day he told me that he was feeling more at ease; and to all appearances he was calmer than before. We arrived at Pochaev in three days and I again insisted that he not break off the prayer either day or night while he was awake, and I assured him that the Most Holy Name of Jesus, unbearable to our enemies, would powerfully save him. In the meantime I read to him a passage from the *Philokalia* which said that although we must say the Jesus prayer at all times, we ought to be especially diligent to do so with the utmost care when we are preparing ourselves to receive the Sacred Mysteries of Christ. And that is what he did. He went to confession without delay and communicated. Although thoughts still beset him from time to time, they were easily dispelled by the Jesus prayer.

On Sunday, in order to rise more easily for Orthros, he went to bed earlier in the evening and said the Jesus prayer unceasingly. As for me, I was still sitting in the corner reading my *Philokalia* with the aid of a night-lamp. An hour passed and he fell asleep. Then I began to pray. Suddenly, about twenty minutes later he roused himself and, wide awake, he quickly leapt up and came running toward me all in tears, and said with great joy, "Ah, brother, what a thing I just saw! How light I feel and joyful! I believe that God does not torment sinners but has mercy on them. Glory to You, O Lord, glory to You!"

Startled and overjoyed by this, I asked him to describe in detail what happened to him.

"Here's how it was. As soon as I dropped off to sleep, I saw myself in the very meadow where I had been tortured. At first I was very nearly terrified, but I saw that instead of a storm cloud the bright sun was rising. A wondrous light flooded the entire meadow and I saw beautiful flowers and grass on it. Suddenly my grandfather came up close to me, looking so fine that you would never tire of looking at him, and he said to me quietly, so fondly and affably: 'Go to Zhitomir, to the Church of Saint George the Victor. There you will be made a sexton. Live there for the rest of your life and pray to God unceasingly. God will have mercy on you!' After saying this he made the sign of the cross over me and vanished that very instant. It is impossible to put into words what joy I felt. It seemed as if a load had been lifted from me and I flew up into heaven.... At that point I suddenly awoke, and I felt very light, my heart not knowing whether to stop or start for joy. What ought I to do now? I shall go straightaway to Zhitomir, just as my grandfather ordered. With the prayer it will be easy for me to go!"

"Excuse me, dear brother, but where will you go at midnight? At least stay for Orthros; say your prayers and then go on your way with God."

After this conversation we went to church, for we didn't sleep. He prayed intently all through Orthros with tears and said that it was very easy and gladdening to say the Jesus prayer with sweetness. Then at the liturgy he received communion again. After dinner, I accompanied him to the Zhitomir road, where we said good-bye with tears and joy.

After this I began to reflect about myself and wondered where I was to go now. Finally I made up my mind to return to Kiev. The wise instructions of my father confessor there drew me in that direction. And besides, if I stayed with him, perhaps he would find some Christ-loving benefactors who would send me to Jerusalem or at least to Mount Athos. I stayed one more week in Pochaev, spending my time recalling those instructive meetings I had experienced on my journey, and making notes of some edifying examples. Then I made ready for the road. I put on my satchel and went to church in order to venerate the Mother of God in spiritual support for my journey, to pray at the liturgy, and then to set off directly.

I was standing at the back of the church, when someone came in. Although not richly attired, he had the appearance of a nobleman, and he asked me where candles were sold. I showed him. The liturgy came to an end and the congregation left, but I stayed to pray at the Footprint of the Mother of God. I said my prayers and then got under way. I had gone a little way along the street when I saw an open window in one of the houses below which the owner was seated, reading a book. I had to go right past that very window and I saw that the one sitting there was the same man who had asked me about the candles in church. Walking by I took off my cap, and when he saw this, he motioned me to come over.

He asked: "You must be a pilgrim, right?"

"Yes," I replied.

He invited me in and asked me who I was and where I was going. I told him everything about myself unreservedly. He offered me some tea and began to speak.

"Listen, my dear fellow. I would advise you to go to the Solovki monastery.[10] You will find there a very isolated and peaceful skete, called Anzersk. That place is like a second Athos and they welcome everyone there. The liturgical duties there consist in reciting the Psalter in turn in the church, about four hours out of twenty-four. I know this for a fact. I am heading there myself, on foot, in accordance with a vow I made. We might go together, and I would be safer with you. They say that the road is very lonely. I will have money with me and will supply you with food the whole way. We could go under this condition, that we stay about six meters from each other so that we do not interfere with each other, for when I am on the road I like to devote myself unceasingly to reading or meditation. Think it over, brother and do say yes! It will be to your benefit too."

When I heard this invitation, given the unexpected circumstance, I reckoned it to be the Mother of God pointing out a path for me, for I had asked her to direct me on the paths of bliss. Thinking nothing more, I agreed at once.

We set out on our trip the next day. Walking for three days as we had agreed, one behind the other, he continually read a book, which he did not set down either by day or by night. Sometimes, though, he would meditate on something. Finally we halted in a certain place to eat. He ate his food with the book lying open before him, and he frequently glanced at it. I saw that the book was a copy of the Gospels, and I said to him, "May I ask you, sir, why do you not let the Gospels out of your hand for an instant, either by day or by night and always keep it with you and carry it around?"

"Because I am learning almost continually from it and it alone...," he replied.

"And what are you learning?" I continued.

"The Christian life, which is summed up in prayer. I consider prayer to be the most important and necessary means of obtaining salvation and the primary duty of every Christian. Prayer constitutes both the first step and the crown of a devout life. That is why the Gospels even command us to *pray unceasingly, always* (1 Thessalonians 5:17). To other works of piety is appointed their proper time, but for prayer there is no time off. Without prayer it is impossible to do any good. Therefore all who have attained salvation by the path of the interior life—the holy preachers of the Word of God, as well as hermits and recluses and even God-fearing Christian lay people—all of them through their unfailing and constant preoccupation had their instruction in the depths of the Word of God. Reading the Gospels was their essential work. Many of them invariably had a copy of the Gospels in their hands, and to those who would ask them for instructions leading to salvation they gave this advice: 'Sit in your cell without speaking and read and reread the Gospel.' That is why I concern myself with the Gospel alone!"

I liked his reasoning and his aspiration for prayer, and I asked him another question.

"From which of the Gospel instructions in particular do you draw your teaching on prayer?"

"From all four evangelists," he replied. "Actually, from the whole New Testament, reading it in order. From my lengthy reading of the New Testament and getting a handle on its meaning, I discovered that there is a step-by-step development and regular chain of teaching on prayer throughout the Gospels, which begins with the first evangelist and goes straight through in a sound order, in a system. For example, at the very beginning is laid out the approach or introduction to the teaching on prayer, then its form or external expression in words, further on the condition necessary for prayer, the methods by which it is learned, and examples. Finally comes the mysterious teaching about interior, spiritual, continual prayer in the name of Jesus Christ, which is presented as being higher and more beneficial than formal prayer. Then follows its necessity, its good fruits and so on. In a word, complete and detailed knowledge of the practice of prayer is laid out in the Gospels in a systematic order or sequence from the very beginning to the very end."

When I heard this I decided to ask him to show me all of this in detail; therefore, I said to him, "Since I like to hear and talk about prayer more than anything else, I am very eager indeed to see this mysterious chain of teaching on prayer in all its details. Show me, for the Lord's sake, all of this in the Gospel itself!"

He willingly agreed to this and told me, "Open your Gospels, look at it, and mark what I shall say." He gave me a pencil. Look at my notes, if you please.

"First of all," he began, "open the Gospel of Matthew to the sixth chapter and read from the fifth to the ninth verse. You see here, don't you, the preparation for prayer or the introduction, which teaches us to begin our prayer not for the sake of vainglory or with fanfare, but in a solitary place and quietly. We are to pray only for the forgiveness of sins and for union with God, and not think up many and superfluous petitions like the pagans. Then read further in this chapter from verse 9 to 14. Here the form of prayer is presented, that is, in what sort of words we must express it. Everything necessary and useful for our soul and our life is wisely brought into one here. After this continue to read the following verses, 14 and 15, from the same chapter and you will see what frame of mind we must preserve for prayer to be effective. For if we do not forgive those who offend us the Lord will not forgive our own sins.

"Move on to the seventh chapter and in verses 7 to 12 you will find the means for success in prayer and for reassurance in hope: *ask, seek, knock*. This powerful expression represents *the frequency of prayer* and the primary exercise of it so that prayer will not only accompany all our occupations but even take precedence over them in time. This constitutes the most important property of prayer.... You will see an example of this in Mark 14:32–40, where Jesus Christ himself repeats one and the same prayerful expression over and over again. The evangelist Luke (Luke 11:5–14) presents a similar example of the frequency of prayer in his parable of the Friend at Midnight as well as in the repeated request of the importunate widow for a decision by the judge (Luke 18:1–15), illustrating the command of Jesus Christ to pray always and at all times, and not lose heart, that is, become lazy.

"After this thorough instruction yet another essential teaching on the mysterious interior prayer of the heart is disclosed in the Gospel by John the evangelist. It is shown first in the profound story of the conversation of Jesus Christ with the Samaritan woman, where the interior worship of God in spirit and in truth is revealed, which God desires and which is true unceasing prayer, like living water flowing into eternal life (John 4:5–25). Further on in the fifteenth chapter, verses 4 to 8, the power, might, and necessity of interior prayer are portrayed still more clearly, that is, the presence of the soul in Christ, in unceasing remembrance of God. Finally, read verses 23 to 25 of the sixteenth chapter of the same evangelist. Observe what kind of mystery is disclosed there! Surely you see that the prayer of Jesus Christ, that is, prayer united with his divine name, is the chief and effectual means to perfection and to the attainment of the fruits of sanctification.

"The invocation of the name of Jesus Christ, or the so-called Jesus prayer, that is, *Lord Jesus Christ, have mercy on me*, when repeated often and over and over again, possesses the greatest power and with great facility opens the heart and sanctifies it. This can be observed for certain in the example of the apostles, who, although they had been the Lord Jesus' disciples for not even one year, already had been taught by him the Lord's Prayer, that is, *Our Father*, which we know through them. At the conclusion of his earthly life, however, Jesus Christ revealed to them a mystery, what they were still lacking in their prayer, so that their prayer would be absolutely successful. He told them: *Thus far you have asked for nothing in my Name. Whatsoever you ask from the Father in my Name, he will give to you.*[11] This is how it was with them, for afterward, when the apostles learned to offer prayer in the name of the Lord Jesus Christ, how many wondrous miracles they produced and how abundantly they themselves were enlightened! Now then, do you see the connection and fullness of the doctrine of prayer so wisely expounded in the Holy Gospel?

"If after this you move on to read the apostles' epistles too, even there you will find the same consistent teaching on prayer. To continue with the preceding remarks, I will show you some places that illustrate the properties of prayer. Thus, in the Acts of the Apostles the practice of prayer is described, that is, the diligent and constant exercise of prayer by the original Christians who were enlightened by their faith in Jesus Christ (Acts 4:31). There is an account about the fruits or results of this constant presence in prayer, that is, the outpouring of the Holy Spirit and his gifts on those praying. You will see something similar in the sixteenth chapter, verses 25 and 26. Then follow along in order in the apostles' epistles, and you will see how necessary prayer is in all events of life (James 5:13–16); how the Holy Spirit helps us to pray (Jude 1:20–21 and Romans 8:26); how we must always pray in the spirit (Ephesians 6:18); how useful tranquillity or interior peace is when praying (Philippians 4:6–7); how necessary it is to pray unceasingly (1 Thessalonians 5:17); and finally we notice that we must pray not only for ourselves but for everyone (1 Timothy 2:1–5).[12]

"In this way, by reading very attentively over a lengthy period, it is possible to find many revelations of mystical knowledge, hidden in the Word of God, which escape us when we read infrequently and cursorily. From what I have now pointed out to you, have you noticed how wisely and how consistently, that is, in a mysterious systematic chain, the New Testament of the Lord Jesus Christ reveals his instruction on this subject that we just now have been tracing? With what marvelous order and how methodically it is distributed in all four evangelists! Here, for example, in Saint Matthew we see the approach or introduction to prayer, its very form, its conditions, and so on. Going further, we find examples in Saint Mark; parables in Saint Luke; and in Saint John, the mystical exercise of interior prayer—although all of this is found in all the evangelists, more briefly or more extensively. In the book of Acts are portrayed the practice and results of prayer; in the epistles of the apostles, as well as in the book of Revelation, there are many properties inseparably connected with the act, with the act of prayer! That is why I am content with the Gospel alone for learning all the paths of a life bringing salvation to the soul."

All this time, as he was showing and explaining these things to me, I was marking the passages in my Gospel, which is in my Bible. The whole thing appeared very remarkable and delightful to me and I thanked him profusely for it.

Then we walked on for about five more days without speaking. My companion's feet caused him a great deal of pain, probably because he was unaccustomed to sustained travel on foot. For this reason he hired a cart and team and took me with him. Thus we reached your bounds and have stopped here for three

174

days. In this way, after pausing for a short rest, we can set out immediately for Anzery, where he is insufferably eager to go.

"This friend of yours is remarkable! Given his devout behavior, he must be well educated. I would like to meet him."

"We are staying in the same room. Please, let me bring him to you tomorrow. It's already late now.... Forgive me!"

The Sixth Meeting

A brother who is helped by a brother
is like a strong and lofty city;
he is made firm like
an established kingdom.
(Proverbs 18:19)

"*A*s I said and promised yesterday when I visited you, I have invited along that revered traveling companion who lightened my pilgrimage with his soul-saving conversation and whom you wanted to meet."

"It is most pleasant for me and, I hope, for my honored visitors, to see the both of you and to hear your helpful and expert words. I have with me a reverend monk of the great habit and a devout priest. Where two or three are gathered in Jesus Christ's name, he promises to be there himself; but there are already five of us gathered in his name, which means, of course, that his grace will be poured out on us all the more generously!

"Your companion's story from yesterday, dear brother, about your burning attachment to the Holy Gospel is quite remarkable and instructive. I am curious to hear in what manner this great mystery of piety was revealed to you."

"The abundantly-loving Lord, who desires everyone to be saved and to come to understand the truth, by his great favor disclosed this knowledge to me in a wondrous manner, without any human intervention. For five years I was a professor in the Lyceum, following a way of life along gloomy paths of lechery, carried away by a vain philosophy based on the elements of the world and not on Christ. Perhaps I would have perished altogether had I not been supported a little by the fact that I lived with my pious mother and my sister, an attentive young woman....

"One day as I was strolling along a fashionable boulevard, I met and made the acquaintance of a beautiful young man. He told me that he was French, a student with certificate in hand who had arrived not long ago from Paris in search of a position as tutor. I very much liked his cultured refinement and, since he was a stranger here, I invited him to my home and we became friends. Over the course of two months he frequently visited me and we sometimes strolled together, did playful things. Together we went out in social circles of the most immoral sort, as you may suppose.... Finally, he showed up at my house with an invitation to one of the aforesaid social circles and, in order to persuade me more quickly, he began to sing the praises of the particular liveliness of the place to which he was inviting me. After saying a few words about it, he suddenly asked me to leave my study where we were sitting and to sit in the drawing room. This seemed strange to me, so I said that I more than once had noticed his reluctance to be in my study and I asked him what the reason for this was. I kept him here even longer, because the drawing room was next door to my mother's and sister's room and it would be inappropriate to talk about matters of this sort there. He bolstered his wishes with various dodges and finally told me openly: 'There is a copy of the Gospels among the books on that shelf. I have such respect for that book that I find it difficult to carry on our dissipated conversation in its presence. Please take it away from here. Then we shall talk freely.' In my frivolity I smiled at these words of his, took the Gospel book from the shelf and said, 'You should have said this long ago!' I placed it in his hands and added 'Well, put it in that room yourself!'

"The very instant that I touched him with the Gospel book he shuddered and vanished. This startled me so thoroughly that I fell unconscious to the floor with fright. When they heard the thud, the household servants came running to me and for a full half-hour they were unable to bring me around. Finally, after I regained consciousness, I felt intense fear, trembling, and restless agitation. My arms and legs were completely numb so that I was unable to move them. The doctor was summoned and he diagnosed paralysis resulting from some great shock or fright. For the whole year after this occurrence, with careful treatment by many doctors, I was laid up and obtained not even the slightest bit of relief from my illness; consequently, I saw the necessity of retiring from my teaching position. My elderly mother died at this time and my sister decided to seek personal holiness as a nun. All of this aggravated my illness all the more. I had but one consolation during this time of sickness—reading the Gospel. From the outset of my illness it never left my hands, like a token of the strange thing that had happened to me.

"One day an unknown hermit, who was collecting alms for his monastery, unexpectedly dropped in to see me. He spoke to me persuasively, urging me not to place my hope in medicine alone, which without divine assistance has no power to heal, but to ask God and pray diligently for this very thing; for prayer is the most powerful means of healing for all diseases, both of the body and of the spirit. 'How can I pray in such a condition as this when I don't have the strength to make a bow or even to raise my hand to make the sign of the cross?' I objected, perplexed. To this he said, 'At least try to pray!' Beyond this he was unable to give a substantial explanation of how I was to pray.... After my visitor's departure, I began almost involuntarily to reflect on prayer, on its power and operations. I recalled some theology lectures that I had heard a long time ago at the institute when I was still a student. This brought me no end of comfort, renewed in my memory that bright religious knowledge, and warmed my soul. Then and there I began to feel some relief from the disease's attacks. Since the Gospel book was constantly at my side, and in view of my faith in it as a result of the miraculous incident, but also because I remembered that the treatise on prayer which I heard in lectures was based in its entirety on the Gospel texts, I considered it the very best thing to study prayer and Christian devotion in the precepts of the Gospel. I got a grasp of it and as if from an abundant spring I drew from the Gospels a complete and regular system for the life of salvation and true interior prayer. I reverently marked all the places and texts on this subject and from that time on I have been trying without interruption to learn these divine precepts and with all my might to put them into practice, even though this is difficult. While I occupied myself with this, the illness gradually subsided until finally, as you see, I completely recovered. Since I was left alone, and in gratitude to God for his fatherly kindness, for his healing me and giving me understanding, I made up my mind to follow my sister's example and the inclination of my soul and seek personal holiness by living as a recluse. In this way I may without hindrance come to know those exceeding sweet words of eternal life shown to me in the Word of God.

"So at the present time I am making my way to a solitary skete known as Anzersk, near the Solovki monastery in the White Sea. I have reliable information that it is a place most conducive to the contemplative life. I will tell you one more thing: it is true, that although the Holy Gospel has greatly consoled me on this journey of mine and abundantly enlightened my undeveloped mind, warming even my cold heart, still, acknowledging my impotence, I openly admit that the conditions for accomplishing the deeds of piety and acquiring salvation, which demand complete selflessness, extraordinary ascetic feats, and the most profound humility, and which the Gospel prescribes, terrify me because of their loftiness and on account of the weak and damaged state of my heart. And so, standing as I now do between despair and hope, I do not know what will happen to me in the future...."

THE MONK OF THE GREAT HABIT:[1] With such a palpable token of God's particular and wonderful mercy and given your scholarly formation, it is unpardonable for you to fall into despondency and even more so to admit into your soul even the shadow of a doubt about God's protection and his assistance! Do you know what the God-enlightened Chrysostom says about this? "No one should lose heart," he begins, "and present as an excuse that the evangelical commandments are impossible or difficult to carry out. In predestining the salvation of human beings God of course did not prescribe the commandments with the intention of making men and women transgressors by the very unfeasibility of the commandments. No! God did so in order that by their holiness and serviceableness they might make us blissful both in this life and in eternity."

Of course the regular and unflinching fulfillment of the divine prescriptions is extraordinarily difficult for our fallen nature, consequently, salvation too is not easily attainable. But the same Word of God who legislated the commandments offers the means not only for their easy fulfillment but also for consolation in the process of fulfilling them. If at first glance this is hidden by a veil of mystery, it is, of course, so that by teaching us immediate recourse to him in prayer and petition for his fatherly help we who practice the commandments may be increasingly turned toward humility and may more easily draw near to union with God. In this is the mystery of salvation, and not in reliance on our own effort.

THE PRIEST: Truly, the Father's help and God's mercy toward his beloved creatures are unlimited! The exceptionally remarkable miracle, so edifyingly related to us by the professor, confirms me all the more in my conviction that there is a self-existing or, as it were, self-operating power outside the conditions known from a human perspective which is implanted by divine grace not merely in words but even in the very things dedicated to God. In the event recounted to us I see a practical illustration of the words of Saint John Chrysostom, who unequivocally proclaimed in one of his discourses that "evil spirits are afraid even to enter a chamber where the Holy Gospels rest" (*Discourse on John* 32). In addition, not long ago I read a similar anecdote in a book with the title *Magnum Speculum*, that is, "The Great Mirror." It described an incident that exerted direct influence on the spirits of darkness, expressed by the presence of the Gospel book. All of this supports the grace-filled incident experienced by the professor. I am sincerely glad that I heard your story. I made a special note of it for my spiritual edification and that of others.

THE PILGRIM: As for me, I noticed above all else that our father monk was beginning to say something about a mystery of salvation that enables us to fulfill God's law with ease. Weak as I am, how I would like to learn this mystery so that using it as a tool, I might set my lazy life straight, to some extent, to the glory of God and for my own salvation.

THE MONK OF THE GREAT HABIT: You know this mystery, beloved brother, from your book, the *Philokalia*. It is summed up in unceasing prayer, which you have so solidly mastered and which you so zealously practice and are consoled by.

THE PILGRIM: I fall at your feet, reverend father! For the sake of God, make me worthy to hear from your lips a useful sermon about this saving mystery and about sanctified prayer. Above all else I thirst to hear about prayer and I love to read about it for the strengthening and consoling of my sin-filled soul.

THE MONK OF THE GREAT HABIT: I cannot satisfy your wish with my own thoughts about this lofty practice, for I am not yet very experienced in it. I do, however, have the manuscript of a spiritual author who treats precisely this topic quite intelligibly. If those sharing our conversation would like, I'll bring it at once, and if you wish, then give me your blessing to read it aloud in your presence!

EVERYONE: Do us the favor, reverend father! Do not deprive us of such saving knowledge.

Reading
The mystery of salvation revealed by unceasing prayer.

How are we saved? This pious Christian question springs up naturally in everyone's mind owing to our awareness of the injured and enfeebled nature of humankind and the remnant of that original tendency toward truth and righteousness. Each of us, although we have some belief in immortality and a reward in eternal life, involuntarily runs up against the thought *how am I saved* when we turn our gaze heavenward. Having difficulty in resolving this problem, we question sensible and experienced people about it, and then under their guidance, we read edifying books by spiritual authors who treat the subject. We strive unwaveringly to follow the truths and rules we have heard and read. In all of these exhortations we are confronted with the necessary conditions for salvation: the devout life, ascetic works, and labors on our very selves for the sake of consummate self-renunciation. This guides us to perform good works and to the constant fulfillment of all of God's commandments, which bears witness to the steadfastness and firmness of our faith.... Further, we are instructed that all of these conditions for salvation must of necessity be implemented with the most profound humility and concurrently, for just as all the virtues depend on each other, so too must they support each other, perfect and animate each other. In this they resemble the rays of the sun, which only then show their power and produce flame when they are focused on a single point through a lens. Otherwise, *the one who is unrighteous in little is unrighteous in much.*[2]

In addition to this, for the sake of giving full force to our conviction about the necessity of this multilayered and concurrent activity, we hear high praise for the excellence of virtue and disparagement for the baseness and misery of vice. All of this is imprinted on us by the certain promise of magnificent rewards and blessedness, or of tormenting punishment and misery, in eternal life. Such especially is the character of preaching in recent times!

Directed in this manner, those who ardently desire salvation set about with much fervor fulfilling the precepts and applying to experience all they have heard and read. But alas! Even at the first step of their striving they do not find the resources to attain their goal, because they foresee and even experience that their injured and enfeebled nature will surmount the convictions of their reason, that their free will is bound, their inclinations damaged, and their strength of spirit utterly exhausted. In the face of such experiential self-awareness of their own impotence, they naturally proceed to this thought: Are no means of any kind to be found that will enable us to fulfill what the law of God prescribes, what Christian piety demands, and what all those who have been made worthy of salvation and holiness have accomplished? Owing to this and in order to reconcile interiorly the demands of reason and conscience with the infirmity of their implementing powers, they turn again to the preachers of salvation with a question:

"How can we be saved? How can conditions for salvation be justified that are beyond our reach? Do those who preach have the strength themselves to accomplish all the things we have been studying?"

Our fellow inquirers are given a firm and general answer: "Ask God; pray God to help you!" "Would it not be more fruitful," they conclude, "if beforehand, or always and in every circumstance, we learned prayer for what it is: the mastermind which fulfills all that Christian piety demands and by which salvation is acquired?" With this thought they go about studying prayer. They read, reflect on, and consider some edifying writers on this subject. It is true that they find in these works many lucid thoughts, much deep knowledge and many powerful expressions. One author reasons beautifully about the necessity of prayer, another writes of its power, its beneficial nature, about the obligation to pray, about the need in prayer for zeal, attention, warmth of spirit, purity of thought, reconciliation with one's enemies, humility, and contrition and about the other things that are necessary for prayer. But what prayer is in and of itself and how a person is actually to pray—with regard to these questions, although they are of the first order and most necessary by far, since very rarely can one find thorough and generally understandable explanations, those who earnestly desire prayer are left under a veil of mystery again. From their general reading a pious but merely external aspect of prayer takes root in their memory, and they reach some such conclusion or outcome as this: in order to pray one must go to church, make the sign of the cross, bow, kneel, read the Psalter, the canons, and akathists....

This is how prayer is generally understood by those who are unfamiliar with the authors of interior prayer and the meditative works of the holy fathers. In the end those who search come across the book called the *Philokalia*, in which twenty-five holy fathers clearly illustrate the complete science of the true and essential prayer of the heart. Here the mystery of salvation and prayer begins to lift its curtain for them slightly and they see what it means to pray in truth: to direct one's intellect and memory toward an unabating recollection of God, to walk in his divine presence, to arouse oneself to his love by means of thinking about God and to unite the divine name with one's breathing and the movements of the heart; in all of this to be guided by the invocation of the Most Holy Name of Jesus Christ with the lips, or by the work of the Jesus prayer, at all times and places and in every occupation without interruption....

After these lucid truths have illuminated the seekers' consciousness and opened to them the path of studying and attaining prayer, they will also convince them to begin at once to put these wise precepts into practice; however, because they operate *in stops and starts*, they will still have difficulties in their attempts until an experienced director discloses to them in all its fullness, from the same *Philokalia*, the mystery that constitutes the mainspring of every soul-saving activity. Their difficulties will persist so long as the director does not explain this mystery: that the sole effective means for them to acquire both the perfection of interior prayer and the salvation of their soul is *the constancy* or incessant quality of prayer, no matter what kind of prayer was initially formulated. The *constancy* of prayer is the basis or foundation supporting the entire range of saving activity, as Saint Symeon the New Theologian affirms. "The one who prays unceasingly," he says, "has accumulated in this one thing all that is good."

In order to present the truth of this revelation in all its fullness, the director develops it in the following manner.

First of all, for the salvation of the soul, true faith is indispensable. Sacred Scripture says, *without faith it is impossible to please God* (Hebrews 11:6). *The one who has no faith will be condemned.*[3] But from the same Sacred Scripture it is evident that an individual cannot give birth within to faith the size of a mustard seed, and that faith is not from us; for it is a divine spiritual gift, given by the Holy Spirit.

What is to be done in such a case? How is one to reconcile the human need with the impossibility of meeting it by human means? The same Sacred Scripture reveals the means and gives examples: *Ask and it shall be given to you.*[4] There you have the means! For, in order to receive and keep any gift at all it is necessary to ask for it; one must pray that it be sent down. *For everyone who asks shall receive.*[5] The apostles were unable on their own to awaken faith within themselves, but they prayed to Jesus Christ: *Lord, add faith to us.*[6] There you have an example of how to win faith! Thus, faith is acquired through prayer.

When true faith is present, good works are also necessary for the salvation of the soul, that is, the virtues. For *faith without works is dead, since a person is justified by works and not by faith alone. If you wish to enter life, keep the commandments: you shall not kill, you shall not commit adultery, you shall not steal, you shall not bear false witness, honor you father and mother and love your neighbor as yourself.* All the commandments must be fulfilled concurrently. *For whoever observes the whole law and yet sins in one law is guilty of them all.* So the holy apostle James teaches.[7]

And the holy apostle Paul, describing human weakness, says *by works of the law shall no flesh be justified. For we know that the law is spiritual, but I am carnal, sold under sin. For to will belongs to me and I do not find how to do good, but the evil I do not will this I do. With my mind I am a slave to the divine law, with my flesh, however, to the law of sin.*[8] By what manner are we to fulfill the requisite works of the divine law when the human race is powerless and has no possibility of making the commandments right within?

Humanity has no possibility until it asks and prays for it. *You do not have because you do not ask,*—the apostle offers this as the cause. Jesus Christ himself says, *Without me you can do nothing.*[9] He teaches us how to do it with him when he says: *Abide in me and I in you. Anyone who abides in me will bring forth much fruit.*[10] Abiding in him means unceasingly to sense his presence, unceasingly to ask in his name. *If you ask anything in my name I will do it.*[11] Therefore, the possibility of fulfilling good works is gained by prayer itself! An example of this is seen in the apostle Paul himself. He prayed three times for victory over temptation, bending his knees before God the Father that he give him strength in his inner being. Finally, he gave the command *to pray* before all else and even *to pray unceasingly* for everything. From all that has been said above it follows that the whole spiritual salvation of humankind is contained in prayer; hence prayer is, first of all, necessary before all other things, for by it faith is vitalized, and through it all the virtues are performed. In a word, with prayer everything contributes to success, but without it no work of Christian piety can be accomplished.

For this reason, unceasing and regular performance belongs exclusively to prayer alone. The other virtues each have their proper time, but in the case of prayer, uninterrupted repetition is commanded. *Pray unceasingly*. It becomes us to pray always, at all times and in all places.

True prayer has its own requirements. It must be offered with purity of thought and heart, with ardent zeal, with steadfast attention, with trembling reverence, and with the most profound humility. But who in good conscience will not agree that they are far from the above-mentioned conditions for true prayer, that they perform their prayers more out of necessity and compulsion than because of attraction to prayer, or enjoyment of prayer, or out of love for prayer? Sacred Scripture bears witness to the fact that a human being does not have the strength to remain steadfast and completely to cleanse the mind of indecent thoughts, *for thoughts incline human beings to evil from their youth*;[12] that *God alone gives us a different heart and he gives us a new spirit*;[13] that *the willing and the doing are God's work*.[14] And this verse asserts the same thing: *we do not know how or for what we pray*.[15] From this it follows that we are unable to pray truly; in our prayer we are unable to display its essential properties!

Such being the impotence of fallen human beings, what remains possible for the salvation of the soul from the side of human will and strength? A person cannot acquire faith without prayer, and the same holds for good works. Finally, even to pray truly is not within human strength. What then is left to the lot of humans? What is offered to their freedom and strengths so that they do not perish but are saved?

Since quality is the chief feature in every act, the Lord has granted this to his own will and giving. But in order to demonstrate more clearly human dependence on the divine will and to immerse human beings more deeply into humility, God has left to the human will and powers only the quantity of prayer, and commanded us to pray unceasingly, to pray always, at all times and in all places. In this fashion the mystical means for acquiring true prayer are revealed, and together with this, how to acquire faith and the fulfillment of the commandments, and salvation itself! Thus, to the lot of humans is given quantity. Constancy of prayer is granted to the human will as its own possession.... The fathers of the church teach about this in precisely this way. Saint Makarios the Great says, "To pray somehow, but frequently, is within our power, but to pray truly is a gift of grace." Saint Hesychios says that "frequency of prayer becomes an acquired habit and turns into nature," and also, "without the frequent invocation of the name of Jesus Christ, it is impossible to cleanse the heart."

Saints Kallistos and Ignatios counsel us to begin praying in the name of Jesus Christ often and without interruption before embarking on any ascetic works and the virtues, for frequency leads even impure prayer toward purity. Blessed Diadochos affirms that if people called upon the divine name as often as possible, that is, prayed, they would not fall into sin.

How experienced, how wise, and how near to the heart these practical instructions of the fathers are! In their time-tested simplicity they shed light on the ways and means of perfecting the soul. What a sharp contrast with the moral precepts of theoretical reason! Reason persuades in this way: do this and that good; arm yourself with courage; use your strength of will; be convinced by the happy consequences of virtue. For example, cleanse your mind and heart of vain imaginings, fill their place with instructive reflections, do good and you will be at peace. Live in the way that your reason and conscience demand. But alas! With all its effort, none of this reaches its goal without frequent prayer, without attracting through prayer the help of God.

Next, let us uncover still more teachings of the fathers and examine what they have to say, for example, about cleansing the soul. Saint John Climacus writes: "When the soul is darkened by impure thoughts, defeat your adversaries with the Jesus prayer by repeating it frequently. You will not find a stronger and more effective weapon than this anywhere, either in heaven or on earth." And Saint Gregory of Sinai teaches: "Know that no one can restrain their mind themselves; therefore in the event of impurity of thought invoke the name of Jesus Christ more often and repeatedly, and the thoughts will fade away of their own accord." How simple and easy, yet how reliable a method, and how contrary it is to the advice of theoretical reason that self-importantly strives to attain purity by its own independent actions!

Having pondered these tried and true instructions of the holy fathers, let us proceed to the truthful conclusion, that the chief, only, and easiest means to obtain both the works of salvation and salvation itself is *the frequency and uninterruptedness* of prayer, no matter what the prayer itself is like.

Christian soul! If you do not find in yourself the power to worship God in spirit and in truth, if your heart still does not feel warmth and a sweet taste for mental and interior prayer, offer in your prayerful sacrifice what you are able, what is within your power, what is in proportion to your strengths. Let the inferior organs, the organs of your mouth become familiar beforehand with frequent, persistent, and prayerful appeal; let them invoke often and uninterruptedly the mighty name of Jesus Christ. This will not be very difficult and is feasible for everyone! In addition, the reliable command of the holy apostle demands this: *Let us continually* (always) *offer our sacrifice to God, that is, the fruit of our lips which confess his name.*[16] Frequency of prayer will produce without fail the acquired habit, and this will be turned into nature; eventually it will attract the intellect and heart to the proper disposition. With this in mind, imagine if we carried out without compromise that one commandment of God concerning unceasing prayer. By doing this alone we would have fulfilled all the commandments. For if we performed the prayer without interruption, at all times, and in every act and occupation, if we secretly invoked the divine name of Jesus Christ, even though initially we did so without spiritual warmth and zeal and merely by compulsion, we would no longer have any time for vain conversations, for condemning our neighbors, for futilely exhausting our time in sinful sensual pleasures. Our every sinful thought would meet with an impediment to its diffusion; no sinful act would be so prolifically mulled over as it is in the idle mind; verbosity and empty talk would be curtailed or entirely eliminated; and each fault would be immediately rectified by the gracious power of the so frequently invoked divine name. The frequent exercise of prayer would regularly divert the soul from sinful works and attract it to its real occupation, communion with God! Now do you see how important and necessary quantity is in prayer? *Frequency* of prayer is the sole means for finding pure and true prayer; it is the very best and most efficacious preparation for prayer and the most reliable path for reaching prayer's goal and our salvation!

To be further convinced of the necessity of frequent prayer, note as firmly as you are able that (1) every impulse and every thought about prayer are the action of the Holy Spirit and the voice of your guardian angel; (2) the name of Jesus Christ, invoked in prayer, contains in itself a self-subsistent salutary power; therefore (3) do not be dismayed by the impurity or aridity of your prayer. Wait patiently for the fruit of frequently calling upon the divine name. Do not listen to the inexperienced, unreflective suggestion of the vain world, as if a single appeal without warmth, even though persistent, is useless verbosity. No! The power of the divine name and the frequency of invoking it will reveal its fruit in its own time!

One of the spiritual authors discusses this topic beautifully, writing, "I know that for many so-called spiritual, pseudo-sophisticated philosophers, who search everywhere for false greatness and practices that seem noble in the eyes of reason and pride, the simple, vocal, unitary but frequent practice of prayer is of little significance, a lowly occupation or a trifle. But they are deceived, unfortunate ones, and they forget the instruction of Jesus Christ: *Unless you are like children you shall not enter into the kingdom of God.*[17] They compose for themselves some sort of science from an appeal to the shaky foundations of natural reason. Does it require a great deal of learning, intellect, or knowledge to say sincerely, *Jesus, Son of God, have mercy on me?* Did not our divine Teacher himself extol frequent prayers of this sort? Have not miracles been solicited and produced by these brief but frequent prayers? Ah, Christian soul! Be vigilant and do not fall silent in the uninterrupted appeals of your prayer! Although this cry of yours may have come from a heart still dissipated and half-filled with the world, never mind! You need only to continue it. Do not let it fall silent and do not be unsettled, for your prayer will be cleansed of its own accord because of repetition. Never dismiss from your memory this thought: *The one who is in you is greater than the one in the world. For God is greater than our heart and knows all things,*[18] says the apostle."

And so, after all these arguments that the frequency of prayer, despite human weakness, is so mighty and certainly within human reach and that it is fully within the power of our will, make up your mind and try it even if only for one day at first. Observe yourself and the frequency of your prayer so that far more time in the course of a day is used for the prayerful invocation of the name of Jesus Christ than for other occupations. And this predominance of prayer over everyday matters will in time prove to you without fail that this day is not lost but has been found for salvation; that on the scales of divine justice, frequent prayer outbalances your weaknesses and transgressions and smoothes over in the memorial book of your conscience the sins of that day. It places you on the level of righteousness and gives you hope of obtaining sanctification in eternal life.

THE PILGRIM: With all my soul I thank you, holy father! You have enchanted my sinful soul with this reading. Everything that you read is so beautiful and comforting, my stupid intellect can grasp it all. Everything is crystal clear, like the *Philokalia*, where the holy fathers discuss the same thing. Here, for example, in the fourth part of the *Philokalia*, John of Karpathos also says that if you do not have the strength for self-control and active ascetic works, know that the Lord wants to save you through prayer. But how beautifully and intelligibly all this is set out in your manuscript. I thank God first of all and then you, that I was found worthy to hear it.

THE PROFESSOR: I too listened with great attention and pleasure to your lecture, most esteemed father! All the arguments, on the basis of strict logic, are correct and for me noteworthy. But at the same time it seems to me that the possibility of unceasing prayer is made primarily dependent on circumstances favorable to it and on perfectly quiet solitude. For I agree that frequent or unceasing prayer is an effective and unique method for acquiring the assistance of grace and the sanctification of the soul, and is accessible to human power; however, this method can be employed only when the person profits from the possibility of solitude and quiet. In getting away from occupations, worries, and distractions he or she is able to pray often or unceasingly. The only thing in store for him or her is the battle with sloth or the boredom of their own thoughts. But if the person is bound by duty and constant business, or is necessarily in the noisy company of people and earnestly desires to pray frequently, it would be impossible to do so by reason of unavoidable distractions. Consequently, since the unique method of frequent prayer requires favorable conditions, it cannot be employed by everyone and does not belong to everyone.

THE MONK OF THE GREAT HABIT: You are wrong to conclude that! During every kind of occupation, be it mechanical or intellectual, and in any kind of noise, the heart trained in interior prayer can always pray and invoke the divine name unimpeded. The initiated person knows this by experience, but the uninitiated requires a gradual training in this. Without even speaking of this, it is possible to state affirmatively that no extraneous distraction can stop prayer in one who desires to pray, for the secret thought of men and women is not subject to any connection with externals and is completely free in itself. At all times it can be perceived and turned toward prayer. Even the tongue itself can express a prayer secretly, without an audible sound, in the presence of many people and when one is outwardly occupied. Besides, our occupations are not so important and our conversations are not so entertaining that it is impossible to find an opportunity periodically to invoke the name of Jesus Christ frequently, even if the intellect has not yet been trained in unceasing prayer. Although, of course, being isolated from people and distracting subjects does constitute the main condition for attentive and unceasing prayer. Nevertheless, when it is impossible to take advantage of this, one must not excuse oneself for rarely praying, because quantity and frequency are within the realm of the possible for everyone, healthy or sick, and are found in the will.

Examples demonstrating this are provided by those people who, although burdened with responsibilities, distracting duties, concerns, worries, and work, not only have always called upon the divine name of Jesus Christ, but by means of this have learned and attained unceasing interior prayer of the heart. So, for example, Patriarch Photios, who was elevated from the senatorial class to the rank of patriarch, continually invoked the name of God while he governed the vast diocese of Constantinople and even trained himself by this means to attain the self-activating prayer of the heart. So too did Kallistos learn unceasing prayer while performing the bustling service of cook on holy Mount Athos. Likewise, the simple-hearted Lazar, who was burdened with continual chores for the brethren, uttered the Jesus prayer without interruption in all his noisy occupations and was at peace. There are many others who similarly practiced the unceasing invocation of the name of God.

If it were impossible to pray during distracting occupations or in the company of people, then of course Saint John Chrysostom would not have prescribed the impossible. In his instruction on prayer he says the following: "No one should offer the excuse that the one taken up in day-to-day cares or unable to go to church cannot possibly pray always. Everywhere, no matter where you find yourself, you can set up an altar to God in your mind by means of prayer. It is easy to pray in the market square and on a journey, and for the one hawking goods or plying a trade it is easy to pray too. Everywhere and in every place it is possible to pray." Indeed, if a man or woman pays close attention to themselves they will find everywhere the convenient opportunity for prayer, provided they are convinced that prayer must constitute their chief occupation and precede all of their responsibilities. In such a case they would, of course, deal with their affairs more decisively. In unavoidable conversation with people they would observe brevity and taciturnity and shun useless verbosity. They would not be overly anxious about troubles. In this way they would find more time for silent prayer. In such a frame of mind their every action would be marked with success by the power of invoking the name of God, and finally they would have trained themselves in the uninterrupted prayerful invocation of Jesus Christ. They would know by experience what frequency of prayer is: that unique means of salvation, granted to the capability and will of man and woman. They would know that it is possible to pray at all times, in all situations and places, and that they may easily ascend from frequent vocal prayer to prayer of the mind, and from this to the prayer of the heart, which opens the kingdom of heaven within us.

THE PROFESSOR: I agree that it is possible and even easy to perform frequent or even uninterrupted prayer during mechanical occupations, for mechanical handiwork does not demand concentration of the mind and a great deal of understanding. For that reason, while this is going on, my mind can be absorbed in unceasing prayer and my lips can follow suit. But when I must devote myself to something exclusively intellectual, for example, to attentive reading, or thinking over some deep matter, or literary composition, how then can I pray with my intellect and lips in this situation? And since prayer is primarily an act of the intellect, in what way can I simultaneously give to one intellect heterogeneous things to do?

THE MONK OF THE GREAT HABIT: The resolution of this question of yours will not be very difficult if we take into consideration that those who pray unceasingly are divided into three classes: beginners, the advanced, and those who have mastered prayer. Now, *beginners* are able to have periodical and frequent elevations of the mind and heart to God and the utterance of short vocal prayer even during intellectual exercises. *The advanced*, or those who have arrived at a constant state of mind, are able to occupy themselves with reflection or literary composition in the uninterrupted presence of God as the foundation of prayer. The following example can express this. Imagine that a stern and exacting emperor ordered you to compose a treatise on some deep subject, set by him, in his presence, at the footstool of his throne. No matter how completely engaged you are in your subject matter, the presence of the emperor, who holds your life in his hands and who has power over you, will not permit you to forget for a single moment that you are reasoning, considering, and composing not in private but in a place demanding particular reverence, respect, and decorum. This awareness and lively sense of the emperor's proximity express very clearly the possibility of being engaged in unceasing interior prayer even during intellectual exercises.

As far as those are concerned who through long habit or divine mercy have acquired from prayer of the mind the prayer of the *heart*, such people as these do not break off unceasing prayer not only when their mind is deeply occupied but even in their sleep, as the All Wise attests: *I sleep but my heart keeps watch.*[19] Among *the most advanced*, the mechanism of the heart receives such a capacity for invoking the name of God that, aroused by itself to prayer, it draws the mind and the whole soul into unceasing prayerful outpourings, in no matter what sort of state the one praying might be found and engaged in whatever abstract and intellectual pursuit.

THE PRIEST: Permit me to express my thoughts. In the article that you read, what struck me was the expression that the only means of salvation and perfection is frequency of prayer "of whatever sort." This is not easy for me to understand, and for this reason: What use is there if I pray without ceasing and call upon the name of God only with my tongue and have no attentiveness, no zeal, and do not understand what I am saying? That will be nothing but idle talk! The result of this can only be that my tongue flaps on and on while my intellect, thereby impeded in its reflections, suffers damage to its active faculties. God demands not words but an attentive mind and a purified heart. Would it not be better, even if only rarely or at a fixed time, to perform a prayer, brief though it be, but with attentiveness, zeal, warmth of soul, and due understanding? Otherwise, if you utter a prayer uninterruptedly day and night, but have neither spiritual purity nor works of piety, you will not acquire anything salutary. Left only with external chattering and finally worn out and bored, you arrive at this conclusion: having completely chilled your faith in prayer, you toss away altogether this fruitless exercise of yours. Furthermore, you can see the uselessness of vocal prayer alone in the accusations made by Sacred Scripture. For example, *These people honor me with their lips, but their heart is far from me.... Not everyone who says to me, Lord, Lord, will enter the kingdom of heaven.... I want to say five words with my mind rather than ten thousand words with my tongue,*[20] and so on. All of this expresses the fruitlessness of superficial, inattentive prayer of the lips.

THE MONK OF THE GREAT HABIT: Your conclusion might have some foundation if constancy and regularity were not coupled with the advice to pray with the mouth, if prayer in the name of Jesus Christ did not possess a self-driving power, and if attentiveness and zeal for prayer were not acquired as a result of making gradual progress in the practice of prayer. But since the matter at hand is the frequency, long-term duration, and uninterruptedness of prayer, although initially it may be accompanied by inattentiveness or dryness, still the erroneous conclusions that you draw are demolished by this very fact. Let's sort this out at greater length.

One spiritual writer, arguing for the paramount benefit and fruitfulness of frequent prayer expressed in uniform words, says in conclusion, "Although many so-called enlightened people consider this vocal and frequent performance of one and the same prayer useless and even trifling, calling it the mechanical and thoughtless occupation of simple people, they unfortunately do not know the secret that is revealed by this mechanical exercise as a result. They do not know how this vocal but frequent cry insensibly becomes the true cry of the heart, how it becomes absorbed in interiority, how it becomes most gratifying, and is made in a way natural for the soul. They do not know how it enlightens the soul, nourishes it, and leads it toward union with God." It seems to me that these reproachful people resemble those young Greenlanders whom missionaries had taken it into their heads to teach the alphabet and to read. Bored with the lesson, they shouted one day: "Wouldn't it be a hundred times better for us to get in our boats and hunt seals, just as our fathers do, instead of spending the day endlessly repeating a, b, c, or scratching a sheet of paper with a quill pen?"

The benefit and enlightenment through learning, which could come their way only from this tedious memorization of the alphabet, was a mystery to them. Similarly, the simple but frequent invocation of the name of God comprises a hidden secret for those who do not possess the understanding and conviction of its subsequent paramount benefit. They measure the work of faith by the strength of their own inexperienced and short-sighted reason and in so doing forget that the human being has two natures, localized in immediate influence of one on the other, that the human being consists of body and soul.

Why, for example, when you want to purify the soul do you purify the body beforehand, imposing a fast on yourself, depriving your body of nourishing and stimulating food? It is, of course, so that the body may not impede, or to put it a better way, so that it may be conducive to purity of soul and enlightenment of reason; so that the unceasing sensation of bodily hunger may remind you of your resolution to seek interior perfection and the God-pleasing pursuits that you so easily forget. And you sense by experience that through the external fasting of your material body you obtain interior refinement of your reason, peacefulness of heart, weaponry to subdue the passions, and a reminder about spiritual exercise. Thus, by means of outward matter you receive interior spiritual benefit and aid.

Understand the same thing about unceasing or frequent vocal prayer, which by its long-term duration develops the interior prayer of the heart, and disposes and promotes intellectual union with God. Vainly do they imagine that, after battering the tongue with frequency and becoming bored by dry incomprehension, they will have to abandon altogether this useless outward prayer exercise. No! Experience here shows the complete opposite. Practitioners of unceasing prayer assure us that those who are resolved to invoke the name of Jesus Christ unceasingly or, what is the same thing, to utter the Jesus prayer without interruption, do of course experience difficulty initially and struggle with laziness; but the longer and harder they practice it, the more imperceptibly they grow accustomed to this exercise. As a result, their lips and tongue gain such direction and self-movement that without any help and effort, they move by themselves unrestrainedly and perform the prayer without a sound. At the same time, the mechanism of the throat muscles is so trained that those praying begin to feel that saying the prayer is a perpetual and essential property of their being and that each time they stop saying it, they sense that something is missing. On this basis, the mind itself begins of its own accord to yield and listen to the involuntary action of the lips and is aroused by this to attentiveness, which is ultimately the source of sweetness for the heart and for true prayer.

This then is the true and beneficent result of unceasing or frequent vocal prayer; exactly the opposite of the conclusion of the inexperienced and those who do not understand this work! Regarding those passages of Sacred Scripture that you brought forward as evidence for your objection, they can be explained by a proper examination of them. Jesus Christ condemned hypocritical reverence for God with the lips, vain display of this, and deceitful praise in the cry "Lord, Lord!" because the proud Pharisees had faith in God only in their speech and in no way justified their belief in their conscience, nor did they acknowledge it in their heart. This was said to them precisely with this case in mind and does not refer to the doctrine of prayer about which Jesus Christ gave direct, positive, and definitive commands. *It befits a person to pray always and not to be weighed down,* that is, to lose heart. In a similar vein, the holy apostle Paul gives preference to five words spoken intelligibly over a multitude of words pronounced in church either without meaning or in an unknown tongue. He intended this for general instruction and not for prayer in particular. Concerning prayer he firmly says this: *I will that they* (Christians) *pray in every place;*[21] and he counsels everyone in general to *pray unceasingly*. Now do you see how frequent prayer is fruitful, even in all its simplicity, and what serious consideration the correct understanding of Sacred Scripture demands?

THE PILGRIM: Truly it is so, most honorable father! I have seen many people without a glimmer of enlightenment and entirely ignorant of attentiveness who simply and of their own accord prayed the Jesus prayer with their mouths and reached the stage where their lips and tongue could not be restrained from uttering the prayer. They were so delighted and illumined as a result that they became entirely different people. It enlightened their minds and transformed these weak and negligent people into ascetic heroes and champions of virtue.

THE MONK OF THE GREAT HABIT: Yes! It's as if prayer regenerates a human being. Its power is so mighty that nothing, no power of passion whatever, is able to stand up against it. If you would like, as a farewell I'll read for you, brothers, a rather short but interesting little article about this, which I brought with me.

EVERYONE: We shall listen with reverent attention!

Reading
On the Power of Prayer.

Prayer is so powerful and mighty that if you "pray and do what you want," prayer will lead you to right and just action.

In order to be pleasing to God nothing more is necessary than to love. "Love and do all that you want," says blessed Augustine.[22] For the one who truly loves cannot and will not do anything disagreeable to the beloved. Since prayer is the outpouring and the activity of love, it is indeed possible to say about it something similar: for salvation nothing more is necessary than perpetual prayer. "Pray and do all that you want," and you will reach the goal of prayer; you will acquire sanctification through it!

In order to develop in greater detail our understanding of this subject, let us illustrate it with some examples.

1. Pray and think what you will, and your thought will be purified by prayer. Prayer will give you enlightenment of mind; it will calm and dispel all inappropriate thoughts. Saint Gregory of Sinai affirms this. "If you wish to drive away thoughts and purify the mind," he advises, "drive them away with prayer, for you cannot control thoughts with anything except prayer." Saint John Climacus says the same thing. "With the name of Jesus vanquish your mental foes; you will find no other weapon than this."[23]

2. Pray and do what you want, and your deeds will be pleasing to God, and useful and saving for you. Frequent prayer, of whatever sort, will not remain without fruit, says Mark the Monk,

inasmuch as the power of grace is in it. *Holy is his name; everyone who calls on the name of the Lord shall be saved.* For example, a man who had been praying for success in his impious ways received understanding and a call to repentance in this prayer. A hedonistic young woman prayed while indulging in debauchery and her prayer showed her the path to a life of virginity and obedience to the precepts of Jesus Christ.

3. Pray and do not make great efforts to conquer the passions by your own power. Prayer will destroy them in you. *The one who is in you is greater than the one in the world,*[24] says Sacred Scripture. Saint John of Karpathos teaches that "if you do not have the gift of self-control, do not be saddened; know, however, that God demands from you diligence in prayer, and prayer will save you." A case in point is the old monk described in the *Paterikon* as one who "when he fell, conquered." That is, when he stumbled in sin he was not despondent but turned to prayer and recovered his balance.

4. Pray and be apprehensive about nothing; do not fear misfortunes; be not afraid of disasters. Prayer will defend you and avert them. Remember Peter of little faith who was drowning; remember Paul who prayed in prison; the monk whom prayer delivered from a temptation that beset him in town; the woman who was saved by prayer from the evil intentions of a soldier; and similar cases. All of this corroborates the power, might, and all-embracing nature of prayer said in the name of Jesus Christ.

5. Pray somehow or other; only pray always and do not be disconcerted by anything. Be spiritually happy and peaceful. Prayer will order everything and lead you to understand. Remember what saints John Chrysostom and Makarios the Great said about the power of prayer. The former asserts that "prayer cleanses at once, even though it is offered by us who are full of sin." The latter speaks in this way about it: "To pray somehow is within our power; but to pray purely is a gift of grace." And so, offer to God in sacrifice what is in your power. If you initially offer him only quantity—and you can do this—God's power will be poured out into your feeble strength. Dry and distracted prayer, though frequent and regular, by becoming a habit and turning

into nature will be changed into pure, bright, flaming, and worthy prayer.

6. Note, finally, that if you spent all of your waking hours in prayer, there would naturally be no time left not only for sinful deeds but even for thoughts about them.

Now do you see how many profound ideas are concentrated in this wise utterance, "Love and do what you want. Pray and do what you want!"? How comforting and consoling for the sinner weighed down by weaknesses, for the one groaning under the burden of warring passions! Prayer is all that is given to us as an all-embracing means for the salvation and perfection of the soul.

And so it is! But prayer is mentioned here in close connection with the condition for prayer. *Pray unceasingly* (1 Thessalonians 5:17) commands the Word of God. Consequently, prayer reveals its all-effective power and its fruit when it is pronounced frequently, unceasingly. For the frequency of prayer belongs without a doubt to our will, just as purity, zeal, and perfection of prayer are gifts of grace.

And so, we shall pray as often as we can; we will dedicate our whole life to prayer, even though initially it is distracted! The frequent exercise of prayer will teach attentiveness; quantity will lead without fail to quality.

"In order to do something well, it is necessary to do it as often as possible," said one experienced spiritual author.

THE PROFESSOR: Prayer is a great thing indeed! And ardor for its frequency is the key to unlocking its beneficent treasures. Yet how often I encounter within me the struggle between ardor and sloth. How desirable it would be to find a means and an aid for gaining the victory that would convince and stimulate me to apply myself unceasingly to prayer.

THE MONK OF THE GREAT HABIT: Many of the spiritual writers present a variety of methods, based on sound reasoning, to awaken diligence in prayer. Let me mention a few. They advise us: (1) to immerse ourselves in meditation on the necessity, excellence, and fruitfulness of prayer for the salvation of the soul;

(2) to be firmly convinced that God undoubtedly demands prayer from us, and that his Word everywhere commands it; (3) constantly to remember that laziness and negligence make it impossible to succeed in the works of piety and to acquire peace and salvation, and that for this reason we must inevitably be subjected both to punishment for this on earth and to torment in eternal life; (4) to inspire our resolution with the examples of those who have found divine favor, all of whom attained sanctification and salvation and the other blessings by the path of unceasing prayer.

Although all these methods have their own merit and derive from true understanding, still the hedonistic soul, which has grown sick through negligence, even when it accepts them and makes use of them, rarely sees their fruitfulness, because these medicines are too bitter for its spoiled sense of taste and too weak for its deeply injured nature. For who among us Christians does not know that we must pray often and diligently, that God commands this and demands it, that we shall bear the punishment for our laziness in prayer, that all the saints prayed zealously and unceasingly? Nevertheless, how rarely all this knowledge shows beneficial results! Everyone can observe within themselves that they actively do justice to these promptings of reason and conscience only rarely or not at all and that by seldom calling them to mind they go on living in the same bad and slothful way.

Accordingly, the holy fathers in their experience and divine wisdom know the weakness of our will and the plumpness of our hedonistic human heart, and take action on this knowledge in particular. In this respect, like physicians who flavor bitter medicine with sweet syrups and smear the rim of a medicine-cup with honey, the fathers reveal the most effective means for extirpating sloth and negligence in prayer. Their method entails hoping with God's help to attain the perfection and sweet ecstasy of prayer, which is the love of God. They advise us to reflect as often as possible on the state of the soul and to read attentively what the fathers say about it, for their accounts give encouraging assurance of how accessibly and easily we can reach these sweet interior feelings in prayer and how much they are to be longed-for. They mention sweetness, which flows out of the heart; delectable warmth and light flooding inside; ineffable rapture, joy, lightness, profound rest, and the utter blessedness and complacency of life, partaken during the operation of prayer in the heart. By entering ever deeper into these reflections the weak and cold soul finds warmth and strength; it is encouraged by zeal for prayer and is seemingly enticed to the experiences of the practice of prayer. Concerning this, Saint Isaac the Syrian says that "joy is an enticement for the soul, and it is produced by hope shedding light in the heart; and meditation on its hope makes the heart prosper" (*Discourse* 4). "For at the outset of each human act," he continues, "and right to the end there is supposed some sort of means and the hope of bringing it to completion...but this stirs the mind to lay a foundation for the task and to continue it. This goal strengthens the mind to bear the difficulties of the task and in its vision of this goal the mind adopts for itself some consolation in the performance of the task." Likewise Saint Hesychios, in describing the word "obstacle" as laziness in prayer as well as the realization of our need to renew prayer, says forthrightly in conclusion that "then there is no other reason that we are prepared to walk in the silence of the heart than for its sweet sensation and happiness in the soul" (chapter 120). It follows from these words that this father submits prayer's sweet feeling and happiness as an incentive for diligence in prayer.... In a similar vein, Makarios the Great teaches that "we must carry out our spiritual labors (prayer) with the goal and the hope of fruits, that is, with enjoyment in our hearts" (*Discourse* 3, chapter 5).

A clear example of this method, as a powerful means, may be seen in a great many places in the *Philokalia* in the detailed descriptions of prayer's delights. One who is struggling with the debility of sloth or dryness during prayer ought to read them through as often as possible!

THE PRIEST: But will not such reflection lead the inexperienced person toward spiritual indulgence, as the theologians call that tendency of the soul which craves excessive consolations and the favor of grace because it is not content to have to perform works of piety by reason of obligation and duty, without thinking about recompense?

THE PROFESSOR: I think that in this case the theologians are warning against immoderation and avidity for spiritual delights, and not repudiating in general the sweetness and consolation that come from practicing the virtues. For if the desire for reward is indeed not perfection, God nonetheless does not prohibit a person from thinking about reward as an incentive to carry out the commandments and to acquire perfection. *Honor your father and your mother.* There is the command! And the reward follows it, inducing us to fulfill it: *so that blessing will be yours. If you wish to be perfect, go, sell your possessions and give to the poor.* There you have the demand for perfection, and immediately after it is the reward, inducing us to attain this perfection: *You shall have treasure in heaven* (Matthew 19:21).[25]

Rejoice on that day when men and women hate you and when they exclude you, revile you, and cast out your name as evil, for the sake of the Son of Man.[26] Here you have the great demand for ascetic feats that require an unusual strength of spirit and unshakable patience. For this too there is a great reward and a consolation capable of arousing and maintaining unusual strength of spirit: *for your reward shall be great in heaven.* For this reason I think that striving for sweetness in the prayer of the heart is entirely necessary and constitutes the chief method both for attaining diligence and for success in it. And so, all of this indisputably corroborates the practical reasoning of our father monk about this topic that he has just told us.

THE MONK OF THE GREAT HABIT: One of the great theologians, Saint Makarios of Egypt, speaks about this topic in a very clear discourse in this way: "Just as when you are planting a vine, your industry and toil are joined with the goal of harvesting fruit, and if they are not there, the whole effort will be in vain, so too in prayer, if we do not perceive in ourselves spiritual fruits, that is, love, peace, joy, and the others, our labor will be useless. And for that reason we must carry out our spiritual labors and our prayer with the goal or hope of fruits, that is, the delight of sweetness in our hearts" (*Discourse* 3, chapter 5). Do you see how clearly this holy father has solved the question about the need for delight during prayer?

Incidentally, a certain spiritual author's opinion, which I read recently, has just come to mind. To wit, the naturalness of prayer for human beings is the principal cause of their inclination to prayerful outpouring. For that reason the examination of this naturalness, in my opinion, can also serve as a means to stir up diligence in prayer, the kind of means for which the professor is so eagerly searching. I shall now tell you what I recall of the things I made a note of in that little treatise. For example, this spiritual author says that reason and nature lead humans to knowledge of God. The first of these, by investigating the fact that there cannot be an action without a cause and by ascending the ladder of tangible things from the lowest to the highest, finally reaches the principal cause of creation, God. The second, by disclosing at every step a marvelous wisdom, harmony, order, and gradation, provides the fundamental material for the ladder leading from finite to infinite causes. In this manner the natural human being naturally arrives at knowledge of God. That is why there is not one nation or barbarous tribe without some sort of concept of God. As a result of this concept, the most savage islanders, without any outside prompting, as it were involuntarily lift their gaze heavenward, fall on their knees, and utter a necessary though incomprehensible sigh; they immediately sense something particular, something that draws them to the heights and urges them toward the unknown.... From this foundation spring all natural religions.

In this regard it is quite remarkable that mystic prayer, expressing itself through some form of movements and obvious oblation more or less distorted by the darkness of the crude and barbarous understanding of pagan peoples, constitutes universally the essence or soul of every religion. The more amazing this phenomenon is in the eyes of reason, the more it demands from it the disclosure of the secret cause of this amazing phenomenon that expresses itself in a natural striving for prayer.

A psychological answer to this is not difficult to find. The root, head, and strength of all passions and actions in the human being is innate self-love. The deep-rooted and general idea of self-preservation clearly confirms this. Every human desire, every enterprise, and every action has as its goal the satisfaction of self-love, the quest for personal happiness. The satisfaction of this demand accompanies the whole life of the natural human being. But because the human spirit is not satisfied with anything sensual, and innate self-love never falls silent in its yearning, desires become more and more intense, and our yearning for happiness grows, filling the imagination and inclining the senses to the same end. The outpouring of this inner feeling and desire, which opens gaping wide of its own accord, is the natural awakening to prayer. It is the distillation of self-love, which attains its goals with difficulty. The less we natural human beings succeed and the more we have our personal happiness in view, the more we desire, and the stronger we pour out our desires in prayer. We turn with our request for what we desire to the unknown cause of being, and this very act fleshes out our desire in our imagination and gives us delight in hope.... Therefore, innate self-love, the principal element of life, is the deep-rooted cause that arouses the natural human being to prayer!

The All-Wise Creator of the natural world has poured into[27] the nature of the human being the capacity for self-love precisely as an enticement, to use the expression of the fathers, which would draw and lead upward to celestial communion the fallen human creature.

Oh, if only human beings did not spoil this capacity or use it in a disorderly manner but kept it in its excellence in relationship with their spiritual nature! Then they would have a powerful encouragement and means on the path to moral perfection. But alas! How often from this noble capacity do they make a base passion of self-love when they turn it into a weapon of their animal nature!

"I sincerely thank you, my dearest visitors! Your wholesome conversation has quite consoled me and imparted much that is instructive to me, so lacking in experience. May the Lord reward you with his grace for your edifying love!"

(They all leave.)

The Seventh Meeting

Pray for one another so that
you may be healed. (*James 5:16*)

*T*HE PILGRIM: My pious traveling companion the professor
and I could not overcome a mutual desire to visit you one last
time and ask for your prayers before setting out on our journey.

THE PROFESSOR: Yes, your candor is memorable as are
those spiritually beneficial conversations that we enjoyed at your
home in the company of your friends. The remembrance of this
will be preserved in our souls as a pledge of communion and
Christian love in that land, remote from this place, for which we
are aiming.

"I thank you for remembering me. And by the way, how
opportune your arrival is! Two wayfarers have stopped at my
house, a Moldavian monk and a hermit who has spent twenty
years in silence in the forest. They want to see you. I'll call them
right now.... Here they are!"

THE PILGRIM: Ah, how blessed life must be in a hermitage!
How convenient for bringing the soul unencumbered into union
with God! A forest without speech, like the paradise of Eden, in
which the sweet tree of life sprouts in the praying heart of the hermit. If I had some means of subsistence, it seems to me that I
would not give up the anchoritic life!

THE PROFESSOR: Everything seems especially fine to us
from a distance, but each of us discovers by experience that every
place has both its positive features and its disadvantages. Of
course, for the person with a melancholic temperament and an

attraction to hesychasm, the anchoritic life will be gratifying. But how many dangers lie ahead on that path! The history of asceticism offers many examples in which it is obvious that many hermits and recluses, who deprived themselves of human intercourse altogether, fell into self-delusion and profound deception.

THE HERMIT: I am amazed how often I hear in Russia, not only in monastic communities but even from some God-fearing lay people, that many who desire the eremitical life or wish to practice the work of interior prayer are kept from following this inclination by the fear of perishing from deception. Insisting on this point, they offer examples in support of their conclusions; because of this they both alienate themselves from the interior life and separate others from it as well. I think that this arises from two sources: either because they have no understanding of the matter and are spiritually unenlightened, or because of personal laziness with respect to the ascetic work of contemplation and because of envy lest others who are at a lower level in comparison with them surpass them in this higher knowledge.

It is a great pity that those adhering to this conviction do not consider carefully the judgment of the holy fathers on the subject. The fathers directly and firmly teach that one ought not to fear or doubt when calling on God. If certain people have fallen into self-deception or frenzy of the mind, this happened to them because of pride, because they did not have a director, and because they took apparitions and dreams for the truth. And even if such a temptation were to occur, the fathers continue, it would lead to experience and the crown. For God's swift help gives protection when such things are permitted. Be bold! *I am with you, fear not!*[1] says Jesus Christ (Gregory the Sinaite, *On Delusion*, chapter 7).

It follows from this that fear and apprehension of the interior life under the pretext of self-delusion are vain. For humble acknowledgment of one's sins, spiritual frankness with a director, and prayer devoid of images are a strong and secure bulwark against the illusion that many people fear so strongly and because of which they do not touch upon prayer of the mind. By the way, in this manner they themselves are found to be in delusion, according to the proven words of Saint Philotheos of Sinai, who says the following: "Many of the monks do not understand the delusion of their intellect that they suffer at the hand of demons. That is, they diligently practice only one activity, the external virtues, but take no care for the intellect, that is, for interior contemplation, because they are neither enlightened nor knowledgeable" (chapter 37). "Even if they hear that grace has been operating interiorly in others, out of envy they reckon it as delusion," confirms Saint Gregory the Sinaite (chapter 1).

THE PROFESSOR: Permit me to pose a question. Of course, acknowledgment of one's own sins is easy for any who are mindful of themselves. But how is a person to act in the case where there is no such director who could expertly lead the individual on the inner path and, listening to the revelation of the soul, be able to communicate correct and reliable guidance pertaining to the spiritual life? In such a case, is it better not to be concerned with contemplation than to attempt it arbitrarily and without guidance? Further, for me it is hard to understand in what way, after placing myself in the presence of God, I can preserve complete "absence of images." This is not natural, for our soul or the intellect cannot conceive anything in the imagination formlessly and entirely without images. And why shouldn't we conceive in our imagination Jesus Christ or the Most Holy Trinity and other things besides, when our mind is sunk in God?

THE HERMIT: The chief condition for the practice of the prayer of the heart for one who labors ascetically in silence is indeed the guidance of an experienced director or elder well versed in spiritual things to whom it is possible freely and beneficially to reveal every day with confidence one's soul, thoughts, and whatever is encountered on the path of interior training. However, when it proves to be impossible to find such a director, the same holy fathers who gave the command also imagine an exception. Saint Nikiphoros the Monk clearly teaches this. "A true and well-versed director is necessary for the practice of the interior activity of the heart. If there is no such person, then you must search for one diligently, and if you do not find one, then, after calling upon God for help contritely, you must draw instruction and guidance from the teaching of the holy fathers and check yourself against the Word of God expressed in Sacred Scripture." In addition, you must likewise take into consideration the fact that the true and sincere desire of a seeker can perceive a useful and instructive word even from the simple. The holy fathers likewise assure us that if with faith and right intention we were to ask even a Saracen, he could communicate a useful word to us. If, however, without faith and just purpose you demand instruction from a prophet, you will not be satisfied. We see an example of this in the great Makarios of Egypt: one day a simple villager made an insightful observation thanks to which he suppressed his passion.

As for "the absence of images" this is so that you do not imagine or accept any apparitions whatsoever during contemplation, neither light, nor an angel, nor Christ or any saint at all, and that you turn away from every sort of dream. The experienced holy fathers command this, of course, because our capacity for imagining can effortlessly make real or as it were bring to life the representations of the mind. An inexperienced person can easily be distracted by these dreams, take them for grace-filled apparitions and fall into self-delusion, though as Sacred Scripture expresses it, *even Satan knows how to transform himself into an Angel of Light.*[2] The mind can naturally and easily be devoid of images and preserve this state even while imagining the presence of God. This is observed from the fact that the power of imagination can represent something for perception "without images" and keep to that representation while attending to objects that are not subject to the sense of sight and have no external shape or form. Thus, for example, our soul's representation and perception of air, warm and cold. If you find yourself in the cold, you can vividly imagine warmth even though it has no form, cannot be seen, and cannot be measured by the touch of the one who is in the cold. Similar to this, the presence of the spiritual and inaccessible divine essence can be imagined in the mind and recognized in the heart entirely without images.

THE PILGRIM: In my travels I too have chanced to hear from devout people seeking salvation that they are afraid to touch upon the interior activity on the excuse of delusion. To some of them I read with profit from the *Philokalia* the instruction of Saint Gregory the Sinaite, who says that "the activity of the heart cannot be deceptive, unlike mental activity, for if the enemy should wish to convert the heart's warmth into his own discordant burning, or to exchange the happiness of the heart for a sensual, phlegmy sweetness, time, experience, and the feeling itself would expose these insidious tricks of his even for the sake of those who do not know his cunning very well" (*On Delusion,* chapter 10).

I have met others as well who to their very great pity used to be familiar with the path of silence and prayer of the heart, but when some sort of obstacle or sinful weakness cropped up, fell into despondency and abandoned the interior activity of the heart that they once knew!

THE PROFESSOR: This is very natural! I myself sometimes experience this in my own person when I happen to wander from my interior disposition into a diversion or commit some fault. For since the interior prayer of the heart is a holy act and a uniting with God, is it decent, or is it not impudent to introduce a holy action into a sinful heart without first purifying it by silent and contrite repentance and due preparation for communion with God? It is better to become dumb before God than to bring forth "meaningless words" from a clouded and distracted heart.

THE MONK: I am very sorry that you reason in this way! This is the thought "of despondency," which is more nefarious than any sin and comprises the principal weapon of the dark world in its relation to us. Our experienced and holy fathers give an entirely different instruction in this case. Saint Nikitas Stithatos says that if you should fall and descend even to the depths of infernal vice, even then do not lose heart and do not despair, but turn back to God all the more speedily and he will raise your dejected heart and give you strength greater than before (chapter 54).

And so, after each fall and sinful wounding of the heart, one ought immediately to place it in the presence of God for healing and cleansing, just as infected things lose their infectious sting and power after being exposed for some time to the sun's rays. A multitude of spiritual teachers speak positively about this. They say that in doing battle with the enemies of salvation, our passions, even if you should receive a thousand wounds every day, you must on no account retreat from this life-giving activity, that is, from calling upon Jesus Christ who is in our hearts! Not only must our faults not turn us away from walking in the presence of God and from interior prayer, thereby stirring up unrest, despondency, and sorrows; they must favor all the more our speedy return to God. A boy who is led by his mother when he begins to walk turns more speedily to her and holds onto her firmly when he stumbles.

THE HERMIT: This is what I think about it: the spirit of despondency and overwhelming thoughts of doubt are awakened all the easier by distraction of the mind and by not preserving the silent plea in oneself. The wise fathers of old maintained their victory over despondency, received interior illumination, and had their hope in God strengthened in peaceful silence and solitude. Indeed, they taught us in this case a useful and wise word of advice: "Sit silently in your cell and it will instruct you."

THE PROFESSOR: Owing to my confidence in you, I am very eager to hear your critical analysis of my thoughts relating to this silence which you praise and the grace-giving use of that seclusion which you hermits so love to keep. Here is how I reason about this. Since all people, in accordance with the law of nature prescribed by the Creator, are necessarily dependent one on the other and hence are obliged to help one another in life, to labor one for the other and to be useful one to another, the well-being of the human race is established by this sociability and reaches its pinnacle in love of neighbor. But how can the silent recluse who has distanced himself from intercourse with people serve his neighbor in his inactivity, and what benefit does he bring for the well-being of human society? He completely destroys in himself the Creator's law regarding the union of love for one's own kind and the beneficent influence on one's sisters and brothers!

THE HERMIT: The degree to which this view of yours about hesychasm is untrue is how wrong your conclusion is. Let's analyze it in detail.

1. The solitary hesychast not only is not inactive and idle, but really and truly acts, and is even more active than a person who participates in the life of society. He works tirelessly with his highest rational nature; he observes, ponders, and keeps watch over the

state and course of his moral existence. This is the true purpose of silence! It is as useful for his own perfection as it is for the development of the moral life of his neighbors, who are deprived of the possibility to plumb their inner depths without distraction. By communicating his inner experiences orally, in exceptional circumstances, or by handing them down in written form, the observant hesychast beneficially promotes the spiritual advantage of his brothers and sisters. He contributes more, and on a higher plane, than does society's private benefactor, because the private perceptible benefaction by the denizens of the world is always limited by the small number of beneficiaries, whereas the person who does good morally by the discovery of persuasive beliefs and expert means for perfecting the spiritual life, becomes the possession of whole peoples. His experiences and edifying words pass from generation to generation, which we see and take advantage of from antiquity down to the present day. This does not differ in any way from the generous alms given for the sake of Christ and realized by Christian love; it even exceeds those alms by reason of its results.

2. The hesychast's benefactory and most useful influence on his neighbors is revealed not just in the sharing of his instructive observations on the inner life. The very example of his life of renunciation profits the attentive denizen of the world by leading the latter toward self-knowledge and a sense of reverence. Hearing about a devout anchorite or walking past his retreat, the denizen of the world feels an excitement for the pious life, recalls what a person can be on earth and how easily humans may return to their primordial contemplative state in which they emerged from their Creator's hands. The silent anchorite teaches by his very quietude, enjoys life itself, edifies, and persuades others to seek God.

3. The above-mentioned benefit flows from true silence that has been enlightened and illumined by the light of grace. But if a hesychast did not have his own gracious gifts in order to be a light to the world, if he entered upon the path of silence with the sole purpose of hiding himself from association with his own kind, by reason of his own sloth, negligence, and base and seductive example, even then he would do great good and have a beneficial influence on the society in whose midst he found himself. He

resembles a gardener who cuts off the dry and barren branches and pulls out the weeds so that the better and useful plants may thrive unimpeded. And this is already a great deal; it is already a benefit to society that the hesychast, by his life of seclusion, removes temptations that inevitably would have arisen from his base and seductive life in the midst of others and would have harmed the morality of his neighbors.

Saint Isaac the Syrian speaks about the importance of silence in this way: "When we place all the works of this life on one side and silence on the other side, we will find that silence tips the scales" (*Discourse* 41). "Do not compare those who work signs and miracles and powers in the world with those who practice silence with knowledge. Love the inactiveness of silence more than satisfying the hungry in the world and converting many peoples to God. You are better to loosen yourself from the bonds of sin than to release slaves from their slavery" (*Discourse* 56).

Even the ancient sages recognized the usefulness of silence. The philosophical school of the Neoplatonists, which had many renowned followers, under the guidance of the philosopher Plato profoundly developed the contemplative interior life, which was attained primarily in silence. One spiritual writer said that if the state were developed to the ultimate level of learnedness and morality, in addition to those active in civil society there would still remain the pains and necessity[3] of having people for other, contemplative purposes in order to uphold the spirit of truth and, having received it from all the ages gone by, to preserve it for future ages and to pass it on to posterity. In the church such people are hermits, anchorites, and recluses.

THE PILGRIM: It seems that no one has estimated the superiority of silence as faithfully as Saint John Climacus. He says, "Silence is the mother of prayer, the return from sinful captivity, the imperceptible success in the virtues and the indiscernible ascent into heaven." Indeed, Jesus Christ himself, in order to show us the use and necessity of silent solitude, frequently abandoned his preaching to the general public and went off to silent places for prayer and quiet.

213

Contemplative hesychasts are like pillars supporting the piety of the church with their mystic and unceasing prayers. Even in ancient times it is evident that many of the pious inhabitants of the world, even the emperors themselves and their officials, went to visit hermits and hesychasts in order to ask for their prayers for succor and salvation. Consequently, the silent anchorite can serve his neighbors and work for the good and advantage of society by solitary prayer.

THE PROFESSOR: Now there's another thought that is not easily resolved for me. All Christians have the general custom of asking one another for prayers. I want another person, especially a member of the church who enjoys my confidence, to pray for me. Is this not simply the demand of self-love? Isn't it just an adopted habit of speaking the same way we heard from others, or of saying what the mind dreams up without any further considerations? Does God really need human intercession? For he foresees all things and acts in accordance with his blessed providence and not with our desires. Does he not know and determine everything before we ask for it, as the Holy Gospel says? Are the prayers of many people really more effective in prevailing over his determination than the prayers of one person? In that case, God would be a respecter of persons. Is it possible that the prayer of another can save me when all of us are praised or put to shame on the basis of our own deeds? Therefore, the request for another's prayer is, in my opinion, merely the pious fruit of spiritual courtesy feigning humility and a desire to please by preferring one person to another, and nothing more!

THE MONK: With outward considerations and natural philosophy it can be presented in this way, but spiritual reason, illumined by the light of religion and formed by the experiences of the inner life, penetrates deeper, contemplates more lucidly, and reveals in mysterious fashion the exact opposite of the conclusion you offer! In order to grasp this more quickly and clearly, we shall explain by example; then we will check its truth against the Word of God.

For example, a pupil comes to a certain teacher to take instruction. His feeble capacities, and not the least his slothfulness and wandering mind, prevent the pupil from succeeding in his

214

studies, and relegate him to the company of the lazy and unsuccessful. Dismayed by this, he does not know what to do or how to contend with his shortcomings. One day he meets another pupil, a classmate who was more capable than he, more studious and successful, and he reveals his trouble to him. Taking an interest in him, this pupil invites him to work together. "Let us learn together," he says, "and we shall be more enthusiastic and happier, and thus more successful." So they begin studying together, the one passing on to the other what he understands. The subject matter is one and the same. And what happens after a few days? The neglectful boy becomes studious and comes to savor learning. His negligence is changed into zeal and comprehension, and these have a beneficial influence on his character and morality. His intelligent companion becomes even sharper, more capable and industrious. By acting on each other they gained a common advantage. This is quite natural, for we are born in a society of people, and through other people we develop our intellectual concepts and our life habits, we refine our feelings and channel our desires; in a word, we receive everything modeled on others like us. Because people live their lives in the most intimate relations and exert a powerful influence on each other, to live among people of any sort is to acquire their habits, activities, and morals. Consequently, the cool can become enthusiastic, the dull can be made sharp, and the lazy can be motivated to act by the lively interest of persons like themselves. The example of personal magnetism expresses this very clearly. In this case observable experiences demonstrate how easily the soul can be unlocked, become attracted, and in particular take action when it is stimulated by the interest and desire of another's soul!

If that is how it is in the natural life, then of course it is all the more possible in the life of the spirit. Being immaterial, the spirit can more easily communicate or assimilate a shared influence, for example, identity, attraction, activity, and strength, to a spirit like itself, having identical properties. Spirit can pass itself to spirit; one can act beneficially in the other, draw it into prayer and attentiveness, encourage it in despondency, divert it from vice, and stimulate it to holy activity. In this way the spirit that assists the other is able to become more pious, more ascetic, and more pleasing to God. There you have the mystery of the benefit of prayer for others that explains the devout custom of Christians to pray for each other and to ask for the prayers of their brothers and sisters! One can see from this that it is not God who finds satisfaction in many requests and intercessions, as is the case among the powerful on earth, but the spirit itself. The power of prayer purifies and stimulates the soul for which prayers are being offered and presents it in a state fit for union with God.

If the mutual prayer of the living on earth is so fruitful then it stands to reason that prayer for the deceased is likewise mutually beneficial because of the intimate connection of the world above with the world below. Such prayer is able to draw the souls of the Church Militant into communion with the souls of the Church Triumphant, or, what is the same, the living with the departed.

Although everything I have said is psychological opinion, we can assure ourselves of its truth by opening Sacred Scripture:

1. Jesus Christ speaks thus to the apostle Peter: *I have prayed for you so that your faith may not fail.*[4] There you see how the power of Christ's prayer strengthens Peter's spirit and encourages him when his faith is tempted.

2. When the apostle Peter was held in a dungeon, *prayer was fervent in the church for him.*[5] This reveals the assistance of a friend's prayer in the difficult circumstances of life.

3. The clearest commandment concerning prayer for one's neighbors is expressed in this fashion by the apostle James: *Confess your transgressions to one another and pray for one another and you will be healed. For the prayer of a righteous person can do much and is effective.*[6] Here the aforesaid psychological conclusion is definitively corroborated.

But what can we say about the example of the holy apostle Paul, given to us in the form of prayer for one another? One writer remarks that this example of the holy apostle Paul must teach us how necessary mutual prayer for one another is, when even this exceedingly holy and steadfast spiritual athlete recognizes his own need for the spiritual assistance of prayer. In his letter to the Hebrews he formulates his request this way: *Pray for us, for we trust that we have a clear conscience, desiring to live honorably in all things.*[7] Hearing this, how unreasonable it would be to rest on our own prayers and successes alone when so grace-filled and holy a man, guided by humility, asks to unite the prayer of his neighbors (the Hebrews) with his own! For this reason, with humility, simplicity, and the bond of love, it is incumbent upon us not to reject or disdain the prayerful assistance even of the weakest members of the faithful, when the clear-sighted spirit of the apostle Paul avoided fastidiousness in this case and asked for the prayers of everyone in general, knowing that God's power is made perfect in weakness. Consequently, it can sometimes be made perfect even among those prayers that seem to be apparently weak.

If we are persuaded by this example, let us further note that prayer for one another maintains the bond of Christian love commanded by God, and bears witness to humility. The spirit of the one who asks seemingly attracts the spirit of the one who prays. In this way, mutual prayer takes fire.

THE PROFESSOR: Your analysis and proofs are beautiful and exact, but it would be interesting to hear from you the method itself and the form of prayer for one's neighbors. I think that if the fruitfulness and attraction of prayer depend on a lively interest in your neighbors and on the primary, constant influence that the spirit of the one praying exerts on the spirit of the one asking for prayer, then will not such an attitude of the soul divert you from standing uninterruptedly in the free-of-images presence of God and pouring out your soul before God in your personal need? But if you manage only once or twice a day to bring your neighbor to mind with concern for him or her, asking for divine assistance for them, will this be sufficient for attracting and strengthening the soul of the one for whom you pray? To say it more briefly, I want to know in what way or how I am to pray for my neighbor.

THE MONK: Prayer about anything at all, when offered to God, must not and cannot lead us away from placing ourselves before God; inasmuch as it is poured out to God, it is of course in his presence. Regarding the method of prayer for our neighbor, we need to notice that the power of this prayer consists in a truly Christian interest in our neighbor and that it has an influence on

217

our neighbor's soul according to the measure of our interest. Prayer for our neighbor also consists in the remembrance of God; thus, when we are remembering our neighbor we ought to pray in this manner: *Lord Jesus Christ, Son of God, have mercy on your servant* X. While praying for yourself it is possible to pray simultaneously for your neighbor: *Lord Jesus Christ, Son of God, have mercy on me a sinner and on your servant* X. And if you wish to pray for several people or for many, you ought to pray this way: *Lord Jesus Christ, Son of God, have mercy on us sinners.* You can offer a prayer like this for your neighbors several times when you happen to remember them, without fixing the time or the quantity. I have learned by experience how beneficially such a prayer works on the one for whom it is offered.

THE PROFESSOR: Your edifying conversation and lucid thoughts, drawn from your points of view and your reasoning, as well as the reverence and gratitude that I owe you for everything, and here attest, oblige me to keep them forever fresh in my memory and to carry them from this place in my grateful heart.

THE PILGRIM AND THE PROFESSOR: And so, the time for our departure has already come. We most sincerely ask for your prayers for our journey and our companionship!

May the God of peace, who brought back from the dead the great shepherd of the sheep, Our Lord Jesus Christ, by the blood of the eternal covenant, perfect you in every good deed to do his will, working in you that which is pleasing in his sight, Jesus Christ, to whom be glory for the ages of ages, Amen.[8]

Notes to Text

First Meeting

[1][In the Russian popular tradition, the day of Pentecost is called Trinity Sunday or the Day of the Holy Trinity. Trans.]
[2]1 Thes 5:17.
[3]See Eph 6:18.
[4]See 1 Tm 2:8.
[5]Lk 18:11 [The Russian differs from the Greek. Trans.]
[6]Ps 108:7 [LXX. Trans.]
[7]See Eph 2:8.
[8]Mt 7:7.
[9]Lk 17:5.
[10]Gn 8:21.
[11]See Ez 11:19.
[12]Ps 50:12.
[13]Rom 7:25.
[14]Eph 6:18.
[15]Mt 6:7.
[16]Eph 6:18.
[17]Prv 3:6; Neh 4:14; Ps 76:12.
[18]Ps 25:2.
[19]Mt 6:7.
[20]See Lk 18:1.
[21]Mt 7:7.
[22]See 1 Pt 4:8.
[23]See Lk 18:7.
[24]Ps 102:22.
[25]Acts 7:48.
[26]Is 55:6–7.

[27][The Russian measurement is a *verst*, which is approximately 1.08 km. Trans.]

[28]Heb 9:6.

[29]See Introduction, n. 88 above.

[30]Sg 5:2.

[31]1 Tm 2:1.

[32]Rom 8:26.

[33][The Slavonic version of the *Philokalia* consists of the texts of only twenty-five instead of the thirty-six authors of the Greek original edition (Venice, 1782). The Slavonic translation was published in 1793 in Moscow and republished in 1822 and 1833. Trans.]

[34][Nikiphoros the Monk lived on Mount Athos during the latter part of the thirteenth century. His teachings may be found in the *Philokalia*, trans. and ed. G. E. H. Palmer, Philip Sherrard, and Kallistos Ware (London: Faber & Faber, 1995) 4:194–206. Trans.]

[35][Orthros roughly corresponds to the canonical hours of matins and lauds in the Roman rite. Though intended to be celebrated before sunrise in the morning, it is most frequently performed after vespers. The service comprises continuous psalmody, the canon, and lauds. See Robert Taft, S.J., *The Liturgy of the Hours in East and West* (Collegeville, Minn.: Liturgical Press, 1985), pp. 277–83. Trans.]

[36][The passage cited here may be found in *The Philokalia*, 4:206 (see n. 34 above). Trans.]

[37]1 Thes 5:17.

Second Meeting

[1]Ps 65:16.

[2][The relics of Bishop Innokenty (d. 1731) were preserved in the Ascension monastery, located approximately 5 km from Irkutsk on the Angara River. Innokenty was canonized for general veneration in the Russian Orthodox Church in 1804. Feast day, 26 November. Trans.]

[3]1 Tm. 2:4.

[4]1 Cor 10:13.

[5][Theoliptos of Philadelphia (ca. 1250–1322) was an important spiritual authority in the late Byzantine empire. His letters of direction to Irene-Evlogia Choumnaina, hegumenissa of Christ Philanthropos Sotir monastery in Constantinople, are regarded as masterpieces. Among his more famous disciples was St. Gregory Palamas. For the

text referred to here, see *The Philokalia: The Complete Text,* trans. G. E. H. Palmer, Philip Sherrard, and Kallistos Ware (London: Faber & Faber, 1995) 4:177–87. Also Robert E. Sinkewicz, *Theoleptos of Philadelphia: The Monastic Discourses* (Toronto: Pontifical Institute of Mediaeval Studies, 1992). Trans.]

[6]Rom 12:20.

[7]Mt 5:44, 40.

[8]See 1 Pt 3:4.

[9]See Jn 4:24.

[10]See Lk 17:21.

[11]Rom 8:26.

[12]Gn 17:1.

[13]Jn 15:4.

[14]Prv 23:26.

[15]Gal 3:27.

[16]See 2 Cor 1:22.

[17]Gal 4:6.

[18][The Russian refers to twelve *sazhen*; one *sazhen* is 2.134 meters. Trans.]

[19][The Russian measurement is *pud*, which is 16.38 kg. Trans.]

[20]1 Cor 12:31; 1 Thes 5:19.

[21]See First Meeting, n. 34 above.

[22][Saint Gregory of Sinai (ca. 1265–1346) was one of the leading teachers and practitioners of hesychasm on Mount Athos in the fourteenth century. After initial monastic training in the Sinai, Gregory traveled to Crete, where he was exposed to inner prayer and the Jesus prayer by a certain Arsenios. He eventually made his way to Mount Athos, but chose to live in the Magoula hermitage rather than a cenobitic monastery. He died in Paroria, near the Bulgarian and Byzantine imperial border. Trans.]

[23][Biographical information and a selection of the writings of Symeon the New Theologian (949–1022) may be found in *Symeon the New Theologian: The Discourses,* trans. C. J. deCatanzaro (New York: Paulist Press, 1980). His authorship of "On the Three Modes of Prayer" is disputed, with some scholars attributing the text to Nikiphoros the Monk. Trans.]

[24][Kallistos and Ignatios Xanthopoulos were monks in the monastery of the Xanthopouloi in Constantinople in the fourteenth century. They authored a book on the hesychast spiritual life, *The Centuries,* which was included in the *Philokalia* of Nikodimos Hagiorites. Kallistos served as patriarch of Constantinople for three months in 1397. Trans.]

[25]Lk 17:21.

[26]Ps 103:24 [LXX].

[27][Missing from the manuscript. Ed.]

[28]Mt 16:26.

[29][Little is known for certain about John of Karpathos (seventh century), a hermit on the island of Karpathos, located between Crete and Rhodes. His principal work, *For the Encouragement of the Monks in India who had written him: One Hundred Texts*, referred to here, is available in an English translation in *The Philokalia*, vol. 1 (1979), pp. 298–321 (see n. 5 above). Trans.]

[30]1 Jn 4:4.

[31]1 Cor 10:13.

[32][Saint Gregory of Thessaloniki, better known as Gregory Palamas (1296–1359), is of fundamental importance not only for the history of hesychasm but also for contemporary Orthodox discussions of trinitarian theology. For information on his life and thought, see John Meyendorff, *A Study of Gregory Palamas* (London, 1964); idem, *St. Gregory Palamas and Orthodox Spirituality* (Crestwood, N.Y., 1974). Selections from a key work by Palamas, the *Triads*, are available in *Gregory Palamas: The Triads*, trans. Nicholas Gendle, *The Classics of Western Spirituality* (New York, 1983). Trans.]

[33][According to Hans-Georg Beck (*Kirche und theologische Literatur im byzantinischen Reich* [Munich, 1977], p. 784), Kallistos (fourteenth century) was known by a number of surnames: Angelikudes Melenikeotes, Meliteniotes, and Telikudes. The Russian surname seems to be a corruption of Angelikudes and Telikudes. He was a hesychast, likely identical with the founder of the Melenikeon monastery, and author of a number of treatises on hesychasm. Beck lists only one edited text, the *Peri isukhastikis tribis*, PG 147, 817–26. Trans.]

[34]See Prv 18:19.

[35]Jer 29:13.

[36]Jn 15:4.

[37]1 Thes 5:17.

[38]Acts 2:1.

[39]Ps 33:9 (34:8).

[40][Literally, "together with her husband she was amazed." The Russian verb was plural in the manuscript and has been corrected. Ed.]

NOTES TO THIRD, FOURTH MEETING

Third Meeting

[1]Ps 50:1 [LXX].

[2][The Akathist hymn is a lengthy liturgical poem sung standing, dedicated to Christ, the Mother of God, and other saints. The Akathist of the Mother of God commemorates the miraculous deliverance of Constantinople from an invasion by Avars and Persians in 626. It is usually said on Saturday of Great Lent during Orthros. An English translation is available in *The Lenten Triodion*, trans. Mother Mary and Archimandrite Kallistos Ware (London: Faber & Faber, 1978), pp. 422–44. Trans.]

[3][Corrected from "dishes" in manuscript. Ed.]

[4][Corrected from "seventeen" in manuscript. Ed.]

[5]See Eph 4:13.

Fourth Meeting

[1]See Ps 72:28 [LXX].

[2][Corrected from "you will decide" in manuscript. Ed.]

[3][Corrected from "and" in manuscript. Ed.]

[4]Phil 2:13.

[5]Phil 3:13–14.

[6]Ps 103:1 [LXX].

[7][Menologies (readings for a month) are collections of saints' lives organized on the basis of the calendar year. There are usually twelve volumes, one volume per month. In the Russian context the two most famous menologies are those compiled by Metropolitan Makary (sixteenth century) and Bishop Dmitry of Rostov (eighteenth century). The latter work was a popular and much more accessible version than the massive and as yet not fully published menology by Metropolitan Makary. Trans.]

[8][The manuscript lacks the necessary preposition for the Russian verb. Ed.]

[9]See 2 Cor 12:9.

[10][See Saint Peter of Damaskos, "God's Universal and Particular Gifts," in *The Philokalia: The Complete Text*, trans. G. E. H. Palmer, Philip Sherrard, and Kallistos Ware (London: Faber & Faber, 1984), 3:173. After Maximos the Confessor, Peter of Damaskos occupies more space in the *Philokalia* than any other writer. Facts about his life, however, are few and

controverted. He lived in the eleventh or twelfth century, though not necessarily in Damascus. Trans.]

[11][The Russian word is *onuchi*, which refers to the cloth wrappings worn about the feet in bast shoes, the typical footgear of peasants. Trans.]

[12][The monk and priest Nikitas Stithatos (ca. 1000–ca. 1092) was a fervent disciple and biographer of Symeon the New Theologian. His surname, "the Courageous," refers to his bold criticism of the illicit romance between emperor Constantine IX Monomachos and Skliriana. He penned a number of polemical tracts against the Latins and was involved in the infamous 1054 confrontation between Cardinal Humbert of Silva Candida and Patriarch Michael Kerularios. In addition to polemics, Nikitas Stithatos composed a number of theological treatises dealing with the soul, paradise, the celestial and earthly hierarchies, fifteen exegetical studies of the Hexaemeron, a homily on penance, and the famous Life of Symeon the New Theologian. See *The Philokalia*, vol. 4 (1995), for a selection of his ascetical writings (see n. 10 above) Trans.]

[13]See Nikitas Stithatos, "On the Practice of the Virtues: One Hundred Texts," no. 52, in *The Philokalia*, 4:92.

[14][Saint Hesychios the Priest (seventh, eighth, or ninth century) was abbot of the monastery of the Burning Bush at Sinai. His chief work, "On Watchfulness and Holiness," reveals him to be strongly devoted to the holy name of Jesus. He is considered an important precursor of the later hesychast tradition. Text in *The Philokalia*, vol. 1 (1979), pp. 162–98 (see n. 10 above). Trans.]

[15]See Second Meeting, n. 24.

[16]1 Cor 12:3.

[17]See Saint Gregory of Sinai, "On Stillness: Fifteen Texts," no. 12, p. 272; "On Prayer: Seven Texts," no. 7, p. 285, in *The Philokalia*, vol. 4 (1995) (see n. 10 above).

[18]Hegumenissa is the Orthodox equivalent of abbess, the head of a monastery of women.

[19][Five rubles. Trans.]

[20][Corrected from "fields" in manuscript. Ed.]

Fifth Meeting

[1][The surname derives from the Russian word for Jew, Hebrew: *evrei*. Trans.]

[2][This prayer is an Orthodox equivalent to the Western "Hail Mary." Its text runs: "Rejoice, Theotokos Virgin, Mary full of grace, the Lord is with you. Blessed are you among women and blessed is the fruit of your womb, for you have given birth to the Savior of our souls." Trans.]

[3][Text in *The Philokalia: The Complete Text*, vol. 1, trans. G. E. H. Palmer, Philip Sherrard, and Kallistos Ware (London: Faber & Faber, 1979), pp. 73–93. Trans.]

[4][This refers to the Kiev Caves monastery, founded in the eleventh century. Its catacombs contain the bodies of many holy monks, hence the name in the text. Trans.]

[5][The Dormition Lavra in Pochaev was an important pilgrimage center in the nineteenth century. According to legend, a group of shepherds near Pochaev witnessed an apparition of the Mother of God accompanied by numerous saints. She left her footprint on a rock from which a spring of water with healing powers began to flow. Oral tradition records that a monastery was built on the site in the thirteenth century; however, documentary evidence begins only in the sixteenth century. In 1720 the monastery became the provincialate for the Ukrainian Catholic order of Basilian monks after a significant number of its residents opted for union with Rome. It was returned to Orthodox control in 1831 during the Polish rebellion. The monastery then served as the residence for the Orthodox bishop of Ostrog. Trans.]

[6]See Introduction, n. 51.

[7][Paisy Velichkovsky (1722–1794) was born in Poltava, Ukraine. One of the most important spiritual authorities of the eighteenth century, Paisy produced a Slavonic version of the *Philokalia* with the title *Dobrotoliubie*, published in 1793. Paisy's text would exert immense influence on Russian spirituality. Later Feofan the Recluse (1815–1894) translated and edited a Russian version of *Dobrotoliubie* that differs in some respects from the Greek *Philokalia*, published in 1782. Trans.]

[8][Nothing certain about the life of Mark the Monk is known. He likely lived in the fifth century, was a hermit in the deserts of Palestine or Egypt, and may have been connected with a monastery in Asia Minor. He wrote important treatises on baptismal grace and penance and combatted the ascetical heresy known as Messalianism. Trans.]

[9][Makarios the Great (ca. 300–ca. 390) of Egypt was an important ascetic master in Sketis. Information about his life and teaching is found in the *Lausiac History* of Palladios and the *Apophthegmata Patrum* (Sayings of the Desert Fathers). Trans.]

[10][Solovki monastery, dedicated to the Transfiguration of Christ, was founded in the years 1429–1436 by Saints German and Savvaty on an island in the far northern White Sea. It quickly became one of the wealthiest and most important spiritual centers in Russia. During the seventeenth-century schism, the majority of monks in the Solovki monastery sided with the Old Ritualists and were violently suppressed by the government. Trans.]

[11]Jn 16:23.

[12][The Byzantine, and, then, Russian order of the books of the New Testament differs from the Western practice. Trans.]

Sixth Meeting

[1]See Introduction, n. 88 above.

[2]Lk 16:10.

[3]See Mk 16:16.

[4]Mt 7:7.

[5]Mt 7:8.

[6]Lk 5:17. The translation "Lord, increase our faith," more familiar to English readers, does not suit the context and is not an accurate rendition of the Russian.

[7]The scriptural references are from Jas 2:24; Mt 19:17–18; Jas 2:10.

[8]See Rom 3:20; 7:14, 18–19, 25.

[9]See Jn 15:5.

[10]See Jn 15:4, 5

[11]See Jn 16:23–24.

[12]Gn 8:21.

[13]See Ez 11:19.

[14]Phil 2:13.

[15]See Rom 8:26.

[16]Heb 13:15.

[17]Mt 18:2.

[18]1 Jn 4:4; 3:20.

[19]Sg 5:2.

[20]See Mt 7:21; 1 Cor 14:19.

[21]1 Tm 2:8.

[22]Saint Augustine, *Homily on 1 John* 7:8.

[23][See John Climacus, *The Ladder of Divine Ascent*, 21 (945C). Trans.]

[24]1 Jn 4:4.
[25]More accurately, Mt 19:19–21.
[26]Lk 6:22–23.
[27][Corrected from "influenced" in manuscript. Ed.]

Seventh Meeting

[1]See Mt 14:27 and Jn 6:20.
[2]2 Cor 11:14.
[3][Corrected from *trebnost'* in manuscript. Presumably a copying error. Ed.]
[4]Lk 22:31.
[5]Acts 12:5.
[6]Jas 5:16.
[7]Heb 13:18.
[8]See Heb 13:20–21.

Bibliography

Readers are referred to the notes for bibliographic information pertaining to the Russian original of *The Pilgrim's Tale* and secondary literature cited by Dr. Pentkovsky and the translator. In addition to these sources, valuable information pertaining to the Jesus prayer may be found in Pierre Adnès, "Jésus (Prière à)," *Dictionnaire de Spiritualité*, vol. 8, cols. 1126–50.

Previous English Translations:

The Way of a Pilgrim and the Pilgrim Continues His Way. Translated by R. M. French. New York: Seabury Press, 1965.

The Way of a Pilgrim and the Pilgrim Continues His Way. Translated by Helen Bacovcin. New York: Doubleday, 1978.

Further Reading:

Crummey, Robert O. *The Old Believers and the World of Antichrist: The Vyg Community and the Russian State, 1694–1855*. Madison: University of Wisconsin Press, 1970.

Pascal, Pierre. *Avvakum et les débuts du raskol*. Paris, 1938. Reprint, The Hague: Mouton, 1963. This is the classic and unsurpassed study of the origins and early history of the Old Believers.

The Philokalia: The Complete Text. 4 vols. Translated from the Greek and edited by G. E. H. Palmer, Philip Sherrard, and Kallistos Ware.

BIBLIOGRAPHY

London: Faber & Faber, 1979–1995. A fifth volume of this fundamental source of Eastern Christian spirituality is in preparation.

Sherrard, Philip. "The Revival of Hesychast Spirituality." In *Christian Spirituality III: Post-Reformation and Modern*. Edited by Louis Dupré and Don E. Saliers, 417–31. New York: Crossroad, 1991.

Spidlík, Tomas. *The Spirituality of the Christian East*. Translated by Anthony P. Gythiel. Kalamazoo, Mich.: Cistercian Publications, 1986. Extensive bibliography.

Index

(References in **boldface** are to material in Introduction)

230

INDEX

Gospels, 73–75, 170–73,
177–79
Gregory Palamas, 139
Gregory of Sinai, St., 61,
126, 131, 187–88, 207,
209–10; Jesus prayer, 81,
83; prayer, 198
Gregory of Thessaloniki,
St., 94
Grolimund, Vasilii, **3–4, 6,
32, 35**

Hesychias, St., 80, 187, 202

Ignatios, St., 61, 82, 83, 187
Ilarion, **31, 34**
Ioann of Moldavia, Elder, **33**
Isaac the Syrian, St., 60, 161,
202, 213

James, St., 216
Jesus prayer, **1, 7–8, 9, 12,
13–15, 17–18, 19, 21,
23–25, 28,** 75, 80, 83–84,
89, 96–97,135–36,
187–89;
instruction on, 156–75
John Cassian the Roman, St.,
155
John Chrysostom, St., 73,
151–52, 153, 179–80,
192, 199
John Climacus, St., 110, 112,
158, 187, 213
John, Gospel of, 172–73
John of Karpathos, 93, 129,
153, 190, 199

"Journey to the Holy Land"
(Daniil), **33**

Kallistos Antelikudis, 94
Kallistos, St., patriarch of
Constantinople, 61, 82,
83, 125, 187, 192
Kharlampovich, K. V., **3**
Kiprian (Kern),
Archimandrite, **5**
Konstantinovski, Matfei, **16**
Kozlov, Mikhail, **3, 4, 7–8, 11,
12, 13, 14, 15, 23, 24, 26,
32, 33–34;** biography, **16**

Lanshakvov, Iakov, **33**
*Letters to my Friends from
Mount Athos* (Kozlov), **16**
Lord's Prayer, 97–98, 113–14,
173

Makarii of Optino, Elder, **17**
Makarios the Great, St., 163,
187, 199, 202, 203, 209
Mark the Monk, 163
Michurin, Petr, **13, 17**
Mikhail, Archimandrite. *See*
Kozlov, Michael
"Mystery of Salavation,
Revealed by Unceasing
Prayer, The," **30–31**

"Narration concerning the
Effects of the Prayer of
the Heart of Elder
Vasilisk the
Hermit, A," **17**
Neoplatonists, 213

231

INDEX

Other Volumes in This Series

Other Volumes in This Series

Other Volumes in This Series